PRAISE FOR
CONSCIOUSNESS MEDICINE

"Françoise Bourzat is uniquely qualified to write this book. She not only has the multicultural training and a deep and real connection with indigenous traditional healing techniques, but she has for decades applied, tested, and extended these techniques, specifically for the training of Western therapists. Her own Western training was first class; perhaps because of that, she is not caught up in idolizing or fantasizing the value of either Western psychodynamic therapies and research or these older systems of indigenous healing. She has no ideological ax to grind, but only to press for effective practice for the healer and for their clients."

—JAMES FADIMAN, PhD, psychologist and author of
The Psychedelic Explorer's Guide: Safe, Therapeutic, and Sacred Journeys

"Françoise Bourzat has been a student and friend of mine for over thirty years. We have shared our prayers for health and help through our breath of life and our heartfelt quest for a healthier world to live in. Our Native American way of life is not a religion; it is a "Way of Life." When I met Bourzat, she was living in the mountains, living in nature, and teaching her students they are one with nature. Bourzat was already connected to our Mother Earth and our Way of Life was not a mystery or difficult to connect to."

—MARILYN YOUNGBIRD, Chief Woman Among Chiefs, Arikara Nation

"Bourzat has an extensive background as a teacher and facilitator of altered states of consciousness, utilizing a variety of techniques including meditation, vision quests, sweat lodges, and entheogens. Regarding entheogens, also known as psychedelics and hallucinogens, Bourzat has done considerable fieldwork among the indigenous Mazatec people of Mexico, who have a vast history and knowledge of the spiritual and healing properties of psilocybin mushrooms and other psychotropic plants, predating the European conquest of the Americas. Having worked closely for many years with these native healers of the Mazatec, Bourzat has acquired considerable insight into these ancient practices that she has transmitted to the many contemporary students and seekers that she has worked with over the past thirty-five years. Given the increasing interest in the range of effects and applications of psychedelic plants in the modern area, Bourzat's knowledge of these ancient practices holds great relevance to today's world."

—CHARLES S. GROB, MD, professor of psychiatry,
UCLA School of Medicine

"Françoise Bourzat has been studying [Mazatec] tradition for many years. Through this study and through her personal experiences, she has acquired an understanding of our ancestral ways and is able to speak about them with respect and the clarity of that responsibility. I support her voice and I trust her approach in combining her psychological angle together with our ancient ways of the ancestral medicines of our Mazatec tradition."

—EUGENIA PINEDA CASIMIRO, guide for the sacred
ceremonies of the Mazatec area, Oaxaca, Mexico

"In *Consciousness Medicine*, Françoise Bourzat deftly pulls together a practical guide for all serious travelers of the inner universe, meant for those who are intent on getting the most out of their journeys with the goal of personal and societal transformation. She draws upon her deep knowledge of indigenous wisdom and techniques for expanding consciousness—combining this with her broad knowledge of contemporary psychological and spiritual practices and thirty years plus of working with people in expanded and extreme mind states—to weave together a multihued cloak of compassionate guidance and loving presence for those brave souls who dare to explore the further reaches of consciousness. Throughout this book, in clear, frank, and humble language, Bourzat's lived experience of the inner landscapes she explores herself and with her clients shines through."

—GARY BRAVO, MD, psychiatrist and coauthor
of *Birth of a Psychedelic Culture*

"A valuable resource for anyone using 'altered states' in their practice of psychotherapy. Françoise Bourzat is not only experienced in how to integrate material gained while in these states into one's daily life, but in addition she is an experienced and insightful psychotherapist. She also has many years of training psychotherapists in how to deal with difficult situations. Bourzat's depth of understanding is unmatched in the work with psilocybin. Her many years as an apprentice to a Mazatec healer has given her both a depth of experience and an appreciation for the origins and purpose of this work. This book is clearly written, with valuable specific examples of clients' work and experiences to illustrate salient points."

—PADMA CATELL, PhD, author of *Drugs and Clients:
What Every Therapist Needs to Know* and a contributor
with Ralph Metzner to *Through the Gateway of the Heart*

CONSCIOUSNESS MEDICINE

CONSCIOUSNESS MEDICINE

*Indigenous Wisdom, Entheogens, and
Expanded States of Consciousness
for Healing and Growth*

FRANÇOISE BOURZAT

WITH KRISTINA HUNTER

FOREWORD BY RALPH METZNER

North Atlantic Books
Berkeley, California

Published by   Cover art by Jacques Roussow
North Atlantic Books   Book design by Happenstance Type-O-Rama
Berkeley, California

Printed in Canada

Consciousness Medicine: Indigenous Wisdom, Entheogens, and Expanded States of Consciousness for Healing and Growth is sponsored and published by the Society for the Study of Native Arts and Sciences (dba North Atlantic Books), an educational nonprofit based in Berkeley, California, that collaborates with partners to develop cross-cultural perspectives, nurture holistic views of art, science, the humanities, and healing, and seed personal and global transformation by publishing work on the relationship of body, spirit, and nature.

North Atlantic Books' publications are distributed to the US trade and internationally by Penguin Random House Publishers Services. For further information, visit our website at www.northatlanticbooks.com.

DISCLAIMER: The following information is intended for general information purposes only. The publisher does not advocate illegal activities but does believe in the right of individuals to have free access to information and ideas. Individuals should always see their health care provider before administering any suggestions made in this book. Any application of the material set forth in the following pages is at the reader's discretion and is his or her sole responsibility.

Library of Congress Cataloging-in-Publication Data
Names: Bourzat, Françoise, author. | Hunter, Kristina (Certified Hakomi practitioner), author.
Title: Consciousness medicine : indigenous wisdom, entheogens, and expanded states of consciousness for healing and growth : a practitioner's guide / Françcoise Bourzat with Kristina Hunter ; foreword by Ralph Metzner.
Description: Berkeley, California : North Atlantic Books, [2019] | Includes bibliographical references. |
Identifiers: LCCN 2019017407 (print) | LCCN 2019017884 (ebook) | ISBN 9781623173500 (E-book) | ISBN 9781623173494 (trade paper)
Subjects: | MESH: Spiritual Therapies—methods | Psychotherapy—methods | Hallucinogens—therapeutic use | Consciousness
Classification: LCC RZ401 (ebook) | LCC RZ401 (print) | NLM WM 427 | DDC 615.8/52—dc23
LC record available at https://lccn.loc.gov/2019017407.

4 5 6 7 8 9 10 MQ 26 25 24 23 22 21

North Atlantic Books is committed to the protection of our environment. We print on recycled paper whenever possible and partner with printers who strive to use environmentally responsible practices.

For Jacqueline and Julieta

I am a woman who looks into the insides of things, I say

I am a woman who investigates, I say

I am a woman wise in medicine, I say

I am a mother woman, I say

I am a woman wise in medicine, I say

—MARÍA SABINA[1]

CONTENTS

FOREWORD

Amidst the current plethora of books on shamanic and entheogenic healing practices, *Consciousness Medicine* is a rare and precious contribution. It is a woman's book, using the ancient metaphoric language of weaving. It speaks of the author's multi-year apprenticeship with the Mazatec medicine elder woman Julieta Casimiro, herself a unique example in a field dominated by men. Julieta calls Françoise "the interpreter," whose task it is to translate the indigenous way of women healers into the modern world. She weaves together stories of medicine healings in Mexico, with stories of how these teachings can be applied in the contemporary world, using experiential modalities such as dance and movement, sweat lodge, breathwork, meditation, sensory awareness, Hakomi therapy, and others. Throughout her book, Françoise emphasizes the need for clear intentions and integration of altered state experiences into everyday life, giving many detailed suggestions for ongoing practices. I especially appreciate the conscious attention she gives to two factors often omitted or neglected in groups that emphasize individual enlightenment experiences—the integration of the new insights into community life and the integration with environmental concerns. The healing stories shared in this book, by both men and women, radiate with the author's infectious enthusiasm and *joie de vivre*.

RALPH METZNER, PHD
Psychotherapist, Professor Emeritus at the
California Institute of Integral Studies and
author of *The Unfolding Self* and *Allies for
Awakening*
October 15, 2018

PREFACE

We are in the midst of a psychedelic renaissance in which we have finally come to recognize the potential of consciousness-expanding compounds in the fields of medicine, innovation, and spiritual transformation. However, as we're coming to see, powerful technologies that can shift our reality applied with neither wisdom nor conscience can be profoundly destabilizing to culture as well as nature. In working with expanded states of consciousness, perhaps the most important consideration is to refine the intention with which we approach them and to cultivate a healthy respect for the context within which they have been used skillfully for thousands of years.

I met Françoise Bourzat at one of her first public talks in San Francisco. With her characteristic vivacity, she was sharing about her experience with the healing tradition of the indigenous Mazatec people, who have ingested the psilocybin mushrooms as their primary sacrament in ceremonies for millennia. Her joy was infectious. Françoise's emphasis on bringing realizations gained from expanded states of consciousness into daily life deeply resonated with me. Over the years, I have found her approach, which combines psychological understanding and plant medicine wisdom, to be both life-affirming and deeply healing.

This book began from a genuine need within our community of clinicians and healing practitioners for a comprehensive resource and guidebook for working with the preparation and integration of expanded states. It's been an honor to deepen my apprenticeship and assist Françoise in the endeavor of bringing this book to life. We began by compiling transcripts and notes from her lectures, interviews, and trainings. Gradually, the book found its own breath and directed us as to how to proceed.

The practical wisdom contained in this book comes from Françoise's rich life experience as well as her dedicated study and apprenticeship with her teachers, and in turn, her teachers' teachers.

A living lineage travels to us through the generations, manifesting as the alchemical relationship between teacher and student, passing from heart to heart, lovingly tended through time up to the present. As we are touched by such a living lineage, we are connected to the original wellspring of our shared human inheritance.

The love and potency of these ancient medicine ways are now emerging and rippling out into the wider community. What we do now, how we hold and apply the gift of this precious technology, is of utmost importance if it is to guide us and our world toward deeply needed reconnection, regeneration, and reunion with ourselves and all of life.

KRISTINA HUNTER
January 1, 2019
Berkeley, California

INTRODUCTION

Weaving Worlds

It was an October morning in 1976 that I arrived on my motorbike at the campus of Paris 8 University to utter pandemonium. Hundreds of students were rushing around the central courtyard while others sat perched high above, along a wrought iron fence. Some held signs, and others were shouting into megaphones, urging us to organize. The outrage and euphoria in the air were palpable. I asked a passing student what was happening, and she explained that the government had broken their agreement; funding to our university had been dramatically reduced. "We've been lied to! All the faculty is on strike!" she exclaimed and walked off. I felt the pain of this betrayal yet invigorated by the collective fervor, as I stood in the courtyard surrounded by the throng of empowered young people demanding their rights.

I was twenty years old and had been studying psychology at the experimental university that was gifted to the students following the French social revolution and consequential reform of May 1968. The student protests and faculty strike continued for weeks, rendering me unable to continue my studies. At the time, many young Europeans were leaving their homes to explore North Africa, Asia, India, and Central and South America, and, feeling inspired and curious, with no school to return to, my boyfriend and I decided to take the opportunity to travel the world. We got jobs at the post office for a few months in order to save for our trip, intending to journey across the Americas until we ran out of money.

We bought one-way tickets to New York City and hitchhiked through North, Central, and South America for nine months, exhilarated to encounter new lands and cultures. By the spring we had arrived in Tarabuco, Bolivia, a small Andean village on a high valley floor, 11,000 feet above sea level. The town was modest, the streets lined with low, simple adobe homes. Most of the roads were dirt, and the evening winds from the mountains would blow swirling clouds of dust along the market stalls. Men and women walked around in traditional woven clothes: colorful, striped ponchos and head coverings reminiscent of sixteenth-century Spain. Everyone would gather in the cobblestone plaza at market time to sell produce, often walking miles from their family farms in their multicolored outfits. I quickly fell in love with the vast landscape of hills, the warm weather, and the friendly Yampara people with their flute and *charango* music.

We were two of only a few tourists in town and decided to rent a room with a local family for two months. At the market, people soon began to recognize me as I shopped for a few tomatoes or a dozen eggs. In the mornings, I would meet with the women in the plaza as they taught me how to spin wool. Their native dialect was incomprehensible to me, so we would simply speak a few words of Spanish and smile at each other. They braided my hair and giggled among themselves, as the beaded headdress they tried to balance on my head would fall off. They complimented the long skirt I wore, which I had sewn myself from African fabric. I was aware of the cultural differences and contrast between us, with my European background and education, my unusual appearance and mannerisms, and I took care to be polite, doing my best to respect their reserved nature.

A week into our stay, while dining at a local cantina, we befriended Rene, a young man of indigenous Bolivian and Spanish descent. He was tall with wavy hair resembling Che Guevara, and home on break from university in La Paz to visit his family. One day Rene invited us on a daylong hike to visit the seasonal quinoa-threshing ritual the Yampara were conducting in the hills surrounding the countryside. He suggested that we ingest some San Pedro cactus as a deeper introduction to the native tradition, and we agreed, although neither of us had taken such a powerful mind-altering substance and were naïve to what such an experience might entail.

In the Andean mountains of South America, the San Pedro cactus *(Echinopsis pachanoi)* has been revered for over 3,000 years as a sacrament capable of inducing expanded states of consciousness through the mescaline alkaloid contained under its skin. The indigenous peoples of the Andes use the San Pedro cactus to enter non-ordinary states of consciousness to access knowledge for healing, guidance, and spiritual practice; and to tend their relationship with the natural world.[1]

As soon as we were out of town, Rene gave us each a dozen small balls of brownish paste to swallow with some water. Two hours into the hike, I noticed I was breathing deeply and easily despite the altitude. My body felt strong and vital, and hiking seemed effortless. Everything around me became vivid and alive with color. The grass appeared lusher, the earth beneath my feet more firm. The sky was so close it was as if I were being enveloped in a cloak of cerulean blue. The air was pure and the vista was vast. To my expanded consciousness, the mountains felt like living beings. I could sense their presence. Their communication to me was as sure as their round summits and rolling shapes. They met my curious eyes as if to say, "We see you seeing us."

I described to Rene what I was seeing and feeling. He walked ahead of me, nodding silently in agreement.

When we arrived at our destination in the mountains, we found dozens of women in bright layered skirts spinning llama wool while watching over pots of cooking potatoes. I recognized a few of them from our wool spinning at the town plaza. They gestured for me to join them, and I approached with a wide grin. As soon as I sat beside them, the women started braiding my hair, this time with satin red ribbons. They giggled, and this time I happily laughed along with them. They gave me a hand spool and fleece and we began to spin yarn while cooking the potatoes. Meanwhile, the men formed two large concentric circles. Between the two circles, five horses galloped over piles of quinoa as the men cracked their leather ropes in the air. Their high-pitched shouts urged the horses on, as the wind blew the chaff away in white clouds. The men would place more bundles of quinoa in the circle and the process would begin again.

The whole scene was astounding. I had the impression of being inside a painting: the horses galloping, the wind carrying away the chaff, the men yipping away, and the mountains surrounding us in complete stillness. Though I was speechless and in awe, I felt that this was all completely natural: being with these people on their land and sharing a universal experience of being human together. On that day, in my mescaline-enhanced state of consciousness, I experienced a profound connection to the living world that left a lasting impression on my young psyche.

✳ ✳ ✳

Despite the inspiring experiences of my travels, I returned home to familiar internal anguish. My father had died suddenly from cancer the previous year, soon after I turned nineteen, and my heart was full of grief, my challenging relationship with him left incomplete. I also suffered from anxiety, which I only later connected to my mother's history.

My father was born in 1924 to a Catholic family of peasants who lived in scarcity, in an isolated hamlet named La Rouchonie, "the rock of the nest," in rural Southwest France. His family had lived in the region for over twenty generations. Our family name, *Bourzat,* means "of the village" in the local dialect that was my father's first language. The villagers of La Rouchonie included bonesetters, herbalists, and traditional dowsers who raised livestock and tended small gardens. The cooking took place in cauldrons hanging in the fireplace, and the milk was picked up daily from the local shepherd, who would ladle it fresh into our small tin pails.

When I was young, our family would spend a month of every summer in my father's village. Every day my grandmother would make fresh cheese and the baker would arrive with a large wheel of bread, cutting off a piece for each family. My sisters and I would fish for minnows in the river, gather wild hazelnuts along the edge of the fields, and walk the village roads collecting dried cow dung to fertilize my grandmother's garden.

Although my childhood was idyllic in many ways, there was a darker side to my family. In rural parts of France like the village where my father grew up, adults routinely used physical punishment to discipline their children. There was a wooden-handled switch that hung above our kitchen door and my father considered this a normal aspect of child-rearing. Regardless of his deep devotion and love for his family, his bouts of anger often turned into fits of rage that frightened me, due to the intensity of his expression and the physical violence that would follow. Even after I grew older and the violence subsided, his stern approach to life never matched my spirited disposition.

My mother was born in 1920 into a very different way of life, yet had suffered in her own way. Her cosmopolitan family lived on the outskirts of Paris and was reasonably well off, although not part of the aristocratic milieu of the late 1800s. My grandmother, who was born the same year that the Eiffel Tower was built, had died soon after my mother's birth of the Spanish Flu, which decimated millions in Europe. As a young woman, my mother survived the Second World War, forced to leave her home as part of the Parisian Exodus. She walked miles with her siblings and thousands of other refugees, while bombs dropped all around the long line of people escaping the war-torn city. My mother's challenging childhood was compounded by the painful rejection she experienced from her often-cruel stepmother.

When my mother met my father, and they chose to marry in 1950, some of her family members disapproved. She came from a Parisian class of financial ease, and my father was four years her junior, from a poor farming family. Each had suffered in their own way; he through the poverty of his childhood, and she through the loss of her mother and the hardship of the war. My mother was thirty years old—an older marrying age for the time—and was determined to create a solid marriage and a family. They went on to have three daughters—of which I was the youngest.

The combination of depression after my father's death, and what I now know to have been an underlying anxiety inherited from my mother, contributed to my feeling quite lost. At twenty-one, after returning from my travels through the Americas, I moved to Northern Italy with a new boyfriend who turned out to be a heroin addict. Seeking relief from my own confusion, I eventually joined him in his reckless drug use, snorting the seductive white powder daily. Soon we were buying and selling heroin, spending time in abysmal environments with subhuman conditions. At the time, I was completely disconnected from my emotions, as our life oriented around heroin and addiction had become normal to me. In retrospect, I see that I was in a traumatized state, numbing my unresolved grief however I could.

Fortunately, one day, five months into my destructive lifestyle, a good friend arrived and physically removed me from my dangerous situation, bringing me back to the South of France and supporting me to get clean.

Once I was sober and stable enough, I moved to Switzerland, and after a few months of working odd jobs, I decided to travel again. In 1979, three years after my trip across the Americas, I went to Thailand for four months—this time alone. It was on this trip that I experienced a trauma that profoundly impacted the rest of my life.

As I was returning to Bangkok from the north of the country, I decided to visit the Buddhist temples of Sukhothai. My first day there I met a young South Indian man named Ramesh. He was at the end of his contract in Thailand as a civil engineer, and was enjoying a final visit to the temples before returning home to his family. Though we had just met, we decided to continue exploring the nearby temples together. As we were walking down a wide country path toward a more remote temple, I felt a sense of unease as I realized that two young men were following us. I considered running, but just seconds later they caught up with us and tapped me on the shoulder. Overcome with dread, I turned around to face them.

Suddenly, there were gunshots and time slowed to a crawl. In that fraction of a second, I saw my mother's torment and despair over her daughter's unexpected disappearance. I thought how senseless it was that I would die at this moment and vanish from existence so young. I was not ready to die. Then came the impact of the bullet into my body, though I couldn't tell where. In the blink of an eye, I tossed my bag behind me and threw myself into a ditch, where I lay completely still, holding my breath. I heard the men walk toward me. Feeling their presence and sure they would now kill me, I screamed at the top of my lungs. A scream for life. I felt their hands grabbing at my wrist to remove my watch, then heard them run off, leaving us both for dead.

I thought I had been shot in the belly and was holding myself tightly with my hands, sure of my imminent death, until I realized the blood was coming from my thigh. I crawled over to Ramesh to see he had been shot in the forehead. There was blood, bones, brains, and hair all around him. He was barely breathing as I frantically tried to think how I could help him. A few minutes later, a farmer passed by on his bicycle and emphatically gestured for me to sit behind him, delivering me to the main road. I was hot, my leg was burning, and I was terrified that the bandits would be waiting in nearby bushes to shoot me again. Once at the main road, my rescuer waved down a car, which drove me to the nearest hospital. I was rushed into the operating room, and just as the doctor began to remove the bullet from my leg, my Indian friend was delivered to the same room and died right beside me.

A few days later, the chief of police reported that they had found some of our stolen belongings. He asked me if I would come view possible suspects and identify the one who had shot us. I arrived to a room of six men standing against a wall opposite me. I could see them, and they could see me. I looked at each of them carefully. Then I spotted him, the one who had shot me; his image was branded in my mind. My eyes lingered, and I moved on to the next man. I looked at each of them and returned to the eyes of my attacker. We held one another's gaze. I saw distress and fear in his eyes, and in that moment I realized my word would determine his life or death. I imagined his mother and family. I considered my life ahead of me. I did not want to carry the burden of his death on my soul. I did not want to perpetuate any more suffering. Something softened inside of me and I shook my head. I did not name him.

It wasn't until I later returned home to Europe that deep, existential questions began to arise.

I was left not with anger, but rather an intense sadness. How could the young men who had killed Ramesh and nearly killed me not have seen us as fellow human beings? In an instant they had stolen my friend's life and changed mine forever. It had been so quick and mindless. I felt heartbroken, imagining how disconnected these young men were to have lost all regard for human life. At the same time, I realized how fragile life was. The tragedy in Thailand woke me from my trance of directionless drifting. I asked myself, what would be the most worthwhile way to spend my precious human existence? I was filled with a sense of fearless determination, intent on pursuing a meaningful and fulfilling life.

I spent the next couple of years living in Switzerland, recuperating from my travels, working in a restaurant, and once my leg had healed, returning to my passion of studying modern dance. During this time, I met a masterful physical therapist who helped me heal a chronic back pain condition from childhood scoliosis. Inspired by his skill, I decided to study the craft. Some dancer friends of mine living in California told me that there were many massage schools in San Francisco; and eager to create a new life for myself, I saved my money, packed my bags, and moved halfway across the world.

In 1981, at the age of twenty-five, I arrived in San Francisco. Once settled in my new life, I was very active meeting new people and studying massage, but beneath the surface I had yet to deal with the emotional challenges of my past. My painful relationship with my father, his sudden death, my days of heroin use, and my horrific experience in Thailand all remained unexplored and unresolved. Lacking the language or tools to heal myself, I suffered a string of unstable relationships. In retrospect, I was using activity and busyness as a way of avoiding deeper layers of trauma in my body and mind. Slowly, I became fed up, longing for relief from my inner agitation. Though I was determined to take an honest look at my life, I didn't know where to begin.

One afternoon four years after moving to San Francisco, I was at a party with friends on Baker Beach when I met the man who would become my future husband. Upon meeting him, it was his interest in psychology and spirituality that resonated with me. I shared my traveling adventures with him, and he turned out to be impressed and attracted to my precocious French style! After a period of dating, he introduced me to his mentor, with whom he had been doing psycho-spiritual work for two years.

Pablo Sanchez was in his sixties, a Chicano–Native American medicine man of Tiwa and Navajo ancestry who was the dean of the newly formed school of social work at San Jose State University in California. Prior to his work in academia, he had worked as a social worker for the Bureau of Indian Affairs, living and working on Navajo and Ute reservations in New Mexico, Colorado, and Utah. As a young man, Pablo had been in the Second World War in the Army Air Force photographic corps, and, while stationed in Europe, he had been given the heartrending task of documenting a concentration camp immediately after liberation. He later shared that the horrors he witnessed in that concentration camp had propelled him along his life path, devoting himself to human transformation and healing. Years later, Pablo befriended and became a student of Dr. Salvador Roquet,[2] a renowned Mexican psychiatrist who had been initiated into the world of traditional mushroom healing ceremonies by María Sabina, the well-known Mazatec *curandera* from Mexico.

At my first session with Pablo, we spent a few minutes casually chatting before he stood up and shuffled over to his bookshelf. He had recently had a tumor removed from his pituitary gland, which left him with impaired sight. He rummaged through books and papers, mumbling to himself while I wondered, "What is he doing over there? What sort of therapist is this? I am NOT in the right place here!" He returned to me with a sly smile on his face as he handed me a small book entitled *The Greatest Salesman in the World*. He pointed to a particular chapter and instructed me to read it aloud. He smiled as I read, "Since the beginning of time never has there been another with my mind, my heart, my eyes, my ears, my hands, my hair, my mouth. None that came before, none that live today, and none that come tomorrow can walk and talk and move and think exactly like me."

Two lines into the passage and I was sobbing, feeling myself dissolve into a strange soup of grief, terror, courage—and hope. I continued reading, "All men are my brothers, yet I am different from each. I am a unique creature. I am nature's greatest miracle." Sitting there in his office, I felt a spark of optimism within my despair, and a desire to heal myself and manifest my human potential awoke within me.

The ways Pablo supported and guided his clients were creative and varied. Beyond the individual hourly consultations he offered, he also facilitated individual and group healing sessions, during which he employed various psycho-spiritual methods such as guided breathwork, drawing, or reading specific books; as well as sending people out into nature, dancing, or spending time in a flotation tank. When he deemed it appropriate, he would guide his clients into inner journeys with consciousness-expanding substances such as MDMA, MDA, LSD, mushrooms, or ketamine. Guided by his intuition and his personal connection with the client, Pablo would choose the modality he felt most fitted with their healing. Rather than being hedonistic adventures, these journeys were conducted with the intention of doing psychological work in a setting of a sacred ceremony.

Pablo placed great importance on the meetings immediately following a journey. He aimed to support the ways these experiences could change people's lives and encouraged his clients to bring ritual into everyday activities. Pablo taught me how to bring intention to every gesture, to give it presence and meaning. If I were to pick a leaf from a tree for my altar, he would instruct me to speak to the tree before taking it, to intentionally acknowledge the leaf's sacrifice for my healing. He once instructed me to snap a small twig in half as a symbol of commitment to my healing and in preparation for a group mushroom ceremony. I felt the gravity of the moment as I chose a small twig from the ground, spoke my prayer, and snapped it in two to punctuate the moment. These two small pieces of wood remain in a small cloth pouch on my altar to this day, honoring my long commitment to the healing path.

As a painter, Pablo complemented his psychological intelligence with the creativity he would bring to assignments he gave. Looking at the world with the eyes of an artist was at the heart of his approach. To support the integration of material that came up in my journeys, he instructed me to work with clay, to improvise dances, and to honor my relationship with nature at all times. As I fulfilled these practical assignments, I felt more inspired and aware, noticing tangible shifts in my life. Pablo was excited to hear about my successes and the changes I reported. When there was resistance on my end, he lovingly challenged it. In retrospect, a huge part of the equation was that there was someone genuinely interested in my development and healing.

After a few months of working together, Pablo invited me to begin assisting him. His style was such that after a short period of being a participant in his groups, his clients would be invited to assist them. This gave everyone a chance to learn from both sides. I joined him in individual medicine sessions with other clients and also helped him organize group journeys. During the same time, I had the opportunity to join a few of Dr. Salvador Roquet's *convivials*, intensive retreats that led participants through a series of psycho-spiritual processes including art, movement, psychodrama, sleep deprivation, and confrontational experiments. The goal of Salvador's work was to expose people to the deepest levels of fear and shadow in their psyche, in service to their psychological and spiritual evolution. I also began to participate in sweat lodges guided by Taos ceremonial leader, Richard Deertrack, and eventually became a long-term student of Marilyn Youngbird, an Arikara–Hidatsa Lakota teacher and sweat lodge leader. As I became more involved in these healing explorations, and my massage clients began to share their personal life stories with me during their sessions, I decided to enter a graduate program in somatic psychology, followed by training in the Hakomi method of body-centered psychotherapy.[3] I wanted to acquire a solid psychological education in addition to my background as a dancer and a bodyworker, in order to have a more balanced foundation from which to help others. During this same time, I became a wife and mother.

Several years into motherhood and after I had begun to see individual clients as a somatically oriented counselor, I was introduced to a man named Juan. Juan had spent ten years in Huautla de Jiménez, a small town high in the Sierra Madre Mountains of Mexico, participating in guided ceremonies with an indigenous Mazatec elder named Julieta Casimiro. Beginning early in life, Julieta had been trained in the knowledge of the sacred mushroom ceremony, a tradition that had been kept alive in her region for thousands of years. Because we had been using mushrooms in our ceremonies with Pablo, I was enthusiastic about the possibility of connecting with the roots of the tradition. Juan felt that Julieta's and my destiny were intertwined and that it was necessary that we meet. He told her about my interest in the work and she invited us to visit.

On a crisp fall day, Juan and I met in Oaxaca, Mexico, for the treacherous six-hour drive up into the mountains. At that time, most of the roads in Huautla de Jiménez were full of potholes and unpaved with rivers of muddy water running down them. Very few buses made it into town and there were only a few other cars around. Vendors walked through the streets selling their fruit and vegetables, and old women shuffled about wearing traditional *huipil* dresses, hand-embroidered and embellished with pink and blue ribbons. There were a couple of phone booths in the streets, no internet, and no one had a cell phone.

We finally arrived at our destination; a two-story compound constructed of cinderblocks and plastered adobe. Full of trepidation, I was almost shaking.

It was as if the mushrooms were already activating my psyche and body, unleashing strange sensations of apprehension and joy. Julieta answered the door, offered her hand, and introduced herself before inviting us in. She was wearing a printed dress and red sweater, her two long, black braids hanging on either side of her chest. She had a warm smile and a playful twinkle in her eye.

Once inside, I saw that the compound was built around an open-air kitchen and patio. There were buckets strewn about the ground collecting rainwater, and others overflowing with bouquets of flowers. I later learned that fresh flowers were delivered daily, destined to adorn Juliet's massive altar or to be offered at family gravesites in the cemetery. We were guided into Julieta's living room, the walls covered with photos of her grandchildren, her husband Lucio making beeswax candles, and a faded black-and-white photo of her wedding—showing her mother, Maria Petra, and her teacher and mother-in-law, Regina Carrera, guiding a ritual procession through the streets.

Julieta spoke with Juan as I sat on the couch, taking in this woman's laughter and gestures. I felt incredibly fortunate to even sit in the room with her, sensing that this was a new beginning for me and that my life and work would change in ways I could not yet articulate.

Julieta and I spent several days together. She took me into the countryside, to the market, to the church, to local sacred spots, and to visit her birthplace. We ate traditional meals and drank her homegrown coffee. She told me that the Mazatec people, descendants of the Maya, call themselves the people of the eagle. She lovingly referred to sacramental mushrooms as *Los Niños Santos*, explaining that they are Mother Earth's holy children. She explained how the act of ingesting them is a sacred moment of communion.

During my stay with her, Julieta guided me in three mushroom ceremonies. Like a night bird in full alertness, she sat beside me lovingly, watching and listening with complete attention. Julieta held my body while it shook out old hurts and instructed me to give my sadness to Mother Earth, who would compassionately receive what I no longer wished to carry. She spoke to the mushrooms and instructed them to clean me inside, to leave only light and the force of creation, for I too was to guide others along the path of healing. She prayed for my family, asking all the saints to protect them from harm and illness. She grinned and said she saw the Virgin of Guadalupe watching over me with her infinite embrace and we laughed together out of sheer joy. I felt reborn, held in such love by this woman and her ancient tradition that I had come to like a pilgrim.

After all my years of studying with male teachers, it was a blessing to finally study with a woman. Pablo and Salvador were amazing visionaries, pioneering a path that brought together indigenous healing and a Western psychological framework. They had encouraged me to take my place as a woman healer in a culture of mostly men, and for that I was grateful. Yet, arriving in this remote mountain town in Mexico and meeting Julieta felt like a homecoming. To have an opportunity to learn from a woman elder who was also a mother, with well-developed intuition and a feminine sensibility, was a miracle to me. As I returned home from that first visit to Mexico, it was clear that I would be back soon and that my relationship with Julieta would deepen.

Over the years, Julieta and I formed a lifelong bond through our personal affection and love for the mushroom healing rituals that were central to both of our lives. I returned to Huautla de Jiménez often. Additionally, Julieta would come visit my family and me in California and we would travel internationally together. Sitting by her side during numerous ceremonies and rituals in Mexico, I readily absorbed as much as I could of her elaborate and beautiful tradition. She taught me in a style that was foreign to me at the time, but that I now know to be common among indigenous teachers: not through words and explanations, but rather through her presence as an embodiment of a living tradition. Over time our work developed into collaboration, integrating her traditional knowledge with my psychological training. I finally understood the cryptic words that Juan, the man who had introduced us, had said to me at our first meeting, "She will pour herself into you and you will serve her well."

Though my primary apprenticeship has been in the Mazatec tradition with Julieta as my teacher and guide, I have a broader appreciation for ways of life that have been nurtured and sustained by indigenous peoples. I recognize that I have a unique perspective, being very much of the industrialized world yet also familiar with the simple, earthy life of the countryside, my father's family and ancestors having lived on the same land for hundreds of years. My deep love for earth-based ways of life has guided me over the years to visit and learn from other indigenous peoples.

I have spent time with the Otavalans and Huaorani people of Ecuador, the Aymara people near Lake Titicaca in Bolivia, and the Maya in Guatemala. My travels have taken me to visit the Raramuri people of Copper Canyon in Northern Mexico, the native people of Uzbekistan, the Hamar and Afar peoples of Ethiopia, and Tibetan communities in Northern India. I have returned many consecutive years to visit the Mosetén community who live in the Madidi National Park of Bolivia. Yet, it is the small town of Huautla de Jiménez in the mountains of Mexico that has called me back year after year. I go to immerse myself in the Mazatec way of life and all the subtle nuances of its unique cosmology and, most importantly, to nurture my precious relationship with Julieta and her family.

During one particular night of ritual, five years into my apprenticeship with Julieta, we were together in her ceremony room. She was reciting a prayer for my family and me when she referred to me as "the interpreter." I remember hearing her words and understanding that this was indeed my role. When I later asked her if she would say more about what she meant, she replied, "You know our ways. You know what your people can hear. You know what you can tell them about our tradition." She saw me as a liaison between her ways and my own.

With Julieta's permission and her blessing, I have attempted to combine my understanding of her approach to healing together with my understanding of the human psyche and psychology. As a person of European descent living in the United States, it is important for me to acknowledge the danger of cultural misappropriation in my counseling practice. Sometimes to act with humility is not enough. A living relationship of mutual respect with my teacher, who could correct my course if I went astray, has been vital.

I understand the importance of weaving these worlds together. While the last century has seen the development of a comprehensive field of psychology and various skillful psychotherapeutic approaches, we need more than an intellectual understanding of our psyche to truly heal and transform. Through my decades of counseling work, I have come to see how people living in industrialized societies are hungry for the ancient knowledge carried by indigenous peoples. They specifically seek the kind of healing and teaching accessed through rituals such as the Mazatec mushroom ceremony.

Without fully understanding these traditions and their wisdom, outsiders often take sacred sacraments, such as mushrooms, absent of ritual or trained guidance. I feel it is a mistake to consume a sacrament without understanding its cultural context. These sacraments can initiate experiences that are confusing or overwhelming, and lack of knowledgeable support can leave someone disoriented or even traumatized. Furthermore, the inner riches of insight and understanding that one can encounter in these spaces often fade quickly without support to integrate them as "life as usual" promptly returns. Ceremonies and rituals of any kind belong to specific cultural philosophies and unique geographic environments. They are integral parts of a whole way of life.

It has thus become my life's work to introduce the healing ways of indigenous rituals to people living in industrialized societies. I believe that experiences of expanded states of consciousness are not enough on their own, so I bring my psychological training in to support the integration of these experiences into daily life in practical ways. Because I want to share this work widely, and the use of the sacred mushroom is illegal in the country in which I live, I have developed alternative methods to effectively guide my clients into expanded states of consciousness. My long-term immersion in the Mazatec tradition has allowed me to share the wisdom of their medicine through rituals, songs, and prayers, which transport people into similarly potent spaces of healing and growth.

After guiding clients into expanded states of consciousness for these last thirty years, my observations have sharpened, my work has evolved, and my synthesis of methods has distilled itself into an approach I feel is imperative to share, here and now. In the scientific world, this is called anecdotal data. In the indigenous world, it is called wisdom.

I call my work "Consciousness Medicine." Consciousness Medicine is the art and science of exploring the infinite dimensions and manifestations of consciousness—the foundation of life. Consciousness Medicine uses varied theories, tools, and techniques to access specific states of expanded consciousness. These state experiences and the insights they bring, when integrated into one's life, offer a path of transformation and healing. As our consciousness grows, we become more aware of ourselves, each other, and the world we belong to. With increased awareness we become healthier and more fulfilled. It is consciousness that heals us. That is why I consider consciousness to be the ultimate medicine.

I have adapted the indigenous ways of approaching expanded states of consciousness into a threefold process consisting of the preparation phase, the journey, and the integration phase. Over the years, when I feel that my counseling clients are ready and would benefit, I invite them to travel with me to Julieta's home in Huautla de Jiménez to partake in the mushroom ritual, which is legal there. Before any journey to Mexico, I take great care to support my clients' readiness on the psychological level through regular counseling sessions prior to the trip, making sure I am as aware as I can be regarding their past and what might be evoked by the work. I also make sure that they have a nurturing environment in place for their return. Upon going home, I actively support their integration process by meeting regularly to support them as they weave the insights gained in their ceremony experiences into their lives.

This approach to spiritual journeying, which emphasizes preparation and integration, brings expanded states of consciousness into connection with daily life. To understand the approach I am presenting, consider pivotal initiatory moments of life such as birth, marriage, and death. These are special events in our lives that, by nature of their intensity, bring us into an expanded state of consciousness. Ideally, these events should be thoroughly prepared for and followed up with appropriate integration. For example, in our culture, the preparation for a wedding—which can take months—includes choosing the location, the clothing, the food, and inviting the guests. The actual ceremony then takes place, with an officiant leading the ritual of exchanging vows. The dinner and celebration bring the families and community together. The integration includes the honeymoon, creating the photo album, opening the gifts, and sending thank-you notes to all the guests.

Another example would be a meditation retreat. Preparation and integration are of utmost importance, and the practitioner might read certain books, choose a specific location, and connect with a teacher to discuss aspirations and intentions. The practitioner then begins the retreat under the guidance of a teacher, whether with a group or in solitude. Once the practitioner completes the retreat, they perform closing rituals, break their silence, and prepare their return to normal life. The practitioner reenters the community, observes how they changed, and weaves those changes into their daily life. Intentional journeys into expanded states of consciousness should be approached in the same manner.

This book offers a roadmap for journeys into expanded states of consciousness, whether it is a ceremony with an entheogenic or psychedelic sacrament, a vision quest, a drumming ritual, a sweat lodge, or a dancing retreat. Whether or not we access these expanded states of consciousness by way of a sacrament, what is important is *how* we approach these states. We can receive much more by relying on the knowledge that indigenous cultures have maintained and passed down for thousands of years of how we can best approach and incorporate these experiences into our lives.

The seed of this book was a series of lectures I gave during university courses, seminars, and conferences. This compilation of knowledge and wisdom developed into this guidebook for practitioners—whether a guide, facilitator, therapist, or participant. It offers therapists and facilitators the necessary tools and techniques to guide and support their clients or ritual participants in maximizing healing and growth. This book also offers participants resources to assist their preparation for and integration of their inner journeys into their daily life. I share what I know to be true from my experience and the techniques and practices I am personally familiar with.

Today, with the natural environment and culture in a state of extreme imbalance and crisis, it is my prayer that each of us do the internal work necessary to move through our personal suffering to a place of greater creativity, clarity, and compassion. We in the industrialized world lead very different lives than those living with original practices and intact traditions anchored in a strong connection with the earth. Life in this world is overrun by technology and the erroneous belief that we can extract resources from the earth at will with no reciprocity. This behavior is harming *all* life on the planet. Additionally, most people living this way are disconnected from their ancestral roots and traditions, lack community, and don't know how or where their food is grown. This results in a profound disconnection from one's self—which manifests as depression, anxiety, negative self-image, compulsive and addictive behaviors and actions, illness, and so on. I see the core imbalance to be an illusion of separation that impacts every level of life in the modern world.

It doesn't matter where on Earth we are. North, south, east, or west; in my experience, every seeker has a similar wish at the core of their being: to heal our relationship with our partner, parents, family, community, ancestors, and ultimately with ourselves and the greater world to which we all belong. Industrialized societies can learn much from earth-based wisdom and the practices of indigenous cultures that fortunately still exist today. Of course, the conversation would be incomplete without acknowledging the ways in which the industrialized world has been extremely aggressive and exploitative toward First Nations peoples. That being said, if we want to create peace and global healing, we need to build bridges between cultures. Indeed, it is also true that some technological developments can be life-saving for people in developing countries. Water purification technology can save lives. Indigenous communities in the Amazon have been able to defend their land from oil drilling using Google Earth's map technology. By pursuing mutual and respectful exchanges of knowledge and technology, we can learn from and help one another.

The aspiration to bring greater harmony to the world, *one person at a time,* is at the center of my life's work and is the core motivation for sharing what I have learned. I have witnessed countless people heal old wounds and current relationships, reconnect with the natural world, reclaim self-respect and self-love, and create community. It has been the inclusion of expanded states of consciousness as a healing modality that has allowed my clients to access a much greater intelligence than what their limited ego identity could possibly have fathomed.

May this book offer you tools toward your own empowerment and give you the courage to pursue your unique path of transformation. May your curiosity and even your suffering be the fuel for your commitment to healing and growth. May you feel validated in your quest to explore the infinite abundance of mystery and beauty that lies just beyond your ego identity and conscious mind. May you liberate your creative energy to be a dynamic force, actively contributing toward the evolution and renewal of our precious world. May you fulfill the life you came to Earth to live.

1

ORIGINAL RITUALS

Expanded States of Consciousness for Healing and Growth

Like all explorers, we are drawn to discover what's out there without knowing yet if we have the courage to face it.

—PEMA CHÖDRÖN[1]

Over many millennia, humans have explored the vast reaches of our planet: its deserts, oceans, mountain ranges, and forests. Throughout our evolution we have developed numerous civilizations, cultures, languages, weapons, and foods. We have discovered and studied animals, plants, fungi, and minerals. Meanwhile, for as long as we have been exploring our external world, we have pursued the equally fascinating realms of our inner world. There is evidence that humans have been exploring consciousness for thousands of years.[2] Yet, despite centuries of speculation and investigation into the origins and nature of consciousness, this most intimate basis of our being remains elusive to modern science.

Many contemporary philosophers and scientists propose that consciousness arises from the brain, beginning at some point in utero and ending at death. This perspective views our consciousness as a result of chemicals and electrical impulses responding to internal and external influences.[3] In another view, the brain and nervous system serve as organic antennae, picking up information like a radio receiver as we move through an ocean of consciousness.[4] Eastern traditions propose that consciousness arises from an empty yet cognizant field of awareness that is the source of all phenomena.[5] Perhaps surprisingly, the physicist Max Planck also held this belief in some form, famously saying: "I regard consciousness as fundamental. I regard matter as derivative from consciousness. We cannot get behind consciousness. Everything that we talk about, everything that we regard as existing, postulates consciousness."[6]

There is a vast spectrum of state-specific experiences available to our consciousness. Most often, we each feel contentedly separate, as though we are individual organisms moving through space, alternating between comfort, discomfort, or boredom depending on whether we feel attraction, aversion, or indifference in the moment. Sometimes we feel tight in our bodies, mentally contracted, unable to connect with others or even ourselves. We might feel isolated from other people, even those close to us. At other times, we find ourselves feeling open and loving, connecting easily with other people, animals, plants, and our natural environment. We feel a sense of effortlessness and flow and receive understandings and insights, feeling the warmth of compassion toward all of life. We are in a constant dance of experience, depending on our state. No wonder people have been investigating consciousness—and ways to shift it—for millennia.

In the more archaic quest to explore consciousness, humans developed ways to shift their states of consciousness by employing various techniques and practices. Humans have likely been drumming, rattling and chanting together, creating art, fasting, sweating and cleansing, meditating, exploring sleep deprivation, going on vision quests, spending extended time in isolation alone, dancing, and singing together for ritual, rites of passage, and spiritual purposes for thousands of years. The famous caves at Lascaux in southwest France, which are less than forty kilometers from my family home, appear to show humans participating in shamanic rituals 17,000 years ago.[7] This spirit of exploration was likely the inspiration for people to ferment fruits and grains into alcohol, as well as to ingest plants and mushrooms with psychotropic compounds in their seeds, bark, leaves, flowers, roots, and flesh. Consciousness-changing compounds have even been found in the venom and excretions of certain amphibians.[8] People explored whatever was growing in their local environment. Mescaline-containing cacti grow abundantly in hot, arid climates. Ayahuasca vines and leafy plants grow abundantly in the jungle, while psilocybin mushrooms grow in damp or forested climates.

There is evidence of ritual ingestion of psychoactive plants and fungi-based practices from nearly every place where humans have lived on this planet. Carved stone mushroom effigies have been found throughout Mexico and Central America dating back to 1000 BCE.[9] There are cave murals in Algeria, Spain, and Bulgaria depicting psilocybin mushrooms that date back to Neolithic times, according to ethnobotanical research.[10] The use of the fly agaric mushroom, *Amanita muscaria,* has been documented as part of the indigenous shamanic traditions of ancient Siberia, Lithuania, and northern Scandinavian Lapland.[11] Africa has many indigenous psychoactive plant medicines that have yet to be studied. The most well-known, iboga, has been used for initiations in central Africa for possibly thousands of years, including most recently the Bwiti society centered in Gabon.[12] While no one knows how long ayahuasca has been central to the indigenous and mestizo healing traditions of South America, archeological evidence for the use of DMT—a tryptamine molecule that occurs naturally in many plants and animals—goes back to 2000 BCE.[13] Mescaline-containing cactus has been used throughout South America and Mexico since pre-Columbian times,[14] while documented use of cannabis in India goes back to 2000 BCE.[15] In medieval Europe, henbane, belladonna, and other psychotropic plants were used for divination and astral travel by herbalists and medicine women.[16] While there is no formal research, anthropologists have documented the presence of stained glass windows in Renaissance period European churches depicting Jesus and saints with mushrooms thought to be in the psilocybe genus.[17] Including psychotropic plants in the exploration of consciousness is nothing new at all.

In addition, there are numerous modalities for altering consciousness that do not depend on plants. Lakota people have included sweat lodges as a cultural practice for thousands of years.[18] Sweat lodges are conducted by a group gathered in a dome-shaped hut made of canvas or cloth blankets and branches, built upon the earth. Stones are heated in an outdoor fire then brought in and placed in a central pit. The entrance of the dome is shut, and water is poured over the hot stones while the leader guides the group through songs and prayers. The flap is opened occasionally for fresh air, and water is passed around to drink. The physical intensity of the heat, the disorientation of the darkness, and the potency of the prayers initiate a state of internal softening and emotional surrender, shifting the participants beyond habitual states of functioning.

Music has long been used to access expanded states. Flutes have been found in Europe dated over 30,000 years old, while the practice of drumming has a long history throughout the world.[19] African drumming and dance rituals are an ancient form of group journeying. A large group of people dances to rhythms played by several drummers. As the rhythms slowly accelerate, and after a period of dancing, people begin to enter trance states. In brain imaging studies on long-term meditators, researchers have noted characteristics of altered states of consciousness, including changes in perception of space and time, and spontaneous visions of light.[20] These various techniques, when practiced intentionally and for an extended period of time, shift brain activity—some of them releasing specific chemicals into the brain and body—and temporarily change the activity of the nervous system. All of this combined directly affects the internal and external experience, as well as the perception of the practitioner. It is in these physiological states that consciousness expands, awareness increases, and healing can occur spontaneously or with guidance.

Accessing expanded states of consciousness requires these specific techniques, tools, or practices to journey beyond an ordinary state of being. These states and the knowledge they make available are used by indigenous communities to connect with the spiritual realm and their ancestors, manage their relationships with one another and their environment, and make important decisions that affect the long-term health and happiness of the group. They are used for divinatory purposes, for rites of passage rituals, to find water, and to decide where to migrate. Through the power of expanded states of consciousness, native peoples strengthen their connection with the local plants and animals they need for survival. Most relevant to our purposes for the subject of this book is how expanded states support healing and growth for an individual or an entire community.

Indigenous cultures that include these states of consciousness tend toward animistic earth-based spiritual practices that honor the local environment and elements. This earth-based "shamanism" predates organized religion, making it the earliest expression of spirituality.[21]

Tragically, many indigenous peoples around the world who carried the knowledge of these original, earth-based rituals and traditions have been killed or colonized over the last five centuries. Although colonization and the domination wrought by expanding kingdoms and empires have existed for thousands of years, the last five hundred years have seen the most brutal destruction of native ways of life in all parts of the world. This colonization has been fueled by the agglomeration of land ownership by European kingdoms, expanding their reach across the world by extracting resources in the form of objects, precious metals, rubber, and worst of all—human beings as slaves. At the same time, Christian missionaries arrived in the newly colonized lands. Under the guise of education and healthcare, they disrupted indigenous traditions and aggressively imposed their belief system on native people. This disregard for indigenous traditions and blatant devastation of earth-based ways of life continue to this day through the unbridled growth of capitalism and its resulting destruction of forests, rivers, and mountains where many indigenous peoples live. Thus, many people have been severed from their original ways of tending their connection with one another, their community, and the living earth.

Although original earth-based practices have been mostly abandoned by industrialized culture, as human beings we all share indigenous roots that tug at us from within. Through our relationships with the people around us, our environment, and the divine, we inevitably encounter suffering and discord. Every problem in life seems to challenge us to find a solution. We naturally seek healing, knowing on some level that our challenges hold potential for us to learn from, yet we wonder how we can see the big picture of our life from a more compassionate perspective. To put it in psychological language, we strive for mental and emotional well-being. We seek the resolution of the traumas we have endured in our life along with old family wounds and the inheritance of transgenerational trauma due to war, slavery, genocide, famine, and so on.[22] Ironically, many of the descendants of the European colonizers are now hungry to reconnect with indigenous ways of life in their desperate search for healing and purpose.

In reality, the evolution of human civilization has been shaped by insights drawn from expanded states of consciousness through the mystical states of prophets, art, and spiritual practices—though the history of these practices in many parts of the world has been eradicated, their methods forgotten. Rather than solely borrowing from or copying other cultures, we can be inspired by still-living traditions to reach back into each of our own ancestral lineages and see what we can find.

Beginning with the advent of Western psychology and psychiatry in the nineteenth century, psychologists and other scientists reinitiated the exploration of expanded states of consciousness. William James, considered the father of American psychology, was known to experiment with various mind-expanding substances, including the study of "mystical states," among his many interests.[23] In the 1960s, the psychologist Abraham Maslow introduced the term "peak experience," which took away the religious overtones and suggested that anyone could access these transcendent, egoless, awe-inducing states.[24] In the late 1960s, Maslow, along with Stanislav Grof and Anthony Sutich, coined the term "Transpersonal Psychology," which proposed a discipline that would include such states and experiences existing beyond the quantifiable reality of our biology and biography.[25] Transpersonal psychology draws from dreamwork, cross-cultural myths and archetypes, Eastern wisdom practices, and indigenous healing traditions.

These days, it is easy to find countless books, websites, and courses on yoga, meditation, hypnotherapy, shamanic practices, or guided imagery. Stress and tension have been discovered at the core of many illnesses, and people are more and more willing to explore new and ancient modes of healing, seeking relief from uncomfortable symptoms. Practices that support relaxation and healing are sought after to the extent that they now have a capitalist sector of their own: the wellness industry.

Perhaps due to this willingness, beginning in the early 1990s, contemporary psychology and psychiatry experienced a widespread resurgence of interest into the healing potential of expanded states accessed by psychedelic medicines after decades of prohibition following the 1960s.

Medical research has resumed after a long hiatus, with many major universities exploring the usefulness of psilocybin mushrooms, MDMA, ketamine, and other compounds for the treatment of anxiety, depression, addiction, and Post-Traumatic Stress Disorder, as well as exploring how these medicines can support people with social anxiety.[26] There has also been research with healthy volunteers, meditators, and clergy, investigating how mystical states induced by psilocybin improve one's quality of relationships, creativity, and spiritual practice.[27] It is clear that interest has boomed with the Multidisciplinary Association for Psychedelic Studies (MAPS) drawing over 3,000 people to San Francisco for its annual conference in 2017. Other organizations interested in the clinical benefits of psychedelic substances and medical legalization are also conducting research while more and more articles, studies, and books are reporting the beneficial potential of psychedelic compounds and entheogenic plant medicines for healing.[28]

So, how do these modalities shift consciousness and activate healing? As I described above, the shifts begin by bringing the body out of its normal homeostasis. Psychedelics and entheogenic plant medicines can initiate these shifts quickly and directly. MDMA increases the activity of serotonin, dopamine, and norepinephrine in the brain and has been shown to decrease activity in the amygdala, the region of the brain associated with fear and the physiological processing of traumatic memories.[29] Psychoactive mushrooms contain psilocybin, which converts to psilocin in the body and binds to serotonin receptors, which in turn increases dopamine levels.[30] Ayahuasca contains DMT, which is molecularly similar to psilocin, and also attaches to serotonin and dopamine receptors in the brain. Brain imaging has shown that both psilocin and DMT facilitate communication between regions of the brain that do not normally communicate, as well as dampen activity in the default mode network region of the brain.[31] This is a region of the brain that is thought to maintain a sense of separate self, and a region that, when overly active, is associated with depression, ruminations, and obsessive-compulsive thought patterns. When activity in the default mode network is reduced, many people report a decreased sense of separate self-identity and an increased feeling of oneness with their surroundings. They report novel insights, an ability to perceive previously unseen connections, and increased access to raw emotional states and memories without the normal tendency to analyze them.

Techniques that do not include psychotropic medicines work similarly. Meditation practices typically include slowing the breath, which slows the heart rate and affects brain activity and biochemistry in the body. Brain imaging on experienced practitioners engaged in meditation has also shown decreased default mode network activity, along with increased growth in the hippocampus, the learning and memory center of the brain, as well as decreased brain cell volume in the amygdala, the part of the brain connected with the fight, flight, or freeze fear response.[32] Drumming has been studied and shown to change brain chemistry as adrenaline is released, blood glucose levels are lowered, and adrenochrome is released. Endorphins are released, which increase alpha waves in the brain and induce synchronous brain activity, with brain waves entering a synchronized rhythm.[33] This can initiate an entirely different state of consciousness replete with visionary experiences. Vision quests with minimal food or water, sweat lodges that increase the body's internal temperature, dancing, and sports all have their unique effects on the body and brain. Many athletes report flow states and peak experiences while immersed in their sport.[34]

Although it is often through physical practices that expanded states of consciousness are accessed, those entering find themselves able to transcend the normal restrictions of the body and the habitual patterns of the ego. Though it is difficult to measure scientifically, many people report a sense of merging with something larger than themselves and encountering aspects of themselves beyond their normal identity.[35] Many report expanding beyond their human conditioning and even beyond their current human incarnation. From a psychological perspective, we might say these techniques open the doorway between the conscious and unconscious dimensions of the psyche. Many earth-based cultures equate the expansion of consciousness with the lifting of the veil between the human and spirit realms. They say that by reconnecting with the eternal, formless dimension of our identity, we are able to heal and discern the original purpose and wisdom of our soul.

In my years of supporting clients who explore these expanded states, as well as through my personal experience, I have studied how expanded states of consciousness initiate healing from a psychological perspective. As bodily tensions and their corresponding psychological defenses begin to relax, the first thing that often happens, especially if we are new to this realm of experience, is that we may feel fear or even terror. There is a sensation of contraction and a primal concern for our safety. Our layers of meticulously crafted defense strategies that have maintained our physical and psychological survival (i.e., our ego structure) begin to soften. These self-protective layers and the corresponding fear are extremely intelligent. They serve an invaluable purpose of managing and organizing the inflow of external information and responding in ways that allow for our greatest safety and well-being. These strategies have developed in response to the specific physical and social circumstances of our childhood and adult environment.

Expanded states amplify deeply held patterns and tensions, their effects akin to bringing a magnifying glass to one's inner world. Along these lines, Stanislav Grof has referred to psychedelics as amplifiers of the psyche.[36] Due to this amplification effect, a journeyer is brought into intimate contact with the total reality of the moment. As the body relaxes, so do the mind and discursive thoughts. Normally filtered sensory gates open, and more information begins to enter the perceptual field of awareness. When these filters dissolve, we are able to understand patterns and see connections that were previously unseen. What is normally unconscious begins to flow into the conscious mind.

Repressed emotions or long-forgotten memories can surface. Grief and sadness or overwhelming love and compassion can arise, sometimes right after one another. Profound insights, visions, and intense somatic expressions can come through. During this inner unfolding, we are able to perceive the symbols, images, visions, and archetypes that live in our unconscious. One fascinating characteristic of this process is that different layers of insight can happen simultaneously. As the body becomes sharply aware of the state of its tissues, muscles, joints, bones, and fluids, and calcified energy begins to melt, we begin to perceive the connections between the visceral layers and the more complex psychological dimensions of our consciousness.

We can perceive how our protective strategies have resulted from our belief systems and our buried wounds. We can make contact with our shame. We can experience wounds in their purity, understanding their causes, and seeing them for what they truly are. They may derive from feeling unseen, unloved, or disconnected from others. Looking at our original wounding from an adult perspective allows us to empathize with what our younger self endured and the complex strategies that we constructed to survive. The direct experiences of previously unconscious memories, thoughts, tensions, and emotions enter into our conscious mind allowing us the opportunity to process and integrate them into the wholeness of our psyche and life.

In this relaxed state, the body and mind are free to follow their deepest impulse: to seek wholeness and flow. The resolution of inner conflicts is possible through accessing a more resourced state than the one in which a conflict or pattern of tension was created. I find that when someone enters an expanded state of consciousness—whether accessed via an entheogenic plant medicine, a drumming journey, a meditation retreat, or any other modality— what is most imbalanced in the overall person is revealed. The psyche, like all things natural and wild, strives for balance, and when attended to and listened to, will intelligently communicate and move toward what it needs to reestablish the highest level of health possible.

✳ ✳ ✳

In the last thirty years, psychology has given due attention to the topic of trauma. Physical, emotional, and sexual abuse have become central topics addressed in the privacy of the psychotherapy office as well as on the public stage. Numerous books, testimonies, and interviews have recounted the terrible tragedies children, men, and women have endured due to rape, war violence, deaths of loved ones, and domestic violence. Accidents and even medical procedures and surgeries can leave a traumatic imprint. Following these events, survivors may be left with symptoms of anxiety, nightmares, a high startle response, eating disorders, or substance abuse habits and addictions. The symptoms fall under the name Post-Traumatic Stress Disorder or PTSD. Many techniques and approaches attempt to address these life-crippling PTSD symptoms, sometimes successfully and sometimes not. In the last twenty-five years, research has demonstrated that MDMA can be useful in the treatment of PTSD; and the prospect of legal status for the administration of this medicine, outside of a research context and under proper supervision is, more than ever, a real possibility.[37]

It should be noted that people with unresolved trauma should seek a well-trained practitioner for intentional exploration of consciousness with psychedelics or other powerful modalities: the connection with a trained guide can help mitigate the potential overwhelm that people with unresolved trauma are at higher risk of encountering.

People who have had psychotic episodes or have a history of psychosis or bipolar disorder should proceed with extreme caution when employing any technique that expands consciousness, especially when ingesting a psychotropic compound that affects brain chemistry. These experiences could lead to challenging states and should be avoided. If a person is determined to pursue this path of exploration, they should do so under the supervision of a medical professional. Techniques such as art, earth-based ritual, sound healing, or meditation would be more appropriate access routes to non-ordinary states of consciousness than any method involving entheogenic medicines.

Whether we are able to maintain a fairly stable life or whether our suffering is such that it warrants a specific diagnosis, everyone has the capacity for emotional healing and psychological growth with the right support and conditions.

If it is not obvious yet how expanded states of consciousness are such an effective and potent healing modality, let me explain a little more. These states expand our awareness of ourselves on a personal level, allowing us to engage in a deeper relationship with our history and the many layers of our lives. This exploration can help us to psychologically as well as physiologically metabolize our traumas, childhood wounds, addictive patterns, relational issues, health imbalances, and psychological blockages. As an adult we can re-parent our inner child who did not receive the much-needed nourishment it sought. But before we can do that, we need to become aware of the wounds and belief systems that resulted from them. If, for example, we are compulsively active, then it is likely that in an expanded state, we may gain insight into the reasons behind our hyperactivity. We have the opportunity to see our patterns, our avoidance behaviors, and our strategies for survival. By taking the time to look at ourselves in this deeper way, we can more clearly perceive what we are doing and why. Compassion can then naturally arise. Thus, our simple awareness, directed by our intention, begins the process of liberation. The truth can set us free.

However, most of us have such a backlog of unprocessed unconscious material that when the gates are opened, a flood of content rushes through—memories, sensory impressions, thoughts, and emotions. Some of it is repressed energy that simply needs to be released and flushed out of our nervous system. When we are in a place of stagnant tension, with little movement, there is almost always agitation in the center. One of the most common concerns I hear from a new client is, "I feel stuck." It is this absence of fluid movement that they are feeling.

Natural law is one of constant change. Nothing stays static in the natural world. Continual movement and cycles of change lie at the heart of all life. Experiencing the movement of energy in our body restores our health, melting away blockages that have reduced our vitality, and dramatically catalyzing the healing process. As this backlog is processed, it allows for more space and movement in our physical, emotional, and psychic layers.

However, much of the stuck energy or tension that gets flushed out needs to be psychologically processed by the ego once it returns to its normal state, which can be challenging. It is crucial to have support in this process and to take time and care with the integration phase.

Perhaps the greatest gift expanded states of consciousness offer is the opportunity to reconnect with the aspect of our self that is always already whole. Beyond the wounds and belief systems exists an original, essential being. This is the self that remains unscathed, wise, and healthy despite all we have endured. It is the innocent self that entered childhood, expecting the environment to be safe and loving and caretakers to be respectful and kind. Through our healing process, expanded states can teach us to have compassion and love for the child who endured and to invite our healthy, original self out to trust in life again.

It is true that personal exploration can be quite rewarding through a commitment to regular psychotherapy. However, expanded states of consciousness tend to open people up to a level of deeply visceral and direct experience that is difficult, if not impossible, to reach through regular therapy. It is my experience that the healing accessed in expanded states goes swiftly to the core of the issue needing attention, making it an extremely effective modality. It is especially useful for addressing preverbal trauma, which talk therapy can barely access. However, it also means that this therapeutic approach calls for an extra level of caution and attention with aftercare and integration. The content of our experience in expanded states is almost always pointing us toward more balance. Though we do not always get what we ask for, we always get what we need.

Some people might argue that healing through expanded states of consciousness and, in particular, the use of entheogenic plant medicines is a shortcut; that it truncates the slow, intricate unfolding of a psychological narrative that long-term psychotherapy offers. I agree that the daunting task of meticulously sorting through our childhood suffering, of figuring out who we are and why we are here, makes it tempting to find a quicker way to attain inner peace. After all, who would want to revisit the fear of their inner child in the grasp of a violent mother or reexperience the feelings of disgust at having had their body touched in abusive ways? Who wants to remember the loss and grief of their dream family being split apart after a bitter divorce? It is understandable why no one would want to return to their most painful memories, and it is quite all right for someone to respect their limits for as long as they feel they must.

Yet, paradoxically, it is my experience that by revisiting these painful memories with love and compassion, liberation from their haunting is possible. An intentionally guided journey into an expanded state of consciousness is the fiercest, most honest way to explore the roots of suffering that I have thus far found. It brings us face-to-face with our psychological wounds and the way they appear in our body as tension, numbness, and dissociation. An inner journey encompasses the multilayered experience of our human life. We can reach the undiscovered corners of our psyche in a way that remains unmatched by other therapeutic modalities. Perhaps it is a shortcut, but if we are suffering so much that it prevents us from having a healthy, happy life, what is wrong with a quicker and more efficient way to heal?

Another argument against entheogen-assisted journeywork relates to its spiritual component and is called spiritual bypassing.[38] A feeling of oneness with the universe may temporarily take precedence over negative or uncomfortable emotions, but once the feeling recedes, the person returns to their previous state. To avoid feeling our discomfort, ennui, or despair, we may try to "bypass" it with more heightened states. However, I would argue that it is advantageous to include a spiritual dimension to our healing. The long-held position that we are only a collection of confused emotional processes is neither helpful nor accurate.

Connecting with a spiritual dimension of a transpersonal nature does not necessarily signify a pattern of refusing to face our psychological reality. It can actually offer a glimpse of hope to people in a state of despair as they prepare themselves to process challenging memories or experiences. Of course, it is crucial to return to the personal in a healthy and integrated manner after connecting with the resource of the spiritual or transpersonal.

I want to emphasize the fact that one is not absolutely required to ingest a psychotropic substance in order to reach an expanded state of consciousness; there is a diverse array of techniques that can access subterranean layers of the psyche, release long-held physical tensions, and open someone to a profound spiritual experience. That said, within the variety of techniques that function to expand consciousness, the depth that is accessed directly corresponds to the chosen technique.

For a person who is just beginning to explore in this way, a seminar in intuitive painting or a one-day meditation retreat might be an appropriate introduction to their inner world. Other people who may be more familiar and at ease with experiences of inner exploration might benefit from a daylong sweat lodge[39] or a weeklong dance retreat.[40] For those who are prepared to dive into the vast regions of their unconscious (assuming they have access to adequate guidance and support), an inner journey supported by a psychotropic plant medicine can guide them into deeper layers of their unconscious and possibly to a place of transformation.

As we heal our immediate circumstances and create more ease in our lives, we directly influence future generations. Our equilibrium and health will greatly affect our children and grandchildren. Paying it forward is obvious, but paying it backward is more difficult to understand. However, in expanded states of consciousness, many people have the experience of traveling back to their ancestors or dead relatives to offer healing. These experiences can leave us questioning the linearity of time. On the most basic level, the willingness to explore the inner worlds contained in our consciousness can bring us healing. It is not so much about what we will see or whether we will completely resolve our issues; it is that we are willing to look inside ourselves and reestablish contact with the abundant dimensions we contain. The courage to go in and look deeper into ourselves is our liberation. It is in the journey that we find redemption, not in the destination. The courage we gather to face the fear of our vastness is what sets us free. We are never guaranteed that we are going to "get somewhere," but we make the attempt to show up for ourselves, and this is often what heals us.

My teacher Pablo used to say there are two essential fears in life: fear of madness and fear of death. These are the two primary fears that we face when we turn toward the inner layers of our psyche, especially in explorations that include ingesting psychedelic substances. We are all afraid that we will lose control and go crazy or enter some vast unknown space and simply cease to exist. He used to say that the two virtues to hold when entering our infinite inner world are faith and surrender. If we want to know the courage that is contained within our being, we are going to have to engage with the fear that we encounter as we approach the unknown. Even if we are fortunate enough to contact an inner space of peace, the habitual ego structure with its strategies of control and protective mechanisms reconstructs itself, even after experiences of extraordinary opening. I believe there is no simple solution besides going inward and facing this fear over and over. It is through cultivating the courage to meet our self that we are liberated.

Expanded states of consciousness teach us about surrender—for regardless of the modality chosen, our normal defenses, self-protection, and control mechanisms are encouraged to relax. If the technique used includes the ingestion of sacred medicines, it will inevitably bring us to a surrendered state. It is difficult to resist their effect on our physiology. We can fight and resist the experience or we can surrender to it. Surrender includes not lying about passively giving in or giving up. Surrender is a combination of active receptivity toward and curiosity about whatever shows up. Acceptance does not mean that we have to like what appears, but it means that we stay present with it anyway.

There are infinite layers of surrender. Surrendering to life means accepting life no matter what it brings—joy, sadness, ecstasy, or pain. Pain becomes suffering when there is no meaning to it. When we find the meaning and understanding of why we are in pain, it ceases to be suffering. When a mother gives birth, there is immense pain, but she knows why she is doing it, so it is not meaningless suffering. There is a purpose, which changes her relationship to it. Pain is, by definition, unpleasant. It is not pleasurable. We live in a culture where we are told we are supposed to be joyful and comfortable all the time, but that is not the reality of life. Surrender means that regardless of the quality of our experience, we engage with it. We let go of expectation and open ourselves to the present moment, whatever it holds. We walk into the unknown without attachment to the outcome.

Each time we surrender, we see that we receive exactly what we need. We begin to understand how our personal predicaments may be our intelligent cocreation. We perceive how our unconscious seeks healing and wholeness by creating situations that push us to grow. We begin to see the ultimate perfection of our life's path and that there is a mysterious plan at work. We might not believe that there is a divine entity guiding us, but we may come to realize that there seems to be an intelligence and benevolence to the unfolding of our life. Through practicing surrender, we begin to develop faith in the moment and trust in the unknown.

Some people are born with faith or are raised to have faith. If this is the case, we can pray to our specific god or to whatever it is that we believe in. Faith can be an active surrender to a greater spiritual dimension, or it can be a deep knowing that our intention will unfold into our healing. Faith can simply be a belief in the goodness or intelligence of life. If a client comes to a guide seeking healing through expanded states of consciousness, they may or may not have faith in the process. Part of the guide's job is to bring the faith by remembering his or her own certainty in the healing potential of the work. Through communicating this sense of faith verbally and energetically, they hold the light that the client might not yet be able to see. It helps to cultivate a basic level of faith before entering a process that can bring up heavy psychological material. A practice of stillness or prayer and being able to ask for support are central to the healing process.

Fortunately, faith is where we naturally arrive after surrendering again and again. When we go through a difficult experience and survive it, we begin to learn that there is something within us that can endure even the most challenging situations. Even if our life feels stuck, we now know that there is still movement and growth, learning and understanding. Even if we are still confused, we are certain that we are in the process of evolution. Something inside us knows it and feels it. It might take three months or three years of hard work, but things eventually move with intention and attention. The more we practice surrender and cultivate faith along our healing path, the more we cultivate it in our life.

Exploring the unknown is not always easy or blissful. Shamanic initiations and rite of passage rituals that bring initiates into expanded states of consciousness are not devised to be easy. Transforming a person into a warrior takes a hero's journey, including arduous preparation, the ordeal of facing fear and absolute darkness, the dissolution of reality, the mysterious and elusive return, the slow reintegration, and the reawakening to a newly transformed existence.

I tell people who come to work with me, "This work is not about being happy, it is about being whole; it can be difficult and it can be intense, but ultimately, it is fulfilling."

Traditionally, techniques for accessing expanded states of consciousness are practiced or facilitated by trained leaders in their communities. Indigenous cultures know the magnitude of what can be accessed in these states and they respect the role of the guide as the intermediary for the community. As these ritual practices are being revived in our culture, it is imperative to remember that the presence of a trained guide is crucial to the safe and effective exploration of expanded states. With a skillful and well-supported approach to these transformative healing states of consciousness, we can safely tune into our unique purpose and path toward healing and wholeness. Expanded states of consciousness contain an impressive potential for healing, but it is the guide who encourages us, keeps us on the path, and welcomes us home.

2

MIDWIFING THE SOUL

The Role of the Guide

Whoever travels without a guide needs two hundred years for a two-day journey.

RUMI[1]

Macario walks in front of me, Feliciano behind. They hold their machetes, their green and blue woven bags strapped behind their backs. They wear red plastic flip-flops. We are surrounded by a thick jungle buzzing with the sound of insects. The heavy moisture in the air is stifling, smelling of wet earth and leaves. We walk in silence.

I am in a remote region of the Amazon, outside a small gathering of huts. It is a two-day ride in a dugout canoe to the closest town. Every year or so, I travel here for the sheer joy of being among my friends, the Mosetén of the Bolivian jungle. We pick açaí nuts, gather palms for the chicken coops, string seeds for our necklaces, and cook fish caught by bow and arrow. When we go walking in the jungle, Macario carves the path with his machete while watching for danger, animal tracks, ant trails, or snakes in the trees. Feliciano keeps "an eye on his back," as he says.

Macario stops suddenly and looks at the ground, listening. I stop behind him. He gestures to the left and says, "A hundred wild pigs, one minute away." How does he know? He explains: "No birds are singing that way. The ground is trampled; you see the way the leaves are bent. Here are the tracks." He points to the messy ground though I see nothing. He knows where the wild pigs have been and where they are going. Wild pigs are big, and if a hundred of them stampede toward you, you are in serious trouble. I am grateful to have Macario guiding my way through the unpredictable paths of the jungle.

* * *

A guide is someone who walks ahead and knows the territory, aware of the potential perils of the terrain. Like the jungle, our inner self is an environment full of beautiful complexity. In many cultures, rituals that invoke expanded states of consciousness for transformation and healing are guided. An appropriate guide is trained in specific techniques that aid the experience of inner exploration. If we visit an African community to participate in a multiday trance dance, there is someone holding the rhythm and drumming us into the trance. If we go on a vision quest, a guide will help us prepare for the experience with prayers, fasting, and a sweat lodge. The guide will then stand over the sacred fire throughout the quest and signal the time to return when the period of solitude is complete. The guide will then help us break our fast with water and ceremonial foods and assist us in interpreting the experience we had.

A guide who accompanies people into expanded states of consciousness has been trained from early youth and has spent many years in apprenticeship under a teacher's supervision. Traditionally, only after someone has cultivated the capacity to navigate these states and demonstrated a commitment to the process are they allowed to guide others through complex healing rituals. Sometimes this guide is called a *shaman*. The word originates in Siberia and means "spiritual healer."[2] The term connotes a medicine person of power, community leadership, and mystery. Shamans traditionally use expanded states of consciousness to connect with other entities and realms of reality. In this way, they channel healing and bring back insights and guidance for individuals or the community at large. Today, the word "shaman" has been appropriated by the neo-shamanic movement and carries with it the burden of colonialism.

The neo-shamanic movement claims an approach inspired by ancient earth-based wisdom, while being led by non-native people with no ongoing reciprocal relationship with an actual indigenous lineage. This shows up as sweat lodges, ayahuasca circles, mushroom ceremonies, and Native American rituals of various kinds being led by people with limited knowledge or experience. For those who have an actual relationship with a living tradition, it is learned early on that the way to carry the gifts we have been given is through reciprocity and with acknowledgment. It is indispensable to honor and express deep gratitude to the lineages that share their practices. As practitioners, we thank the people from whom we each have learned, tracing back through our lineage of teachers as far as we can, as well as the lands that have inspired them. It is important to cultivate a link to the original place of the tradition we choose to follow by giving back to the people of that region in the form of supporting healthcare, land protection, children's education, or contributing to sustainable projects organized by local people. Otherwise, we are extracting from a tradition for personal gain without being invited in or offering anything back, which becomes a form of cultural misappropriation.

I make it a priority to support children's education, provide medical care funding, and buy the local art and crafts of the people I visit or study with. I make sure to support the local economy when I bring groups to Huautla de Jiménez by hiring drivers, cooks, and guides who in turn can support their daily life with dignity and resources.

Unfortunately, there are many people in the neo-shamanism subculture who are ignorant of the cultural origin of shamanism and call themselves "shamans." It is challenging to call oneself a shaman in any specific tradition, if one has not been raised in that tradition. There is a transmission that takes place as a young person grows up in a culture, immersed in their unique cosmology, rituals, and celebrations. One can be spiritually adopted, as has been my case, but I would never be so arrogant as to say that I am a full-fledged shaman or curandera of the Mazatec tradition. Even after twenty years immersed in the tradition, spending time with the people and the land, the dialect is still foreign to me; there are customs that I do not understand, and many of the ways that people relate remain a mystery to me.

Other words for someone who is trained in journeywork are guide, healer, doctor, priest, or teacher. Each culture has a title for someone who does this work, which may include physical healing and doctoring assisted by plants, minerals, animal or spirit guides; music, spiritual teaching, or prayer; and working with the ancestors, elements, or the earth.

In the modern industrialized world, the psychotherapist or counselor holds the role most similar to a shaman or curandera. It is the therapist's job to facilitate and support their client's inner transformation. The therapist integrates psychological understanding with personal growth. Most often, when a client comes to see me, they complain of pain, confusion, unresolved trauma, or emotional dullness, and they seek healing and support.

My healing practice combines the role of a counselor with the approach of a curandera. My training in somatic-based psychology helps me understand the ways our physical body holds emotions, how it expresses symptoms of tension, and how our physical experience can be a pathway to healing. The field of psychology contains vocabulary, theoretical maps, and methods that significantly enhance my understanding of what clients share with me.

Similar to transpersonal psychotherapy, my work also includes the exploration of realms of the psyche beyond ordinary consensus reality. When I guide a client into an expanded state, my psychological knowledge helps me connect the impetus behind an inner journey with its contents, and to skillfully support clients as they create new habits during the integration process.

Furthermore, I also take into account the indigenous worldview founded on animistic beliefs: that the natural world is alive and in constant communication with us. This includes the presence of the elements, cardinal points, and the philosophy of interdependence—the understanding that we are all connected through the web of life. We can take care of others by taking care of ourselves, and we can take care of ourselves by taking care of others. My work with clients emphasizes balance. I encourage my clients to translate the teachings from their experiences in expanded consciousness into actions that will improve their quality of life.

I work as a counselor, so in this book I often refer to my clients. In a shamanic healing ceremony, the person being healed is called a participant or a journeyer; hence, I also refer to them as journeyers. I use the term "guide" to indicate the role of a counselor or therapist who is also trained to support someone before, throughout, and after an experience in an expanded state of consciousness. For an actual experience, I will use the terms "journey" and occasionally "ritual."

Often used in counseling and healing work, the term "container" is the setting in which a healing journey or ritual takes place. It refers to the space where healing happens, and it includes both the physical space and the interpersonal space: the relationship between client and therapist or guide. In a safe and appealing setting, with someone well trained guiding the process, the journeyer can relax.

Due to the illegal status of most consciousness-expanding substances, people often end up experimenting on their own. The absence of a guide with no established container can lead to disorientation and fear. Many people get high together and go to a concert or to the beach, where, out of ignorance, they may be putting themselves in situations of physical or psychological danger. Many people have been startled by an unguided journey that took them into strange and frightening realms they were not able to manage alone. Perhaps they were not adequately prepared, or were in an unsupportive setting, or took an inappropriate dose for their body weight or level of experience. Perhaps they went into a vision quest by themselves and became lost or frightened or went into a sweat lodge that was not guided correctly and got heatstroke.

A guide's job is to keep a journeyer safe and protected as they enter an expanded state, trusting that in a secure and contained environment, a person's psyche will only go as far as it can manage. It is also the job of a guide to discern what the appropriate level of exploration is for an individual journeyer. If substantial fear is present, it is best to approach expanded states of consciousness gradually in order to build trust and comfort. At first, the guide might introduce the journeyer to gentle introspection through mindfulness, journaling, and self-reflection.

If someone intends to explore an expanded state of consciousness and does not have a guide, at the minimum they should have a sober friend at hand and should thoroughly educate themselves of the potential risks and outcomes of the choices they are making. This is relevant not only when ingesting a psychedelic substance, but with any practice that can bring one into an expanded state of consciousness. With a well-trained guide, a journeyer has a safe environment in which to release their strategies of self-protection and surrender to deeper transformation. It is vital that a journeyer choose the right guide. This is an important decision and should be based on a sense of the guide as a person, along with their training and experience. In the process of choosing, it is helpful to talk with others who have worked with the guide.

If a guide intends to include these timeless healing modalities in their work, they should have extensive personal experience and should have completed a thorough training, as well as have an ongoing relationship with their teacher or supervising practitioner. Thorough training would include a solid understanding of human psychology, training in body awareness, and some understanding of spirituality. This basic grounding and knowledge help the guide track the many dimensions that can open in an expanded state and best support the interpretation and integration of the material that emerges.

When I began this work, I quickly realized that to become a well-rounded and creative guide, it was essential that I acquire an understanding of various modalities. I needed direct experience with more techniques and approaches. I attended 5Rhythms dance retreats with Gabrielle Roth[3] and later studied flamenco with Rosa Montoya. I sat in numerous sweat lodges with Richard Deertrack and Marilyn Youngbird. I painted for hours with French–American art teacher Michele Cassou. I studied Sensory Awareness with Charlotte Selver and practiced breathwork with Stanislav Grof and Ilse Middendorf.[4] I sat in meditation retreats with Jack Kornfield and went to teachings by Tibetan lamas. I studied plant lore and flower essence making. I took singing lessons and attended yoga classes of many styles.

Some of these approaches touched me profoundly and remain part of my daily life. Some were simply enriching experiences. My earnest curiosity immersed me in an array of possibilities and taught me various ways to explore the inner landscape of the self. When I suggest that one of my clients go dancing or on a meditation retreat, I make that suggestion from an embodied sense of how that particular practice will support their growth.

In this way, a guide makes a commitment to be a renaissance person: to create, to be in their body, to stay in process with their emotional material, to nurture their spiritual life, and to cultivate community. It is not about being perfect and knowing everything. It is about having a wide range of experience and continuing to expand one's toolkit.

While I have acquired many skills over the years, I realize there are topics in which I am not knowledgeable. I do not keep up with the variety of medications and their possible interactions with plant medicines. If someone wants to travel with me to Mexico and is on any kind of medication, I have them consult with a psychiatrist or MD. Although I have studied various forms of movement, I have not deeply explored specific practices such as Continuum or Authentic Movement. I happily refer clients to another teacher or to a nutritionist, herbalist, acupuncturist, or meditation teacher if health issues arise or I feel that an adjunct practice would benefit a client at any point during our work together. I feel that as practitioners, it is vitally important to recognize the areas that we are not expert in and have the humility and sense to refer onwards appropriately.

My teacher Julieta's role as a healer and ceremony leader did not keep her away from everyday activities. She grew her own coffee plants, kept bees, and collected her own honey. She carried wood down from the mountain until the age of seventy. She employed many of the women who lived in the countryside by providing them with cloth and yarn. They would return with embroidered dresses and shirts that she would buy back from them and sell to visiting tourists. She would regularly collaborate with the community to create spiritual celebrations, and every day she would take time for prayer in solitude.

A guide makes a commitment to be as balanced a person as possible and to continue recalibrating their natural rhythms. Overworking, under-exercising, or squeezing in spiritual practice as an afterthought is not reflective of a balanced life. A guide should have a normal life with relationships, friends, embodiment practices, a relationship with nature, and ways of having fun. It is a daily practice to manage the equilibrium of work and health with self-care. In a world where time is consumed by constant activity, maintaining life balance takes intention and determination.

Acting as a guide or ritual facilitator also carries responsibilities and risks. Stepping into the role of guide means curating an environment for a client or participant's consciousness to expand within. That space ought to be safe, supportive, and skillfully held. This safety is maintained by the quality of boundaries held by the guide. Because a guide or ritual facilitator is taking participants into expanded states of consciousness where normal ego defenses relax, it is crucial to develop and uphold a high ethical standard. Clients and participants may look up to a facilitator for their role of leadership. They may access childhood material and feel vulnerable, sometimes projecting their own parental dynamics onto the guide in an unconscious attempt to resolve old wounding.

For these reasons, all counselors, and especially those offering psychotherapeutic work that includes guiding clients into expanded states of consciousness, should be in supervision or have an ongoing relationship with a mentor. Moments of error and misjudgment do occur, and mentorship offers a place for any practitioner to explore unresolved personal material.

Over the years I have seen many spiritual communities struggle or even dissolve when a leader breached boundaries. These transgressions often relate to money or power. Some leaders demand immense sums of money with no transparency concerning its use. Sometimes participants are told to abandon their normal lives in order to devote themselves to their spiritual teacher and are then treated as servants. Other leaders abuse their position of power by seducing clients or students into entering sexual relationships with them under the guise of it being customary of the lineage.

A trustworthy guide or facilitator asks for a reasonable amount of money for their services and is transparent about their costs. A trustworthy facilitator holds clear sexual boundaries and does not engage in a relationship that benefits them at the expense of anyone else. If a specific tradition includes sexual or sensual practices between teacher and student, these should be clearly stated and all parties should be psychologically and emotionally healthy enough to understand the details of the exchange. To verify if a leader has healthy boundaries, a potential client, participant, or student should feel comfortable asking to speak with other clients, participants, or students. They should feel welcome to ask candid questions on the topics of boundaries and power dynamics before entering into a relationship with a new teacher or facilitator.

One young friend of mine went to a group retreat in Costa Rica some years ago. The woman leader was lovely, and the ritual was held skillfully with love. However, an assistant approached my friend as the ritual ended, walked her back to her sleeping area, and seduced her into having sex. She was confused afterward, wondering if this had been planned or intended by the leader. She felt unsafe and betrayed in a setting she had hoped to feel safe in. When she approached the leader, the leader minimized the incident. She was doubly hurt. It is never okay for sexual boundaries with a participant to be breached by a leader or assistant. When there are psychedelic substances involved, personal defenses drop, which nullifies one's capacity to give consent. Explicit boundaries and agreements should be discussed and defined beforehand and upheld by the facilitators.

Often, leaders follow a code of ethics appropriate to their own tradition or lineage. Sometimes, a code of ethics is tacit and unspoken and inherited from time spent with elders. Other times a code is explicitly written out and enforced by a council of elders.

The following excerpt from the Code of Ethics for Spiritual Guides, written by the Council on Spiritual Practices, proposes a clear and concise summary of the ethical commitments a guide or facilitator can adhere to for maximum benefit.[5]

Preamble

In any community, there are some who feel called to assist others along spiritual paths, and who are known as ministers, rabbis, pastors, curanderas, shamans, priests, or other titles. We call such people 'guides': those experienced in some practice, familiar with the terrain, and who act to facilitate the spiritual practices of others. A guide need not claim exclusive or definitive knowledge of the terrain.

Spiritual practices, and especially primary religious practices, carry risks. Therefore, when an individual chooses to practice with the assistance of a guide, both take on special responsibilities. The Council on Spiritual Practices proposes the following Code of Ethics for those who serve as spiritual guides.

*1. **Intention:** Spiritual guides are to practice and serve in ways that cultivate awareness, empathy, and wisdom.*

*2. **Serving Society:** Spiritual practices are to be designed and conducted in ways that respect the common good, with due regard for public safety, health, and order. Because the increased awareness gained from spiritual practices can catalyze desire for personal and social change, guides shall use special care to help direct the energies of those they serve, as well as their own, in responsible ways that reflect a loving regard for all life.*

*3. **Serving Individuals:** Spiritual guides shall respect and seek to preserve the autonomy and dignity of each person. Participation in any primary religious practice must be voluntary and based on prior disclosure and consent given individually by each participant while in an ordinary state of consciousness. Disclosure shall include, at a minimum, discussion of any elements of the practice that could reasonably be seen as presenting physical or psychological risks. In particular, participants must be warned that primary religious experience can be difficult and dramatically transformative.*

Guides shall make reasonable preparations to protect each participant's health and safety during spiritual practices and in the periods of vulnerability that may follow. Limits on the behaviors of participants and facilitators are to be made clear and agreed upon in advance of any session. Appropriate customs of confidentiality are to be established and honored.

*4. **Competence:** Spiritual guides shall assist with only those practices for which they are qualified by personal experience and by training or education.*

*5. **Integrity:** Spiritual guides shall strive to be aware of how their own belief systems, values, needs, and limitations affect their work. During primary religious practices, participants may be especially open to suggestion, manipulation, and exploitation; therefore, guides pledge to protect participants and not to allow anyone to use that vulnerability in ways that harm participants or others.*

6. Quiet Presence: To help safeguard against the harmful consequences of personal and organizational ambition, spiritual communities are usually better allowed to grow through attraction rather than active promotion.

7. Not for Profit: Spiritual practices are to be conducted in the spirit of service. Spiritual guides shall strive to accommodate participants without regard to their ability to pay or make donations.

8. Tolerance: Spiritual guides shall practice openness and respect toward people whose beliefs are in apparent contradiction to their own.

9. Peer Review: Each guide shall seek the counsel of other guides to help ensure the wholesomeness of his or her practices and shall offer counsel when there is need.

It is also of ethical importance that a guide is familiar with a journeyer's background and the resources they have in place before facilitating any work together. A guide's practical responsibilities in the preparation phase include completing a comprehensive intake with a client and gathering personal, medical, and family history. This preparatory intake can help the client and guide acknowledge challenging past events and how they may contribute to imbalance in the client's life. The guide needs to be aware of any events in the client's life that are traumatic enough to potentially take them into a place of fear or panic during a journey. If a client has been raped or abused, the guide should be aware of this. The guide should be aware that when someone enters an expanded state, previously repressed or unprocessed trauma could come to the surface. However, a guide should be aware that the client may claim in the intake process that they have no trauma, only to remember forgotten events during a journey.

In cases of trauma such as rape, physical, or sexual abuse, a guide should have psychotherapeutic training and ideally advanced experience in methods of addressing trauma. If they do not, they should refer the journeyer to a trained professional.

If a journey evokes intense emotions or memories, it is helpful to know that there are people, practices, or structures in place that will help soothe and support the journeyer afterward. It is better to work with resources that have already been cultivated—good friends, creative expression, or connection with nature—rather than create new ones out of thin air. After a journey, a person might be depleted and overwhelmed and unable to create new resources.

A thorough preparation also includes guiding a client physically, emotionally, and spiritually, toward their readiness for the inner exploration that a journey provides. Of course, the guide is also responsible for preparing the physical location for the ritual, providing the necessary objects and supplies, and describing the framework to the journeyer. However, in indigenous cultures, even though people might be led through specific preparations, the framework of a ceremony is not necessarily described to the participants. Often, people are only told what to bring and when to show up. Not knowing how long a ritual will last or what will take place increases the sense of being in "unknown territory" and invites deeper faith and surrender. In a society where these rituals are new and are not part of the dominant culture, participants may feel easily disoriented or scared. Informing them about the framework and logistics of a ritual creates a sense of basic safety.

The skill, expertise, and emotional state of a guide strongly affect a journeyer's experience. Throughout a journey, a guide should maintain an attitude of curiosity and care. A few basic qualities that a guide should bring to this work are respect, humility, and service. These qualities translate into how a guide establishes safety, holds clear boundaries, and supports a client's process in its entirety. While in an expanded state of consciousness, people have a heightened awareness of their physical and energetic surroundings. This means that a guide should be well rested, emotionally available, and gently attentive to their client's needs. The guide's internal posture should be open to the journeyer, with no expectation or investment in any particular outcome. Although the guide comes knowing what was shared before the journey, the unconscious is vast, and one cannot know in advance what will be revealed.

The most valuable support offered to a journeyer is one of available presence. The guide should validate the journeyer's personal agency. At the same time, it is their responsibility to track signs of fear, sensory overload, or isolation and to offer reassurance even when the journeyer does not ask for it. Sometimes merely making one's presence known as a solid support helps someone. At other times, in a vulnerable state, a journeyer may need the touch of a hand or a reassuring gesture, such as a mother might give. A guide should be ready to work with anything that comes up.

The way a guide holds the container varies, depending on the client. Does the client need nurture and ego strengthening or do they need to confront and soften their defense strategies? Some clients come in raw, with a less constructed ego. There is an innocence and childlike energy to them. If they are tender and defenseless, they need to be parented and comforted. This helps their ego development catch up with their chronological age. Once this happens, they can begin to nurture themselves. Other clients come in tough and defended with well-developed strategies of protection. Those with stronger strategies often have a more developed ego. It is more skillful to support these clients as they identify their coping mechanisms so as to find their way to the tenderness that lies within.

During a journey, a guide is entirely responsible for their client's physical safety, which includes hydration, warmth, and possible danger from intensified expressions of emotion. The guide's attention should be on their client, taking enough time at the end of a journey to provide support for whatever emotional material has surfaced. The return to a normal state of consciousness is supported by the guide offering food, water, and respectful, loving presence. The guide is responsible for deciding if and when a journeyer can go home, especially if that includes driving a car.

In the days and weeks after a journey, the guide then supports the integration process, meaning that they facilitate the time and place to meet to discuss and decipher the content of the journey with their client. The guide should then support the application of any insights or healing into the client's everyday life. In later chapters, we will explore the key points of integration in detail.

Above all, a guide must continually practice self-care. We cannot help others if we are in a depleted state. The most crucial ingredient in showing up as a sensitive and efficient guide is to be self-resourced and centered. This means a guide needs to be well rested and cultivate a foundation of inner stillness through whichever practices work best for them. Additionally, a guide should be continually cultivating wisdom, creativity, and love. I will describe the relationship these qualities have to this method of work in more detail in the next chapter. Suffice it to say that they are the foundation on which everything else rests.

Having worked in this field for many years, I am part of a large community of practitioners who integrate expanded states of consciousness, accessed through various techniques, into their practice. Considering these people as a population, I can say that they have an exceptional degree of compassion and acceptance of one another and themselves. However, some people, whether guide or journeyer, do develop an inflated ego through this work. The difference between those who have an inflated ego and those who do not is often how much healing they have done. As long as an unmet need for validation remains unconscious, ego strategies and defenses will engage to protect this inner insecurity. People can stay caught in a state of ignorance regarding underlying wounds and lack capacity for self-nourishment. This keeps them in constant need of receiving that self-nourishment from external sources.

A common romantic fantasy in neo-shamanism is that the shaman's role is to journey into a person's inner world and rescue their soul like some kind of superhero. A genuine guide is someone who has the courage to face fear and is full of humility. The role is one of humble service. Cleaning up poop and vomit, wiping snot, and managing terror are just as much the work of a guide as is facilitating a ritual. A guide's integrity stems from humility. If you feel that the path of guiding and supporting others calls you, be ready for less than glorious hours in the pit of someone's unraveling. You may watch someone unravel during an innocent bathroom break, uncertain of how and when the re-gathering will take place. Depending on the nature of the ritual, the process can sometimes include aggressive expression and anger—even toward the guide. As for grace and rapture, even if they sound lovely at first, they are not necessarily easier to witness, as they too can include dramatic catharsis.

I once watched over a man in a mushroom ceremony in a state of paranoia and anger that lasted for hours. His fear was an unmistakable presence in the room, tangible and all-encompassing. I had to tread very lightly, aware that my presence was triggering childhood memories that were surfacing and bringing up waves of terror and rage. Somehow, mysteriously, his state eventually changed and he broke into the sobs of a young child, slowly softening the incredible armor that had become rigid around his heart. He reached out for my hand and allowed himself to connect with my compassion, receiving support even though he had always "held it together" alone before. He now speaks of this journey as a pivotal moment in his life.

Upon first meeting with a guide, a client will present certain symptoms and mental states, such as anxiety, depression, or insomnia. They might share specific emotions, bodily tensions, habits, relationship patterns, childhood memories, visions, or dreams that seem to be unrelated at first glance. Many indigenous cultures that incorporate expanded states of consciousness in their healing practices understand that these seemingly distinct aspects of life are intimately connected to one another. For example, our bodies affect our emotions, which affect our spirit, which then affects our families and communities, which affect our environment, which then affects our bodies. Every dimension of life inevitably affects the others, and life is experienced as an interwoven tapestry of these many dimensions. The guide should notice connections and understand that what we call "symptoms" are often the intelligence of the organism communicating a state of imbalance.

In order to interpret this wisdom for therapeutic application, I have developed what I call "The Holistic Model for a Balanced Life." The Holistic Model for a Balanced Life provides a categorization of human experience, grouping the various expressions of our life into five main aspects infused with three main qualities. During the threefold process of preparation, journey, and integration, a guide can use the model to effectively track the multifaceted expression of a client's process. Recognizing the interdependence between all aspects is at the core of this method of healing work.

3

ILLUMINATING
THE PATH

The Holistic Model for a Balanced Life

*Change is not something that we should fear.
Rather, it is something that we should welcome. For
without change, nothing in this world would ever
grow or blossom, and no one in this world would
ever move forward to become the person they're
meant to be.*

—B. K. S. IYENGAR

Through my desire to effectively integrate expanded states of consciousness with psychology, I realized the need for a model that draws from an integrated way of life. Intact indigenous communities often consist of close-knit groups that span generations and extend beyond the nuclear family. Frequently, these communities have lived on the same land for centuries.

Individuals labor upon the earth, grow the food they eat, live closely with the elements, and engage in spiritual practices and rituals that connect them with the natural cycles and seasons.

The changes that have produced the modern industrialized world have resulted in the loss of this integrated way of life. Life in cities is much more compartmentalized than village life, and results in feelings of isolation. Even though people are people and every community has its share of conflicts and personality clashes, many aspects of these indigenous communities offer lessons for us to draw from. I am not suggesting that we all need to return to premodern standards of living and reject the benefits and comforts of the modern era, but rather that we can look to earth-based cultures and learn from some aspects of their ways of life.

Drawing on my experience with Julieta and the Mazatec tradition, as well as the other indigenous, earth-based communities I have spent time with over the years, I developed the Holistic Model for a Balanced Life. By using the Holistic Model for a Balanced Life as a tool for self-inquiry, one can thoroughly examine the many aspects of their life and determine whether they are in balance or not. This model also helps those who live in the modern industrialized world prepare for a journey into an expanded state of consciousness—including the formulation of an intention—as well as navigate the integration phase that follows.

The Holistic Model for a Balanced Life divides life into five aspects: body, mind, spirit, community, and environment. These five aspects are infused with three qualities: wisdom, creativity, and love. The entire perspective is held in the embrace of Pure Being.

By using the Holistic Model for a Balanced Life as a tool for self-inquiry, people can effectively assess the current state of their lives and navigate the preparation process, including the appropriate formulation of their intention. The Holistic Model for a Balanced Life—which I will henceforth refer to as the Holistic Model—is also useful for decoding the material that emerges during an experience of expanded consciousness, and serves as a practical map for developing integration practices.

Origins of the Holistic Model
for a Balanced Life

In post-Socratic Western philosophy, the thinking mind was believed to be the source of human experience, disconnected from the physical body. René Descartes summed this up with his infamous saying, *Cogito ergo sum:* "I think, therefore I am." In the last fifty years, the physical, embodied dimension has been recognized as being intimately connected with the psyche. More recently, spirituality, with its increasingly popular teachings on mindfulness and meditation, has been recognized as an invaluable component of overall well-being. These aspects of human existence have been popularized as the body-mind-spirit triad. Even though the concept of body-mind-spirit suggests a more integrated approach to well-being than the mind alone, it is limited to an individual's personal life, without including his or her social or physical environment. It is clear that community—including our family and friends, our romantic relationships, and our ethnic and cultural identity—has a major influence on our development. Additionally, humans are learning more and more how much we are affected by our physical environment, whether our immediate home, our workplace, the wild and natural places near us, or the earth as a whole. These two additional aspects of community and environment reflect the shamanic as well as the Buddhist and Taoist views that all life is connected in an interwoven web of relationship. Community and environment are essential to the Holistic Model.

The Holistic Model facilitates self-knowledge and self-reflection. The five aspects of the Holistic Model weave into and out of one another in a pattern unique to every individual. Yet, to fully appreciate the complex way these aspects work together, we must first pull them apart. Just as various aspects of our planet's ecosystem can be individually studied—the ocean, the soil, a certain species of plant or animal, or the climate of a particular region—we can see their obvious interdependence.

In the Mazatec tradition, the animal totem of the mushroom healing ceremony is the eagle. The name of Huautla in Mazatec is *Tejao,* which translates to "eagle's nest." The eagle flies high in the sky, able to perceive the vast landscape of a place. It sees the interrelationships between zones: hills, rivers, canyons, and forests. At the same time, the eagle's superb vision can perceive the most minute details of a specific location on the ground. This capacity to hold a broad view while tracking the nuances of a situation is one of the principles on which healing stands.

How to Use the Holistic Model for a Balanced Life: An Inventory

Expanded states of consciousness invite us into a more complete state of being, granting us the ability to explore blockages or weakness in our life from a superior vantage point. I have found in my work that when clients hold the intention to heal or grow, they begin to notice specific points of imbalance in their lives—which then direct their discoveries during a journey.

In this chapter, I define each of the five aspects of the Holistic Model and offer a sample inventory to help determine a person's current situation. The inventory is a checklist of specific questions one can go through in an effort to collect pertinent information.

A guide can use the Holistic Model as a comprehensive intake tool and lens to guide the preparation process and integration phase with a journeyer or participant. It can also be used by a journeyer to engage their own preparation process. The inventories assist someone as they examine and reflect on their life in order to increase their understanding of their present reality. Through one's responses, one can see where imbalances lie. As a guide, my role is to help a client identify the state of psychological, emotional, or spiritual material they are currently aware of and working on. I then help them formulate an appropriate intention, one that will shed light on their specific areas of blockage.

When one explores an inventory, they should tell the truth while approaching the process with gentleness. It is not helpful to take an inventory with an attitude of judgment or condemnation. Taking an inventory of one's life is simply a way of increasing self-awareness. Whether you are a guide or a journeyer, I invite you, the reader, to engage with these questions.

Body

> When I was fifteen, during a modern dance class, my dance teacher choreo-graphed a piece around the four elements. I was chosen to be water. She played a piece of music and asked the water people to simply "be water." I remember feeling my body move into a state of liquid; I let myself fall to the ground and roll around, over people and objects. I was no longer made of flesh and bones. I was fluid. With closed eyes and a watery body, I moved around the floor, sat up, and then fell into a puddle again. I sensed my body as a vessel capable of infinite embodiment.

As a dancer and bodyworker trained in somatic psychology and Hakomi, I am fascinated by how we perceive and express our lives through our emotions and bodies. This includes the ways we experience reality through our five senses: sight, smell, hearing, taste, and touch.

Our physical body is shaped by inner influences—including mental and emotional experiences such as anger, anxiety, confusion, relaxation, or love. It is also shaped by outer influences such as food, stressors, traumas, and disease. The body is a complex and mysterious organism in the way that it functions, including how it heals. Our body holds the story of our life despite how the mind may attempt to repress that story. As we begin to listen to our body's intelligence, we can work toward establishing balance.

BODY INVENTORY

The following questions are designed to help you explore how you are in your relationship with your body.

Breath

- Do you breathe easily and deeply?
- When you exercise, do you feel your lungs expanding?

- Do you know what it feels like to be out of breath?
- Have you explored breathing practices, such as *pranayama* or Holotropic Breathwork?

Food

- How do you nourish yourself with food?
- Do you take the time to prepare food for yourself?
- Is feeding yourself an enjoyable activity?
- Do you eat junk food or sweets?
- Do you forget to eat sometimes?
- In what ways is your relationship with food a healthy one?
- In what ways is it problematic?

Exercise and Movement

- What do you do for exercise and movement?
- Do you exercise too little or too much?
- What physical practices do you want to explore?

Sleep

- How do you prepare for sleep?
- Do you go to sleep early or stay up late?
- How many hours do you sleep per night?
- Is your sleeping environment nourishing to you?
- Do you wake feeling rested?
- What do you dream about?

Sensory Pleasure

- What textures do you like?
- What beautiful things do you surround yourself with?

- How do you relate to your personal sensuality and erotic flow?
- How is your erotic expression with others? Is it inhibited, uninhibited, expressive, happy, too little, or too much?
- How do you express your sexuality?
- How do you express your gender identity?

Clothing

- How do you like to feel in your clothing?
- Do you dress for comfort or for beauty?
- Is it important how people see you?
- What are your favorite things to wear?

Sickness

- What do you do to maintain your sense of health and balance, chemically or hormonally?
- How do you choose to take care of yourself when you don't feel well?
- Are you able to ask for and receive support when you are sick?

Psychosomatic Awareness

- Where and how do you hold fear, stress, or tension in your body?
- How do you deal with stressful situations?
- Do you experience waves of depressive or anxious energy? If so, how do you experience them in your body?
- Do you tend to your physical body and appearance: your hair, your skin, your nails, and your teeth?

As you answer these questions, how do you feel at this moment? Do you feel content with the ways you tend your body? Do you feel motivation toward better self-care or anxiety about how much could be improved? What changes do you feel ready to make in the not too distant future?

Mind

Joseph was well-educated and intellectual, and had read an impressive number of books on psychology and theoretical approaches to therapy. At our first meeting, he sat in my office and spoke for twenty minutes straight. When there was finally a pause, I looked into his eyes intently, and asked him: "So ... what brings you here?" He looked lost, disarmed, yet seen. I nodded my head, and he began to cry softly, like a child. His emotions were there, right under the surface. He just needed someone to invite them to emerge. In this warm and supportive environment, he felt safe to share his story, and we continued to explore his tenderness, sorrow, and vision for his life. Joseph benefited greatly from a sound healing journey during which he connected with painful childhood memories and associated emotions that had lain dormant for years. He was eventually able to create a better routine of self-care for himself, finally feeling in charge of his life.

The aspect of the mind includes ego structure; emotional states; mental activity such as conscious and unconscious thoughts, dreams and fantasies; and intellectual activity.

The mind is a vehicle of awareness and transformation. It is capable of logic, reasoning, and calculation, as well as creativity, intuition, and imagination. Our self-reflective capacity allows us to reflect on emotional states while our thinking mind makes decisions and can seek out the support we need. Our intellect gives us a way to understand our unconscious material after it has been revealed through a journey.

Since most healing modalities—and especially expanded states of consciousness—attempt to bring awareness to contracted places in the body and psyche, repressed energy, memories, and shadow parts of ourselves are brought to the surface and into consciousness. This shadow material has often been repressed until it has become seemingly solid, manifesting as physiological tension. It can be pain, it can be grief, it can be shameful actions, or it can be guilt. Yet, as the body and psyche open up to more awareness, an enhanced flow of energy and stronger vitality is experienced.

Mind Inventory

The following questions are designed to help you explore how you are in your relationship with your mind and emotions.

Intellect

- Can you describe your intellectual strengths?
- What kind of books or podcasts stimulate your intellect?
- Do you find yourself obsessing about the past or worrying about the future?
- Is there a person or memory you constantly think about or a recurring situation that you are trying to "figure out"?
- What practices do you have to calm your mind and manage your stress?

Emotional Processes

- What are your emotional strengths?
- In what ways do you consider yourself emotionally wounded?
- What emotions do you have a hard time feeling?
- How do you express your emotions?
- In what ways do you repress anger, grief, or joy?
- Do your fears affect how you interact with the world?
- When do you feel joy or well-being?
- Could you be more honest with yourself?
- Do you have a supportive environment for your emotional process such as a therapist, bodyworker, or a 12-Step group?

Accessing the Unconscious

- How do you relate with your unconscious?
- Do you record your dreams when you wake up and work with them?

- Are there maps that help you reflect on your life? (astrology, numerology, or the Enneagram[1])

- Do you go to workshops to explore healing and therapeutic modalities?

Spirit

When I was a child, our community church seemed so magnificent: the light streaming through the stained glass windows, the smell of the incense, the painted Jesus with arms open on the ceiling, a dove above his head. I felt the presence of grace, mystery, and an almighty God. I sang in the small choir with a few friends, my voice filling the church with beauty and heart. Then I became a teenager and learned that women could not become priests, sexuality was frowned upon, and actions that were considered sinful were to be hidden away in shame. I felt confined and oppressed.

Then, many years later, I visited the Basilica of the Virgin of Guadalupe in Mexico City. I stood there, bathing in the ocean of all the pilgrims' faith and the mystery of the Virgin's presence, and I wept. I felt how that original foundation of faith had lived in me all these years, waiting to be reawakened. I no longer adhered to concepts of sins or shame, yet I felt spirit still alive within me.

Most techniques that aim to expand consciousness allow us to connect to a spiritual dimension. Going beyond the human reality to a vast transpersonal dimension has been at the core of human inquiry for millennia.

The spiritual aspect I am addressing here has to do with our relationship with the divine and spirit. It includes the parts of life that cannot be experienced by one's senses through everyday states of consciousness. Spirit is that which exists beyond ordinary human perception, beyond intellect, beyond scientific theories; and that which can be measured by quantitative methods. Spirituality enlivens and enriches the other dimensions of life.

As many health professionals are now aware, an imbalance in the spiritual dimension of life can result in limitations and weakness in other parts of life, such as one's health or relationships.

When I myself speak of spirit, I speak of the quality of the divine that resides in every animate being as well as in inanimate aspects of creation. The definition of spirit is left open here, in order to include a vast range of possibilities.

Religion, on the other hand, is structured spirituality that is governed by rules, rituals, and often hierarchies. Religions take spirituality and add structure and protocols. It is possible that through the process of creating an organization, religions can distort the original spiritual experiences of their founders and destroy the authentic spirituality at their origin. Yet, spirituality remains the pure essence of religion.

Spirit Inventory

The following questions are designed to help you explore your relationship with spirituality.

Spiritual Background

- Do you consider yourself to be a spiritual person?
- Did you have a religious upbringing?
- If so, did it impact your life negatively or positively?
- If not, what has shaped your relationship with spirituality?

Beliefs

- Do you believe in a god, many gods, or no god at all?
- Do you believe that life is sacred?
- What is your relationship with the elements, or the local rivers and mountains?
- Do you consider yourself to have faith?
- How do you express your gratitude?
- What do you value most in your life?

Practices

- Do you have a spiritual teacher?

- Do you belong to a spiritual community?
- Do you gather together to meditate, pray, sing, or do acts of service?
- What rituals or spiritual practices do you perform?
- How do you celebrate births, anniversaries, or significant deaths?
- Which spiritual or inspirational books do you love?
- Where do you put images of spiritual teachers, meaningful objects, or special photos?
- Do you meditate, pray, or spend time in nature?
- Do you include times of silence and quiet when you are by yourself?
- Do you take time for spiritual or personal retreat?

Community

When I was eleven years old, I saw in a magazine that, due to the war in Vietnam, the Vietnamese people were in serious distress, and humanitarian organizations were organizing sponsorship for Vietnamese children. I wanted to sponsor a child. I spoke with my mother about it and she thought it was a terrific idea. She said she would even match my allowance to send to the organization. I felt understood and supported as if we were a team. Once connected, I wrote to my faraway friend and received back a letter and a small black-and-white photo. I felt a bond that brought me joy.

Years later, after I became pregnant with our first child, my husband and I decided to sponsor a child again. If I was to offer a child a good life, I wanted to share it with another one in a place where help was needed. Five years later, as my husband and I were contemplating whether to have a second child, we agreed that opening our home and hearts to a child who needed a home would be more aligned with our beliefs than conceiving another biological one. So we decided to adopt a child. Our son has grown up to become a sensitive man and talented artist who has taught our family much about inclusion and generosity.

The fourth aspect is that of community. From a shamanic perspective, community is not limited to the humans in one's life but includes everything one is in relationship with. The sacred Lakota prayer, *Mitakuye Oyasin,* meaning "All my Relations,"[2] acknowledges the interdependence of all life; the humans, animals, insects, mountains, rivers, plants, stones, and everything else. While acknowledging the many beings that constitute community in its broadest shamanic sense, here we will use the term "community" more specifically, as it refers to human community and relationships.

Due to the emphasis on individualism in modern industrialized societies, many of us have lost our balance in relationship with the social structures around us: our family, our neighborhood, our workplace, our school, and our nation. As a result, many people feel isolated and lonely. This is not to say that people in indigenous cultures are never lonely, but that people living in fragmented communities often lack effective solutions for reconnection.

The aspect of community includes intimate relationships with partners and families. These intimate relationships, while sometimes sources of conflict, can be valuable territory for psychological growth. Community also includes our spiritual, political, educational, and work communities, our neighborhood, and the school we attend. These communities often overlap in obvious and subtle ways, forming a variegated, interdependent web of living relationship.

COMMUNITY INVENTORY

The following questions are designed to help you explore how you are in your relationship with your community.

Personal Relationships

- How is your relationship with your family of origin?
- If you need a friend, whom do you call?
- Are you able to cultivate lasting friendships?
- Do you have friends you can trust and depend on?
- How do you share your vulnerability with the people in your life?

- How do you feel when other people express their vulnerability?
- Do you tend to overfocus on others in a relationship, listening and supporting?
- Do you tend to overfocus on yourself, asking for help and seeking attention?

Group Belonging

- What does it mean to you to belong to a community?
- Which work, sports, spiritual, or artistic communities do you belong to?
- If you go to a workshop or a ceremony or are traveling with a group, how easy is it for you to relate with others?
- What qualities or actions do you contribute to your communities?
- What are your ways of connecting with new people?
- How do you maintain a connection with the people in your life?
- Do you have "unfinished business" with any of your friends, family, or other people in your community?
- Do you take an interest in global events?
- Do you empathize with others experiencing suffering or triumph?
- How do you contribute to the evolution of human consciousness?

Giving and Receiving

- Do you feel nourished or exhausted by your social commitments?
- How well do you balance time with others with time for yourself?
- Are you more withdrawn and introverted or are you more outgoing and extroverted?
- How could you be more balanced in the ways that you relate with others?
- In what ways do you give back to your communities through service?

Environment

When I am sad, I go to my garden. When I am happy, I go to my garden. My garden is my refuge and creative palette. I dig holes and transplant seedlings. I cut flowers and create stunning bouquets for our dining room table. I weed the grass that suffocates my favorite roses. There is a pink rose bush dedicated to my friend Elisabeth, who died at forty-one and a white one for my mother, who recently passed away. There are flowers I grow for my bees or to make into tinctures and herbal medicines. My connection with the garden is complex and intimate. It tells the story of my life, my tears and joys. It is like a friend I share everything with, one who has watched me grow over these past thirty years. I am grateful to have a garden as a palette for my creative expression and to live in direct relationship with the earth and her plants.

The fifth aspect is that of the environment, which includes our nonhuman animate and inanimate surroundings. It includes the gardens, rivers, trees, mountains, animals, and other living creatures that inhabit wild places. It also includes the spaces we live and work in, our neighborhood, town or city, and our country. This aspect includes our relationship with the elements of earth, water, fire, air, and space; and the directions of north, south, east, and west, above, below, and within.

Our environment strongly affects who we are. It affects our consciousness and impacts our priorities and ways of thinking. If we live by the ocean, we will have a specific kind of lifestyle, the tide inevitably affecting our activities. If we live in the desert, our daily reality will be shaped by our hot and dry landscape. The external environment directly affects our daily life. We, in turn, affect our environment. Every resource we use comes from the earth and will go back to the earth. Through the ways we live, how we cook, consume and travel, we express our level of ecological awareness, our commitment to a sustainable lifestyle, and our personal connection with the natural world.

How we relate with our living environment and the natural world reflects how we *relate* with ourselves. The state of our home can be considered a reflection of our inner state. The same applies to the greater environment of the planet we inhabit. The way we treat the earth reflects the way we treat ourselves. Healing and transformation happen on macro and micro levels that reflect one another in both obvious and subtle ways.

ENVIRONMENT INVENTORY

The following questions are designed to help you explore how you are in your relationship with your environment.

Relating with the Natural World

- How much time do you spend in nature?
- How do you connect with the mountains, rivers, trees, and plants around you?
- What local flora and fauna are you familiar with?
- Which elements—earth, water, fire, air, or space—do you connect with most?
- In what ways do you consider the natural world to be alive?
- Do you use sustainable and biodegradable products?
- Do you reuse and recycle when you can?
- How do you show your respect for the earth?

Home and Work Environments

- Do you keep your home messy or tidy?
- How does your home reflect your sense of beauty and the things that you love?
- Do you have plants in your living space?
- Do you have artwork, precious objects, or paintings in your home?
- How do you relate to and treat the street you live on?
- How relaxed or energized do you feel in your place of work?

The Three Qualities

The Mazatec curandera María Sabina used to speak poetic words during her evening mushroom ceremonies. In one of her poems, referring to the essential nature of her work, she says, "It is a matter of clarity. It is a matter of tenderness."[3] These qualities are similar to the two principal virtues to be developed through Buddhist practices: wisdom and compassion. Julieta has explained to me that the Mazatec interpret the Catholic cross as symbolic of the union of these two qualities: the vertical axis of clarity-wisdom and the horizontal axis of tenderness-compassion, which meet in the middle. In the middle is where the heart is, and from which we manifest our creative expression in this life.

As the Indian non-dual master Nisargadatta said so eloquently, "When I see I am nothing, that is wisdom. When I see I am everything, that is love. And between the two my life moves."[4]

Infusing the qualities of wisdom, creativity, and love into the process of exploring the inventories makes it more human; it becomes a more embodied practice. These three qualities apply to every level of self-exploration, from working with responses to the inventories to guiding the preparation of a journey, to supporting a journey, to interpreting the material that has arisen during a journey and determining the most beneficial approach to the integration process.

Wisdom

When my client Yosef returned from an ayahuasca retreat in Peru, he was agitated and distraught. He said he had unraveled and had been overtaken by visions of enormous snakes eating him. I asked him what he thought this meant about his life. He was clueless. The symbolism of his visions meant nothing to him. The absence of self-reflection left him with no context to work from. When we looked at his life, he realized that his level of vitality was very low, and his sexuality was repressed. When I asked him again, he admitted that he could see the snakes as symbols of awakening, his life force waking up inside of his body. He realized that instead of trying to kill him, they may have been messengers reminding him of his power. He committed to dance, paint, and attempt to open his sensual energy back up after years of neglect. His experience turned out to be a herald of growth rather than a bewildering nightmare.

Wisdom is the capacity to combine knowledge with concrete life experience. If I read the theory behind a practice that physically releases emotions, but I have never had the actual experience, I cannot validate or say that I know this practice since I have not lived it myself. Life experience turns knowledge into embodied wisdom.

Conversely, a raw experience by itself—while valuable—can be disorienting if we do not have context for it. For example, if I go into a shamanic drumming journey and descend into the lower world, becoming immersed in amazing visions of swimming in the ocean with whales and upon my return simply report, "Wow, I saw whales," how does this serve me? It might be a poignant experience and I might treasure it, but if I do not have a question or an intention before entering the journey, the content lacks context. If I state a prior intention such as, "I want to receive an animal teaching for my present situation," then my visionary experience begins to make sense. I can see how the grandeur and grace of whales offer me a lesson on how to take up more space in my life. It becomes an answer to a question and the lessons become applicable. It is knowledge combined with raw experience that leads to wisdom and guides one toward making appropriate and discerning choices in their life.

Wisdom Inventory

- How do you recognize wisdom in someone?
- In what ways do you consider yourself wise?
- What are your sources of wisdom? People, teachings, living traditions?
- Do you lean more toward gathering knowledge or having direct experiences?

- Do you encounter the same issues or patterns over and over?
- Are you able to assimilate knowledge about these patterns?
- Do you have the wisdom of how to transform them? Or not?
- Do you trust yourself to make necessary changes in your life?
- Can you reach out for support if you feel unable to change difficult patterns?
- How do you integrate your experiences?
- How do you keep yourself learning and growing?
- How might you introduce new wisdom into your life?

Creativity

A few years ago, I reflected on the ways I prepared food and realized how uncreative I was in this domain. I seldom explored new ingredients or recipes. I decided to be more explorative, to enhance the creative energy in my cooking. I bought new spices I didn't know at the market and looked up recipes that included them. I began experimenting with cardamom, lemongrass, and juniper berries. The creative force guided me to explore bolder flower arrangements in my house, add new plants to my garden, and more color to my wardrobe.

We live in a world in constant creation. Creativity is the energy that propels life toward change and evolution. It reflects the way we respond to experience. It is within our capacity to modify, expand, or deepen an experience or a state. Creativity is not a gift that only artists possess. All of us are artists and impart genius in our unique way, simply by authentically showing up in our life. Everything we do, every thought, and every action can be a new creation.

The power of the creative impulse demands that we engage our wisdom to create new, healthy patterns and loving relationships in our life. If I wake up feeling stiff in the morning, joints aching, and cannot sit up well, this is my raw experience. The quality of wisdom leads me to do something about it. Creativity then appears with ideas: "I can do yoga. I can take a walk. I can take a hot shower or spend time in a sauna." In this way, I can creatively change my situation.

CREATIVITY INVENTORY

- In what ways do you consider yourself to be creative?
- How are you creative in the ways you dress, how you eat, or how you express yourself through words and actions?
- What are you curious about?
- Do you practice any expressive art forms?
- What beliefs do you have about your capacity to be creative?
- Do you feel blocked in your creativity?
- What blocks you?
- Could you relate with someone you know in a more creative way?
- What aspect of life would you like to bring innovation to?
- What new thing could you explore?

Love

During one of my group journeys with Pablo, he showed us a variety of slides before we ingested the sacramental mushrooms. We watched children crying in hunger, flowers blooming in a spring meadow, deforested hillsides, a baby being born, and other evocative images. I remember being emotionally flooded by the range of human experience. Then the feelings lifted and I was beyond anger, joy, or sorrow. I was simply open and in awe. I had connected with the essence of all emotions. I was love feeling itself.

I consider love to be a state rather than an emotion. Its presence is naturally caring and concerned with the well-being, growth, and fulfillment of life. Love is a force that compels us to know ourselves more deeply and connect more fully with others. I am not talking about romantic love, nor am I speaking of sexual attraction. The kind of love I am talking about is similar to, but not the same as, compassion. Compassion tends to the vulnerability of humanity with an acknowledgment of the suffering of others, whereas love encompasses the greatness and celebration of all that we are. Love is our capacity to appreciate the complexity of others in all their dimensions. If a process is devoid of love, it is missing the core human element. When we identify a situation in our life that needs changing, even if our response is creative, addressing it without loving care can feel dry. Love brings tenderness to the process. If I am guiding a client through preparation and I know she drinks alcohol regularly and I sense it is having a negative impact on her well-being, then I might gently say, "Before going into this healing journey, it would be appropriate to prepare by reducing the amount of alcohol you are drinking, so that you can be more receptive." If I say, "You need to stop drinking" in a cold tone, my communication comes across as judgmental and results in disconnection between us. I want to offer loving guidance toward what serves her healing process best, even if what I'm suggesting may be difficult or challenging.

Love Inventory

- Do you feel love?
- Where in your body do you feel it?
- Do you love yourself?
- How do you express love toward yourself?
- When have you felt the most loved?
- What does it mean to you to love someone or something?
- What and whom do you love the most?

- Are you comfortable expressing love?
- How do you nurture what you love?
- How could you express your love more?
- What are you here to learn about love in this life?

These three qualities of wisdom, creativity, and love permeate the five aspects of life: body, mind, spirit, community, and environment. Our challenge is to find a dynamic balance between the three qualities in each of the five aspects. Creativity without wisdom can be chaotic and destructive. Wisdom without creativity can be static and lack the energy to manifest itself. Love without wisdom can be overly sentimental or reckless, and wisdom without love can be cool and detached. Creativity without love can be insensitive and mechanical, and love without creativity can become limited and repetitious.

When these three qualities are in balance, they support one another beautifully. In fact, the three qualities are the core of this method of healing. As a guide cultivates and embodies these qualities, they are able to hold a client in a truly supportive field. In this way, the qualities can become internalized by the client. On the most fundamental level, it is the creative transmission of love, sourced in wisdom, that has the power to heal.

Pure Being

The five aspects and the three qualities exist within the realm of Pure Being. This can be called God, source, emptiness, awareness, transcendence, or the Great Mystery. It is not an "it." It is beyond words and can only be defined by our capacity to perceive it. It is the field of pure potentiality that seeks manifestation. It is the spark of the divine within all things, and the space in which our lives unfold.

Pure Being exists everywhere all of the time, including throughout the myriad layers of our human life, and the qualities that infuse those layers. The experience of encountering Pure Being naturally makes us want to live a more sustainable, balanced, and peaceful life.

Pure Being Inventory

- How do you connect with your core essence?
- Who are you when you are not doing anything?
- Are you comfortable simply *being* with yourself?
- Are you comfortable simply *being* with someone else?
- What do you think happens when your body dies?
- Do you relate with the terms Pure Being, God, source, awareness, emptiness, open presence, transcendence, Great Mystery, or the Divine?
- Do you make space for the power of Pure Being to be felt?
- How does this presence inform your life?

＊＊＊

The Holistic Model for a Balanced Life is a compass that can guide us toward a more honest relationship with the five aspects of our lives and toward a deeper cultivation of the three qualities that permeate the aspects. How someone prepares for a journey will be determined by what they discover through their inventories. The content of a journey is easier to decipher when using the model as a lens. Finally, approaching the integration phase following a journey is greatly supported by using the Holistic Model for a Balanced Life.

＊＊＊

The following story is an example of how to use the Holistic Model with a client throughout the phase of preparation, the journey, and the integration.

My client Michelle was a thirty-five-year-old professional woman working in the film industry. She traveled often for work, was relatively disconnected from her family of origin, and had only a few close friends. She had been in therapy for five years, during which time she had uncovered memories of having been sexually abused by her stepfather as a child. Her therapy helped her remain stable in her demanding job and find additional strength in support groups, yet she continued to feel feelings of shame and discomfort in her body as she struggled with her crippling memories.

Michelle came to me because she was suffering from depression and severe anxiety and wanted to try another method of healing. She had heard about studies including psilocybin and its ability to alleviate anxiety and intuitively felt that it might benefit her. After an in-depth intake and screening for possible health contraindications, I decided she was an appropriate candidate for this work.

Naturally, it took us several months of counseling to establish a firm bond of trust, all the while reaffirming the emotional resources that she had already cultivated. During that time, we looked at her life from the perspective of the Holistic Model, exploring the inventories together.

On the physical level, Michelle was uncomfortable in her body; she felt she lacked something essential and pushed her body very hard through exercise. She felt overwhelming shame, at times repulsion, and was afraid to be touched or embraced. Her sleep was agitated. She maintained a reasonably healthy diet but often depended on alcohol to soothe her anxiety. She enjoyed walks in nature as her primary physical activity.

On the emotional level, Michelle had learned to speak up for herself at work, yet she still felt uneasy in social situations. She often felt verbally attacked even when she logically knew it was not the case. She dreaded work functions where she felt she had to appear enthusiastic, while inside she felt overwhelmed and raw.

On the spiritual level, Michelle was angry with God for having permitted her childhood abuse. However, her relationship with nature was a source of tranquility, as she found a spiritual solace there.

On the level of community, she maintained contact with the members of her support group, but she felt that these friendships actually made her unhappier. Michelle had been able to establish trust with her previous therapist, but other relationships, especially romantic ones, were difficult for her. Overall, she felt isolated.

On the level of environment, Michelle kept her home highly organized. Everything had to be extremely clean and in its correct place. Though she enjoyed being in nature, she was afraid of dirt, twigs, or insects on her clothing or skin.

I could see that Michelle's sexual abuse history had impacted all the dimensions of her life. By looking without judgment at these various aspects of her life, she was able to see herself more clearly and holistically. She saw her strengths and accomplishments, such as the support she had sought out. She also saw the areas of fragility that still needed healing. She wanted to feel more loving toward her body and wished for a more spiritual life and more human connection. During our months of dialogue together, Michelle was willing to prepare for her experience by making some changes in her life. She started attending a restorative yoga class, which got her more in touch with her body. She agreed to read a few spiritual books and to attend a couple of meditation practice evenings, which helped her connect to a sense of inner peace. She also drank less alcohol.

Eventually, after we had cultivated a significant therapeutic relationship and she had taken the time to make substantial preparatory changes, it felt right to bring Michelle to Mexico to experience the healing modality of the mushroom ceremony. I described the setting to her, including the various stages of the ceremony, the physical effects of the mushrooms, and the possible presence of visions and unusual sensations. She formulated the intention that she wanted to accept her body more fully, have greater ease in her relationships, and access a more profound spirituality.

Upon arrival, Michelle felt somewhat shy about meeting my teacher and her family. I explained to them that Michelle was seeking to heal through the mushroom ceremony and they all welcomed her warmly. As we got closer to the evening of the ceremony, I suggested it would be good for her to relax, breathe calmly, and surrender to the experience, even if it felt unusual. Julieta and I would be there to sing, pray, and offer physical and emotional support during the entire journey.

At 6:00 PM Michelle ingested the mushrooms and the honey served to her on a small plate. She then reclined on her mattress and covered herself with blankets. We began to conduct the ceremony with songs, prayers, and moments of silence while checking in with Michelle from time to time. At first, she was a bit disoriented. She did not enjoy her lack of mental clarity and was confused with the images she was seeing inside her mind. She saw dark and foreboding colors, transforming into vast spaces of emptiness and gloom. I reassured her, telling her that distorted images and shapes were not unusual in this phase of entry. I offered to hold her hand, which she gladly accepted. After a short while, I could sense that she was relaxing into her experience. She started to yawn and sigh, a sure sign of opening into the effects of the mushrooms. She later wrote the following account:

At first, I was disoriented, seeing weird shapes and colors that did not mean anything to me. My body was scared to let go. But then as Françoise checked in and held my hand, I felt better. I started to feel heat in my body, waves flowing inside me like an ocean. I felt so vast, watery, and free. Waves were washing my fears away as stones, debris, and old, half-decomposed seaweed. I felt my depth as the ocean, my surface as the waves, the fish and sea plants as my children.

At one point I felt the presence of my stepfather. He looked confused, small, and wounded. I almost felt sorry for him. After all, he had to live with what he had done to me. I was innocent, and that was my strength. I was able to sense my fragility and how I had been scared of people. I saw why I had come to see my body as embarrassing and shameful. I could feel my love for myself in that wounded state. I returned over and over to being the ocean, and everything felt different. The possibility of transformation felt limitless. My body was sacred and full of water and life. I have moved on to better things in my life now. I can accomplish whatever I want. I am free.

Once in a while, I could hear Françoise sing, sometimes alone, sometimes with her teacher. She asked me a few times how I was feeling. As the effects of the mushrooms faded, I felt relaxed and cozy in my blankets. The candle at the altar was the most sublime thing I had ever seen; amber light dancing with flowers, creating magical shadow patterns on the walls. There was a sweet smoke in the air and it smelled delicious. After a period of rest, Françoise offered me a mug of herbal tea with some bread and mango. Everything tasted marvelous. I had never eaten anything so incredible in my life!

Obviously, Michelle's journey was a significant and empowering experience. Her vision of being the ocean, her insights, and her heart opening were a radical shift from how she had felt before. As we began the process of integration, it was important for Michelle to narrate the story of her journey to me. That was the first phase; listening to her stories, impressions, and visions. I had her recall her initial intention for the journey. She recalled the expansive sensations she had as a watery being. She felt open, soft, and receptive. She also felt a bit worried about being "too open" and the risk of being hurt. I acknowledged her concern. The strength and personal power she contacted during her journey gave her confidence that she might be able to relate differently to people. However, this was all so new she was not sure how to apply these new insights to her daily life.

As far as Michelle's intention to forge a deeper spiritual connection, she felt that being the ocean during the journey was not only a physical experience but also a spiritual initiation. She had never felt "nonhuman," as she put it. This effacing of her human identity and merge into nature was a genuine spiritual experience. It felt abstract at first, and she was not sure how to integrate it into her life. Even though Michelle's journey had been a healing and blessing to her whole being, she felt sadness after it faded. I told her that was natural. After all, the day-to-day world can sometimes appear flat following an experience like hers. I reassured her that the memories and visions would now live in her and the integration phase would support her ability to stay in touch with what she had accessed.

Michelle's experience allowed her to restore an inner sense of beauty and peace. As a trauma survivor, she could have explored aspects of her pain and suffering, her shame, or anger toward her abuser. Unpleasant though it sounds, an experience like this can be empowering. But instead, she had an experience of resourcing in her well-being. This was the way in which her psyche directed her experience during the ceremony. In that fluid space, Michelle recovered a space of relaxation and safety inside. This journey became a new template for life, granting her the possibility of feeling safe in the world.

The integration was an ongoing invitation to seek experiences in which she would feel safe and relaxed. She decided to bathe often, adding essential oils to her water and surrounding herself with candles. She felt this was a way she could create a supportive environment for her body as it reminded her of the feeling of fluidity she had so profoundly enjoyed in the journey. Michelle continued to take her walks in nature and, over time, realized how much more comfortable she felt. She found herself curious and wanting to touch everything, smell flowers, and lie in the leaves.

Michelle eventually joined a local meditation group, where she began to practice mindfulness meditation. She noted how the practice of calming her mind reminded her of the calm she had felt in the journey. We continued ongoing counseling, during which I supported her renewed sense of emotional stability and the new template she had created for her life. Michelle became a different person. Her inner world continued to develop into a place of refuge. This transformation allowed her to view her history in a new way, not limited to a series of meaningless, painful traumas, but as a path toward a more embodied and empowered self.

4

LEAVING HOME

The Essentials of Preparation

*The winds of grace are always blowing but you have
to raise the sail.*

—RAMAKRISHNA PARAMAHAMSA

Thirty years ago, I gathered some girlfriends of mine for a sweat lodge with a masterful guide, Marilyn Youngbird. The sweat lodge ritual consists of many hours in a low, canvas-covered dome built of willow branches. Hot stones are brought from an outside fire to a pit in the center of the lodge. The flap of the door is closed and the participants sit together in complete darkness. The leader pours water over the hot stones, which fills the dome with intense heat and steam as she sings and prays. In some Native cultures this practice is a powerful ritual of purification and a ceremony for community healing.

> *It was many years ago and I was brand new to the practice, not yet knowing what it entailed. I casually thought, "La, la, la, it is going to be great! We are a bunch of girls about to have a bonding experience. What could go wrong?"*
>
> *Well, it turned out that Marilyn runs long, beautiful, and intense lodges. I went in there completely clueless, and within five minutes, I was a mess. I was panting, feeling frightened by the heat, the darkness, and the intensity of my physical and emotional state. We were in there for four hours. Even though Marilyn opened the door a few times to let in some cool air, I felt as if I were dying. The darkness and heat were overwhelming. I kept wondering what I was doing there; I was floundering in the experience without any sense of personal direction. I was miserable without knowing why.*

As we look at the many traditions that include techniques for accessing expanded states of consciousness, we see that they consistently emphasize the process of preparation. Indigenous people consider these expanded states to be times for healing and communion with spirit; they are entered into with reverence and care. In the countless ceremonies facilitated by Mazatec leaders that I have attended, I have observed that they pay close attention to diet, to their relationship with their guide, and to their prayers and their offerings. They open their ceremonies with specific songs and blessings. As we in the modern industrialized world approach the topic of preparation, we must recognize the import and rigor of these long-standing approaches and adapt them to our lives.

In order to integrate these preparatory practices into my work as a therapist and guide, I emphasize two separate but related tracks. The first track utilizes the wisdom of "set and setting." The second emphasizes the wisdom of the Holistic Model.

The term "set and setting" was coined by Timothy Leary in 1961 during the initial wave of contemporary psychedelic exploration, and has now become fairly mainstream. The first generation of pioneers in the mid-twentieth century studied consciousness-expanding substances such as LSD and mescaline from a scientific perspective, and they anticipated reliable results. However, from their observations, they found that every psychedelic experience was completely unique depending on the journeyer and the environment. This awareness led them to the concept of "set and setting." As Timothy Leary wrote:

> *Of course, the drug dose does not produce the transcendent experience. It merely acts as a chemical key—it opens the mind, frees the nervous system of its ordinary patterns and structures. The nature of the experience depends almost entirely on set and setting. Set denotes the preparation of the individual, including his personality structure and his mood at the time. Setting is physical—the weather, the room's atmosphere; social—feelings of persons present towards one another; and cultural—prevailing views as to what is real. It is for this reason that manuals or guidebooks are necessary. Their purpose is to enable a person to understand the new realities of the expanded consciousness, to serve as road maps for new interior territories which modern science has made accessible.[1]*

Set

The *set* includes the mindset and intention of the journeyer. Mindset is defined as the emotional and psychological state of a journeyer approaching an experience. For example, if someone has had a fight with their partner before entering an expanded state, their mindset is likely to be agitated. If they have just taken a relaxing walk in nature, their mindset is more likely to be serene. Also critical to set is one's worldview. This includes one's religious or scientific cosmology, as well as their personal, social, and cultural perspectives of the world.

Intention is the second component of the set. An intention is like a prayer; it is a statement of one's motivation or direction. Discerning our intention means taking the time to clarify our motivation. It is less about what we are doing and more about why we are doing it. Our intention directs our journey and communicates to our higher self and to our guide what it is that we are seeking. The exercise of determining our intention is an exercise of self-inquiry. What do we want? Where are we going? These questions direct our attention toward the present moment and toward the truth of constant change. What comes next? In which way does our healing unfold now?

Having an intention is akin to having a compass aboard our sailboat. When we enter the vast ocean of expanded consciousness, there can be waves and storms, placid waters, gentle breezes, or intense winds. Having our sail raised high and our compass in hand gives us a point of reference to return to, and a direction to pursue.

By using the Holistic Model, the journeyer has already begun to identify the facets of their life that are in or out of balance. Depending on this inventory, they will then orient their intention toward what needs attention. An intention can be well defined, such as wanting to heal physical illness, exploring the lifelong effects of childhood abuse, seeking resolution of a challenging relationship, or enriching the spiritual dimension of one's life.

Perhaps being vulnerable in relationship with others is someone's main challenge. Consequently, their intention could be: "I want to learn why I am so defensive in my intimate relationships." Or perhaps the main issue is a fear of spirituality because it feels so vast and unknown. In this case, an intention could be: "I am curious to explore the divine."

Sometimes a journeyer may feel ready to explore new territory. In this case, I suggest the formulation of the curious inquiry intention, which is about surrendering to the mystery of the unknown. It is another way of saying, "Here I am. Please teach me."

We will refer back to the intention as a starting point when attempting to interpret the content of a journey.

Setting

The setting refers to the external conditions of a journey, including the location, the time, and all other logistical aspects of the ritual. Another component of the setting is the guide and the other participants.

Humans are dependent upon the environment, as a fetus is dependent on the womb. The fetus is a separate being with its unique constitution, and yet it is in an intimate relationship with the womb it inhabits. Every sound, movement, nutrient, and toxin potentially influences its development during its nine-month gestation. As sensing, feeling beings, we perceive the external world through our sense organs. The environment and the sensory inputs present in a journey have a notable effect on what we are drawn to explore within ourselves. If we go to a ceremony in the Amazon, the sounds of frogs and crickets will bring living nature into our internal experience. Songs, chanting, or silence will affect our experience in different ways. Specific prayers or song lyrics will evoke particular psychological material.

Whether we are lying down outside, feeling the cool earth below us, or sitting on a cushion in a retreat hut impacts our journey. The smell of incense or fresh air or rose essential oil takes us to different places. Whether the guide or facilitator is present and centered or scattered and distracted impacts our experience. If we are with fellow participants, then their emotional state, whether it is kind and loving or angry and fearful, will also affect us.

When we are in an indoor space, the presence of an altar focuses our attention toward the space we are in. Any religious imagery, icons, or statues that are present can impact our experience.

Some indoor spaces give us a womb-like feeling of safety. However, at different times during a journey, the same space can make us feel tight and suffocated. Being outdoors is wonderful for some people, while it can trigger overwhelm and anxiety for people who need containment and predictability.

If one is comfortable being outdoors in a state of heightened receptivity, elements of nature can be more strongly felt and offer their teachings. Whether we are near a river or a mountain will affect our state. Sitting near a tree can evoke a sense of solidity and rootedness. A creek can communicate a sense of flow. In an expanded state of consciousness, we can more readily perceive the simple majesty of earth, water, fire, air, and space.

The guide's power, expertise, and skill will create a certain energy—one of healing through love and clarity. As we receive the songs and teachings of our guide and the greater nature around us, our inner nature awakens. It is the guide's job to discern which environment will be most fruitful for a client's current life situation and overall state. Someone in a fragile emotional state might benefit from a cozy, contained space. Conversely, a guide might suggest the outdoors for someone in need of expression and externalization of emotions. The appropriate environment is the one that will fit a client's needs best. Yet, while the setting greatly affects the journeyer's experience, expanded states can also completely transcend the immediate environment. Transcendence is made possible by a safe container.

Going back to my personal story about the women's sweat lodge at the beginning of the chapter, I consequently realized the importance of asking more details about the actual ritual and the importance of forming an intention. It remains an experience that I continue to learn from, and thirty years later, I still participate in Marilyn's sweat lodges.

Using the Holistic Model for Preparation

In the preparation process, the guide should emphasize the holistic nature of the individual, which includes the physical, emotional, spiritual, communal, and environmental aspects of their life. This approach provides the client with reassurance because they feel that every dimension of their life is being addressed. The guide should acknowledge the strength derived from the resources that have been cultivated, as well as identify the places of challenge with honesty and compassion. Before the journey takes place, the guide can use the Holistic Model to determine small shifts or practices that can be addressed as part of the preparation process. Someone who is generally inactive in their daily life could start taking walks or go to a beginner yoga class. Someone without much relationship to spirituality could read some books on meditation or prayer. By bringing creativity to the preparation process and tracking the impact of these engaged actions, the guide supports the client's sense of agency. During the experience, the journeyer will perceive the impact of the changes they have made. Later, in the phase of integration, they will draw strength from understanding how these shifts support their well-being.

The Afterplan

While the following five chapters discuss preparation in more detail, part of this phase is considering the immediate phase following a journey. The guide should support the journeyer by encouraging them to prepare internally and practically as they will likely be in a more raw, tender emotional state following a journey. The journeyer should have food already prepared for their return. It is a good idea that they secure a calm, safe environment in which to rest after the journey. If they will be participating in an overnight event, they should bring comfortable bedding and adequate hydration. If the experience is likely to be psychologically activating, they will need support for that vulnerable state. Some people want solitude; others want to be surrounded by loved ones. Where a journeyer lands after a journey is as important as where they begin.

The following five chapters discuss the process of preparation as it applies to each of the five aspects of the Holistic Model. For each of these aspects I give examples of how indigenous cultures might approach journeys into expanded states of consciousness, then offer ways to adapt these approaches to life in the modern industrialized world. Each chapter includes practical suggestions for a journeyer as to how they can prepare and create optimal conditions for an upcoming journey. Additionally, there are specific instructions for a guide who is facilitating the preparation process for another.

Powerful moments and breakthroughs can come at any point in a journey, beginning at the first moment of preparation. From the moment we choose to engage in an experience that will take us beyond our ego defenses and agree to receive guidance, a powerful process begins. I have seen many people arrive at a ritual having received an impressive amount of insight in the days preceding, perceiving existent dysfunctional patterns, and gaining clarity on decisions that need to be made. By simply engaging mindful attention itself, we begin the process of transformation.

5

FLESH AND BONES
Physical Preparation

The body is a sacred garment. It's your first and last garment; it is what you enter life in and what you depart life with, and it should be treated with honor.
MARTHA GRAHAM[1]

Hannah had decided to go on a weeklong vision quest and wanted to make the most of it. We sat in my office to discuss her preparation. I asked her questions about her relationship with her body. She responded that she was in good shape, ate healthily, and rarely drank alcohol except at the occasional dinner with friends. It all sounded good. When we started talking about her sleep patterns, she fidgeted in her chair and looked down, avoiding my eyes. She admitted that she was often anxious at night and could not sleep unless she took a sleeping pill.

*I felt immediately concerned that going out on a vision quest might be too chal-
lenging for her. I was afraid she was setting herself up for a panic attack all alone
in nature. To support her preparation, I suggested a few meditative practices she
could try before bed along with an herbal tea recipe to help her relax. I also had
Hannah commit to not use her computer or cell phone for the two hours leading
up to bedtime.*

*Two weeks later, when Hannah came back to see me, she was beaming. With a
big smile, she told me, "It was hell, and then it was heaven." I nodded, waiting
for more. She explained, "I was fine at first, but when the night approached, I
panicked, all alone. I watched my fears, creeping under my skin like an itch, and
driving me crazy. I had memories of being alone and scared in my childhood
home. I was a mess, shaking and curled up in a ball, crying like a small child. Then
I remembered the breathing exercise you recommended and was able to calm
myself down. Eventually, I fell asleep. The same thing happened the second night,
though less intense. The anxiety came, it went, I calmed down, and I survived. The
next two nights were actually enjoyable. I felt calmer and calmer, and as I looked
out at the stars, I finally felt safe with myself."*

The way we physically prepare our body for an expanded state of consciousness is of utmost importance. In the preparation phase, indigenous cultures bring special care to diet, cleansing and purification, sexual intimacy,
sleep, and dress for the specific purpose of enhancing the healing potential
of a journey. Before entering a traditional sweat lodge, a participant is often
asked to fast from food and alcohol for a couple of days preceding the ceremony. This is because the physical intensity of the lodge can induce nausea on
a full stomach. Also, due to the heat of a lodge, it would be unsafe to be under
the influence of any substance, including alcohol. Before a meditation retreat
in the Buddhist tradition, participants are often requested not to eat meat,
as it is at odds with the first Buddhist precept of abstaining from taking life.

In the Amazonian shamanic tradition of ayahuasca, there are strict food
restrictions due to biochemical contraindications, as well as sexual restrictions, in order to calm the physical and subtle body. They teach that keeping

other people's energies out of one's body before a ceremony allows the medicine to enter more profoundly. A guide in this tradition might suggest drinking specific herbal teas to either facilitate purging or to enhance dream states and visions.

In the Mazatec tradition, a light vegetarian diet is recommended before the mushroom ceremony, as the mushrooms reduce digestive activity. They emphasize the importance of refraining from eating animal products to support "cleaner physical energy." Mazatec practitioners consider the realm of the mushroom a realm of divinity where sexual encounters do not belong. Therefore, they instruct participants to hold a strict "sexual diet" for five days before and five days after a mushroom ceremony. They find these restrictions conducive to receiving the teachings and healing of the ritual. I agree that it is best to prepare for a ritual by refraining from sexual contact, before and after, in order to attune to one's own personal energy. Sexual activity is, in its own way, an expanded state. Cultivating a calm state is preferable before entering any ritual, specifically one that includes consciousness-expanding medicine.

Mazatec participants perform rituals of cleansing called *limpias* on each journeyer before a ceremony, to remove energetic disturbances and toxicity from the body. They also visit healers who perform *chupas*, extractions, that pull stagnant energy out of the participant's body through sucking, air aspirations, or using their hands. This allows the journeyer to approach the mushroom ceremony from a state of increased physical purity.

In the Bwiti tradition of West Africa, those who ingest the strongly psychedelic and healing iboga in ceremony drink specific teas to purify their bodies beforehand. They also paint their faces with white pigment to prepare themselves to enter the realm of their ancestors.

It is customary in many indigenous cultures to wear special clothing when entering the space of ceremony, as a way to show reverence for the practice or tradition. Some traditions prefer natural fibers to synthetic or light colors to darker ones. The appropriate clothing might be a specific color, such as the burgundy robes of Tibetan monks, a special hat such as the traditional beaded hat worn by the Q'ero shamans in the Peruvian Andes, or a specific vest, shawl, or skirt.

When integrating expanded states of consciousness into a path of healing and transformation, we want to adopt these ways of preparation the best we can, but ideally in ways that are deliberately adapted for our unique life. We can prepare by abstaining from or restricting certain foods and activities, by adding certain practices to our daily routine, by wearing special clothing, or by taking the time and energy to modify our actions or appearance. Through these actions, we begin to prepare our body and our psyche for an experience that lies outside the normal, day-to-day realm. Some general guidelines apply to almost any type of ritual, especially those that specifically challenge the physical body.

Diet and Substances

It is best that one eats lightly or even fasts the day before a journey and avoids meat or other heavy foods. This takes the burden off the digestive system so that more energy is available for other processes. If the ritual includes intense movement or heat, it is best not to eat beforehand, to avoid the risks of indigestion or nausea.

Since most cultures hold a firm rule against mixing alcohol with expanded states of consciousness (unless alcohol is the specific vehicle to the state as is used in some traditions), a general guideline is to avoid alcohol for at least one week before any journey. Additional drugs, psychedelics, or sacraments are also discouraged, as one should be in a physical state that allows them to perceive the new and unusual sensations that arise during the journey. It is also recommended to avoid cannabis for a minimum of one week before any kind of journey. While cannabis can be a wonderful medicine, it has substantial effects and is best avoided when working with other medicines. Additionally, a journeyer should discuss with the guide which vitamins, supplements, and other medications they are taking. There can be contraindications between certain pharmaceutical drugs, supplements, and plant medicines.

Sexual Activity

Many indigenous cultures impose a sexual diet before the journey. It is best not to engage in sexual activity (even with oneself) for at least five days before an experience. This gives the journeyer's body a few days to sort out what is theirs and what belongs to another. It also allows the body to return to a calm state. Going into an expanded state is an extraordinary opportunity to explore our internal world, with its unique energies and blocks. For this reason, maintaining clear boundaries helps us perceive what is ours. If our intention for healing is around personal sensuality, we can take this time to be with our body and erotic self. If we have a partner, it is an appropriate time to explore tenderness and gentle, nonsexual cuddles.

However, it is sometimes valid to bring sensuality and sexuality into an expanded state experience. In the Eleusinian mysteries of ancient Greece, where it is conjectured that the psychedelic ergot was ingested, some surmise that sacred rituals included sensual exploration.[2] Today, a healing ritual could include tantric techniques, specific breathing practices, or healing sexual touch. In these instances, it is all the more imperative that the container is carefully created and that the people involved are all in agreement with the intention. As long as the ritual is intentional and sacred, this exploration can indeed be extremely healing. However, if the presence of a ritual is necessary to share uninhibited intimacy with another, then the relationship itself might benefit from psychological exploration in a non-expanded therapeutic context.

Rest and Movement

Before entering an expanded state of consciousness, we want to do two seemingly contradictory things. On the one hand, we want to move stagnant energy out of the body, and, on the other hand, we want to quiet the physical system. We want to go into a journey with a sense of vitality, yet be rested enough for the experience. If we are going on a vision quest where we will be sitting still for three days, we want to make sure that we move our energy before and after our quest. If we sit all day at a computer, it is going to be difficult to go inward and expect to expand. It can be helpful to get a massage or go to a sauna to begin the process of relaxation.

The ancient Hindu art of *yogasana*, or yoga postures, has always preceded pranayama and meditation practices, as various postures prepare the body for the deeper practices. To prepare myself, I personally like to practice pranayama and walk in nature. These are the ways I have found work well to open my body. My teacher Pablo used to send me to walk barefoot on dirt paths or grass fields. At the time I was not sure why he was so insistent on this, but I later realized how useful this simple preparation was for me and how it supported my authentic relationship to movement as well as my connection with the earth.

Moving energy in the body as a preparation does not mean getting exhausted and worn out before going into our experience. We do not want to deplete ourselves, as it is equally necessary to create a sense of quietness and rest. At the same time, making time for rest and relaxation does not mean that we need to sleep for three days or not move from our bed. It is a matter of discernment and balance.

Clothing

As for special clothing, some people choose to wear a piece of clothing or fabric that represents the culture the ritual originates from. In the Mazatec culture, they embroider white ceremonial clothes with colorful flowers, birds, and mushrooms. Many people who participate in ayahuasca ceremonies like to wear clothes embroidered by ayahuasca-drinking people in support and appreciation for their traditional craftsmanship. If there is a special scarf or vest that gives a person a sense of connection with their tradition or symbolizes a personal sense of power, they should wear this piece of clothing. Having external reminders of what we are calling forth from within can bring us strength and power. When I first started studying with my teacher Julieta in Mexico, I wanted a *huipil,* an embroidered ceremonial dress, of my own. They are made by hand and could only be bought inside people's homes. I naïvely thought I could find the one I liked and wear it occasionally. I soon realized that it was only appropriate for me to wear it when my teacher told me to do so. I came to understand that the *huipil* was not a costuming item; it was a symbol of an entire culture and way of life. In twenty years, I have worn my *huipil* three times.

Personal Preparation

Depending on what you discovered through your inventory, you can see where you are in or out of balance. You can then give extra-special care and attention to these aspects of your preparation. For example, if someone presents with a pattern of sleep deprivation, it is the guide's job to attend to sleep issues first. They need to be rested enough before entering a ritual. If a client comes with a history of abuse or trauma, I often suggest gentle practices to open the body before undergoing anything more vigorous. If someone presents with physical symptoms or a chronic disease, I will explore their symptoms with them thoroughly and make sure it is safe for them to do deeper work. From a holistic perspective, symptoms are communication from an organism in need of attention and rebalancing. An approach to healing that integrates expanded states of consciousness into daily living is not about solely treating symptoms, but rather restoring health to one's entire life.

To prepare for a journey on the physical level, a journeyer should eat lightly. Try sticking to soups, cooked vegetables, and fruits. Drink plenty of water and light herbal teas. Avoid coffee or strong black tea, alcohol, animal products, fried, spicy, or overly sweet foods. Avoid cannabis and other psychoactive substances. Sleep at least seven to eight hours for three days before and after a journey and take naps if you feel tired from your activities. Take care to cleanse and purify your physical body so that you feel ready for your experience, using sage, incense, and salt baths.

Additionally, take walks or do yoga every day for a week prior to a journey. Practice mindful breathing and body stretching for a few days. If your lifestyle is too static, go jogging or hiking in nature, or swim laps, so that your body is more open and limber and your lungs more open. If your lifestyle is overly active, practice slow and gentle exercise such as restorative yoga to calm your nervous system without stopping your movement completely. Try not to exhaust yourself with too much activity, nor stay static and motionless. Minimize news, computer, and screen use. Plan a few days of decreased activity and fewer responsibilities immediately following the journey.

You can stay in contact with your personal sensuality through loving touch and massage, and relate to your partner with tenderness and gentle, nonsexual cuddles. Avoid sexual intercourse or orgasm with anyone (including with oneself) for at least five days before an experience, to conserve your personal energy.

When we tend to the places that need extra care before entering a journey, we are able to go deeper. By simply giving ourselves extra rest, eating healthier, and nurturing our body, we approach the transformative experience we are about to undergo with increased attention and greater respect.

6

TURNING INWARD

Mental and Emotional Preparation

*Before you know kindness as the deepest thing
inside, you must know sorrow as the other deepest
thing.*

—NAOMI SHIHAB NYE[1]

Greta came to meet with me in a fragile state. The recent death of a friend had triggered old memories of the accidental death of her father when she was a child and the family grief that had followed. Even though she had explored how this tragedy had affected her on many levels, she found herself depressed again and unable to move on. She asked me for guidance, as she was eager to explore other methods of healing besides talk therapy. I invited her to travel with me to Mexico the following month and to take the next four weeks to prepare. She felt that the natural world was her most significant support. So, over the next few weeks, I guided her through a few earth-based rituals.

At first, Greta sat by her favorite tree, a short time initially, and then longer and longer. She was alone, quiet, and present with her natural surroundings and her feelings. Creating a sacred space was previously foreign to her, but with some encouragement, she became inspired and created an elegant altar with photos, candles, and flowers. Then, she wrote a letter to her dad in front of the altar. She buried the letter at the foot of the tree and created a small sculpture with branches, leaves, and stones, dedicated to her father's memory. She then sat beside it and played a song on her flute for her dad.

When we met in my office next, Greta said she felt lighter and less haunted by her father's death. She was ready to go to Mexico and grieve the death of her friend.

✳ ✳ ✳

In expanded states of consciousness, we are granted access to the domain beyond our normal ego structure. The veil that lies between our conscious mind and the vast ocean-like realm of our unconscious becomes more permeable. Because expanded consciousness gives us access to these normally elusive layers of our mind, a journeyer should be thoroughly prepared before entering this space. We can do this by becoming familiar with the ways the mind functions.

The Ego and Intellect

As human beings, we develop defenses and strategies as ways to cope with the painful experience of not getting our needs met or having been violated in any way. These defenses and strategies take shape as coping behaviors, thinking patterns, habits, and fears. On a basic level, their function is to create safety and avoid emotional pain associated with challenging psychological material. It is a basic animal instinct to not want to feel pain and to do whatever is possible to avoid it. Expanded states of consciousness have the effect of relaxing our psychological strategies and defenses and bringing us face-to-face with the content our ego structure normally keeps hidden.

In order to soften the intensity of this encounter, it is best that we develop a familiarity with these protective structures beforehand. We can acknowledge the ways we have been able to survive and then bring awareness to the ways these survival strategies may be outdated or how they limit our current life. For example, if I am in a situation where someone is acting unkind toward me, I may become agitated, unable to feel the pain of rejection. In my defense, I might become aggressive, rejecting the other in order to protect myself from feeling hurt. Pushing the other away is a defense mechanism that puts the attention on the other rather than acknowledging what is taking place for me on an emotional level.

The Emotions

We also want to become familiar with the content and flavor of the emotions that arise in our body and awareness. The more in touch we are with the way these states arise within us, the more profoundly we can engage our core material in expanded states of consciousness. We can cultivate this familiarity through paying attention to our day-to-day emotional states and to our behavioral patterns and tendencies.

In my experience with the Native American sweat lodge, the group prepares for the ritual by standing together around the fire pit, holding stones against their body. One by one, each person shares their current life situation and formulates a prayer based either on their problems or inspired by the gratitude they feel at the moment. In this way, they bring presence to their current emotional state before they enter the space of the healing ritual. Before meditation practitioners begin a solo retreat, they might meet with their teacher to share what is currently present in their inner world. Ideally, the teacher will then give them specific practices, depending on where they are in their process of spiritual development. If they are working with unprocessed anger, they might be given purification practices. If they are feeling uninspired, they may be given practices to cultivate energy and motivation. In this way, attention is brought to the specific situation and needs of the person entering the experience of self-exploration.

What a psychologist might consider to be an afflictive emotion or a psychological imbalance is sometimes understood differently by indigenous cultures. The Mazatec healers I have worked with speak of *envidia,* negative energy that can be shamanically sent to a person. I have been taught that it is critical to create alliances with the spirits of the land to strengthen the psyche against such attacks. Although that perspective does not fit into the scientific materialist paradigm, perhaps it is reflective of a different understanding of "in here" vs. "out there." My Mazatec friend Tiburcio conducts divinations to see if an emotional or psychological issue is due to past trauma, in which a piece of someone's spirit was left at the location of the event, or whether a person's anger comes from within, or is coming from the outside as negative energy. Tiburcio then recommends certain practices and offerings that can be made to regain peace.

Overall, during my time in the Mazatec community, I have observed that my hosts seem to spend less time than I do analyzing their thoughts, feelings, and emotional states. I have noticed that people tend to simply experience emotion with minimal self-reflection. If someone gets angry, they do not ask themselves, "Why am I angry?" They get angry and leave it at that, for better or for worse. They do not tend to dialogue as a way to resolve and explore the deeper roots of the issues that arise. When my teacher's family is experiencing conflict, they sometimes make the decision to journey together as a way to restore peace in the family. It is common in the Mazatec community that a whole family, including the mother, the father, and children from the age of eight, will partake in a ceremony together. The way I have seen my teacher's family prepare for a journey from an emotional perspective is with acknowledgment of the way they feel regarding the specific situation. It is by paying attention to the presence of harmony or dissonance in the family and noticing when there is a need for restoring the peace that they prepare for the experience.

However, over the years that I have been spending time and working in Mexico, I have witnessed what I would call a cross-pollination between our ways of dealing with emotions. Through my ongoing relationship with the family I work with, we have created a vocabulary of naming emotions and discussing difficult situations.

The Unconscious

In working with the unconscious, the approach tends to be different in indigenous cultures. I have observed how different cultures rely on unique cosmologies and certain rituals and prayers—which serve as a basis for the subconscious and unconscious material of their collective psyche. The Mazatec people embroider images of nature—animals, flowers, and mushrooms, as well as ancient symbols for the sun, water, earth, and geometric patterns that go back to ancestral times. Their art expresses subconscious imagery while also keeping them in close relationship with the power of these ancient symbols of their ancestral lineage. What we might call the unconscious, they call the realm of spirit. I have often heard them refer to what I would call the collective unconscious as the "Other Side," the "Place of God," the "Great Sky," or the "Great Book." I have also observed, during my travels around the world visiting different cultures, the unique beauty of creative expressions such as making art and music, that are practiced individually or as a group, strengthening the bond and codified identity of the culture. Thus, they are engaging their creative channels and expressing what comes through from "the other side" by giving it form. Some indigenous cultures take time to discuss their dreams together as a way to delve into the deeper material present in the community.[2]

✳ ✳ ✳

We in the modern industrialized world tend to use our mind mainly for its analytical and reflective abilities. Residing primarily in this analytical function of mind has advantages as well as weaknesses. The advantages include the framework and terminology to look inside and take stock of our emotional states, our fears, and our vulnerabilities. In our culture of healing and self-growth, we have cultivated the capacity to reflect, identify, name, and share. These are some of the wonderful gifts of our culture that we can use to our benefit. We can be honest and say, "I have a weakness around this territory," or "I am kind of lost around this." We have the vocabulary to reflect upon and name our feelings. The disadvantage of this is the tendency to become overly analytical of our inner states and lose contact with our actual raw emotion, our somatic experience, and our spiritual resources.

To best engage the preparation process on the level of the mind and emotions, we begin by bringing mindfulness to our immediate experience. In this way, we begin to prepare our conscious mind through the simple act of becoming aware of our actual state, whatever it is. We can begin by noticing and naming our thoughts and how we are feeling in general. What thoughts, ideas, anxieties, fears, or concerns are occupying our thinking and feeling body? What personal material, memories, or emotions are we conscious of right now? What are we feeling on a raw emotional level? What are the habits, tendencies, or patterns that keep us at a distance from our raw experience?

And specifically, as we approach an expanded state of consciousness experience, what are we feeling? We might feel fearful as we leave for a vision quest. We may feel excited to begin a meditation retreat. We might feel growing agitation before we participate in a breathwork seminar. By bringing awareness to our emotions and thoughts, we are able to encounter our raw experience rather than resist or avoid it. We can also consider unconscious material that may be attempting to reveal itself to us by engaging in practices to open and activate the unconscious. What is in or out of balance for us? What is asking for more nurture?

In order to explore psychological content from an archetypal perspective, a journeyer can explore a system like the Enneagram or astrology. These maps can work as reflections of where we are in relationship with everything else. I find that astrology sometimes shows us the big picture. What planetary transits are happening as we prepare to go into a journey, and what does this mean for us? One can also use divination to access the deeper levels of knowing: tarot cards, the I Ching, rune stones, or similar practices.[3]

For most people, the thought of going inward to explore unknown territories of the mind will trigger palpable apprehension. As we open into an expanded state, we sometimes find ourselves gripped by a complex configuration of fear that is directly related to our biographical material, regardless of how well we know it. This fear often reflects unresolved memories and emotions from our past that have become calcified inside us. Facing the unknown with some apprehension is a natural response. We can consider it healthy respect. In the Mazatec culture, when fear arises for someone going into a journey, it is presumed that they need to deepen their respect for the mushrooms. They are invited to keep faith in divine intervention and surrender to the healing of the medicine. For people new to the mushrooms, faith will develop with time and experience.

Simple meditation or relaxation practices will help to calm the mind and nervous system, which is helpful before entering a journey of any kind. A journeyer should attempt to tend to any agitation appearing in their body and take basic measures to soothe the mind and relax. It is best to minimize stressors. It is suggested that before going into a journey one avoids disturbing movies, intense interpersonal conflict, or watching the news and its drama. One does not want to increase their contraction and fear before entering into an expanded state of consciousness. As one calms the physical body to create a steady baseline on the physical level, it is important to do the same with the mind.

Spending extra time in nature can have a harmonizing effect on our minds as well as our bodies. When we are in nature, the organic coherence around us is soothing. The shades of green, the vibration of the trees, and the earth beneath us all combine to help ground us. Nature helps us slow down so we can notice the thoughts and emotions that are moving through us moment to moment. A calm, steady place facilitates self-awareness.

As for the unconscious, we cannot completely prepare it because, by definition, it is unconscious. Often, though, when we make a commitment and begin to prepare for a journey into an expanded state, the deeper levels of the psyche begin to open on their own. We may feel stronger emotions, have memories surface, experience vivid dreams, or sense a more acute awareness than usual. Perhaps this is because humans have been journeying inward for thousands of years and our psyches know what to do. It is as though we are hardwired for the experience of diving into our inner world, and our psyche remembers.

It is helpful to practice techniques that access the unconscious so that when we encounter our material in a journey we are not completely caught off guard. If we are already utilizing the language of the unconscious and in conversation with our deeper material, we will likely move into an encounter with it more gracefully. In preparation for a journey, it is not our goal to bring the unconscious completely into consciousness. I see the unconscious as an ongoing matrix of gestation where things need to develop before they are born into our conscious mind. There is much that we do not know about ourselves, and that is okay. What is ready to appear will do so at just the right time.

Personal Preparation

Begin by reflecting on your inventory and the state of your mental and emotional experience, as described in chapter 3 of this book.

As you prepare for a journey on the level of the mind and emotions, it can be beneficial to write in a journal or make art, play music, sing, or write as a way of expressing what is coming through. A journaling practice brings your attention to your feelings and internal states—write for fifteen minutes every morning. Read through old journals and reflect on how far you have come. Contemplate old photos of yourself. It is also helpful to have a therapist, elder, guide, loved one, or support group to connect with and share the thoughts and emotions that you are experiencing. Depending on your preferences and your resources, find a therapist and explore core wounds, painful memories and issues, or open up emotionally with a trusted friend and share what you are going through. To gain a broader understanding of trauma, read books by Peter Levine or Bessel van der Kolk,[4] find a Somatic Experiencing practitioner,[5] or join a support group.

If you are not a meditator, beginning a simple daily practice of mindfulness is a wonderful way to begin to pay attention to what is moving through you. You can take ten minutes and focus your attention on your breath. You can chant a mantra. You can be with what is; sit still and notice what is there. You can explore guided imagery, breathing techniques, and Mindfulness-Based Stress Reduction (MBSR).[6] If mindfulness is new to you, watch some videos or read some books to begin with by reputable teachers such as Tara Brach, Bhikkhu Bodhi, Pema Chödrön, Jon Kabat-Zinn, Jack Kornfield, Thich Nhat Hanh, Byron Katie, or Larry Yang.[7] There are now many resources available online from which you can learn a simple mindfulness practice, the first step of a well-tested path that leads to healing and transformation. You can also explore loving-kindness practice, also known as *metta* meditation in the Buddhist tradition, to cultivate compassion, forgiveness, and joy within yourself.[8]

To prepare the unconscious, intend to remember and then record your dreams. Again, it is partly a matter of paying attention and looking for themes, as dreams can be direct indications of the material we are processing. What characters, relationships, disturbances, or emotions show up? You can seek out a dream group to discuss them with others. Explore myth and the writings of Carl Jung,[9] Joseph Campbell,[10] Stanislav Grof,[11] or Michael Meade.[12] Read *The 13 Moon Oracle: A Journey through the Archetypal Faces of the Divine Feminine* by Ariel Spilsbury.[13] You can access unconscious material through practices that work on archetypal and mythic levels.

You can also activate your unconscious through intuitive painting, creative writing, playing music, making sculptures, or creative movement. In your painting or other artistic expressions, how is the unconscious slipping through? You can also be on the lookout for external signs and symbols that seem to jump out at you. Do you keep seeing the same animal, hearing the same song, or having the same thoughts? Why do you notice certain things more than others and how does that reflect the movement of your unconscious?

Because expanded states of consciousness can loosen and liberate long-repressed emotions, memories, and fears, it is wise to familiarize oneself with what is apparent as well as what is lying below the surface. We do not want to blast abruptly into tender memories and places of inner pain. Rather, by taking the time to prepare our mind for a journey, we assure our inner world that we are approaching with care and respect. In this way, we are able to cultivate trust in the path and trust in ourselves.

7

APPROACHING THE ALTAR

Spiritual Preparation

The spiritual path—is simply the journey of living our lives. Everyone is on a spiritual path; most people just don't know it.

—MARIANNE WILLIAMSON

During my trips to Mexico with clients, we often spend a few days preparing for the evening mushroom ceremonies. In the Mazatec tradition, it is customary to make offerings to the local spirits as a way of showing respect and asking permission to partake in any healing ritual.

During one such trip, my teacher's son-in-law, José, took us into an extensive underground network of caves, below the mountain overlooking Huautla de Jiménez. The locals call these caves "the lungs of the earth." We brought headlights, flashlights, hiking shoes, and ropes. We arrived at the mouth of the cave, a huge vault of rocks filled with bats' nests leading to endless, dark tunnels. José stopped us at the entrance. He opened his bag and pulled out a handful of cocoa beans, handing us each a few to offer. We each silently asked permission to the spirit of the cave to allow us into its realm, to keep us safe, and to assure a favorable visit, as we tossed our beans to the ground. Once we were inside, in pitch dark, we stopped again. This time, José pulled out a small ceramic pot and some charcoal. He lit the charcoal and placed a piece of copal resin incense on it. He gently spoke to the spirit of the cave, thanking it for welcoming us and for the mysterious beauty of its ancient formations, lakes, and walls.

Later that evening, as we deepened into the mushroom ritual, I felt how the power of the cave left a distinct impression on every level of my being. I felt in my heart that due to the inner posture of our offering and humility, I was able to receive the gifts of that mighty force.

My teacher Julieta has explained to me that the Mazatec people consider the state accessed in the mushroom ceremony to be the place where their ancestors reside. They emphasize the importance of having adequate spiritual protection for this realm and are careful about how they enter and leave it. Other indigenous cultures also view expanded states of consciousness as thinning the veil between the visible and invisible worlds. In the medicine journey, we cross from this reality and our identification with a specific personality into the realm of the formless, the ancestors, and of spirit.

Beyond the alliance with the ancestors and local spirits, earth-based rituals of preparation on the level of spirit include the creation of altars, the cleansing and purification of the body, making offerings, and silent periods of personal reflection.

The Altar

Most indigenous cultures that perform healing rituals or plant medicine ceremonies use an altar during ritual. An altar is a shrine, table, cabinet, shelf, or platform on which spiritual or religious objects and images are placed together in a way that invokes a sense of the sacred. When all the objects are brought together in a particular arrangement, they create a unique field of energy that represents and reflects those who participate in its making.

An altar can also be a place where religious rites are performed or on which offerings are made to deities or ancestors. Some cultures view the altar itself to be the portal between the physical and spiritual realms. Ayahuasqueros have an altar of healing perfumes, tobacco, crystals, or rocks. San Pedro shamans have a *mesa*, a cloth bundle containing talismans, water jars, and stones. Mushroom curanderas have an altar featuring sacred images, candles, and flowers. Churches and Buddhist temples have their distinct altars as well. An altar creates a focal point where the intention of the guide and his or her relationship with spirit is strengthened.

In my teacher Julieta's ceremony room, there is an altar that extends along the entire wall, arranged in three tiers from floor to ceiling. It is an amazing construction with large images, mostly of the Virgin of Guadalupe and Jesus. Julieta spent the last twenty-five years of her life frequently traveling internationally, and every time she would bring something new back to place on her altar. Over the years, her altar gained images of the Buddha, Native American bowls, and a Quan Yin statue. There were bottles of sacred water from other continents and a photo of His Holiness the Dalai Lama, whom she had personally met in Dharamsala and affectionately referred to as *El Jefe*, "the chief." There were huge vases of flowers, photos of the people she was praying for, and candles that were lit at the beginning and end of each ceremony. I was always awed by the magnitude of her altar.

In 2006, Julieta invited the entire Council of the 13 Indigenous Grandmothers, of which she was one of the founding members, to visit Huautla de Jiménez.[1] A friend of mine and I were asked to help organize it. Each grandmother was invited to guide the group in a ritual prayer according to their respective tradition. When it was the two Lakota grandmothers' turn to offer their ritual, they shared that out of concern that their eagle feathers and other sacred objects would be confiscated at the Mexican border, they did not bring them along. I had set up an area for them to conduct their ritual: the chairs stood in a half circle by the river, and the setting was beautiful. As they were preparing their sacred space, I asked if they needed anything for their altar, and they said no. They looked at the ground and chose four stones. They placed them mindfully on the ground, and then stood in the middle and faced the seven directions with tobacco in their hands. They slowly and deliberately offered it to the sky.

This simple yet moving ritual taught me how to see the divine in everything. An altar can be anything from four stones on the earth to an elaborate church altar rich with esoteric symbolism.

Cleansing and Purification

Another way to approach the divine is through energetic cleansing, which is central to many indigenous and meditative traditions. Extensive cleansing with herbs, called *limpias,* are often done amongst the Mazatec people. They go into the mountains and collect branches of specific herbs. In the evening, as participants enter the space of the mushroom ceremony, the curandera stands at the threshold with a small earthen chalice called a *copalero* where her incense resin is burning. She passes the branches through the smoke then brushes each participant's entire body to accomplish the cleansing process. Other traditions use the smoke of burning sage, sweetgrass, palo santo, or tobacco as a way to cleanse whatever stagnant energy may be clinging to people and to invite them into a deeper state of presence.

I once visited a Buddhist temple in Singapore. At the door of the temple was a huge bowl filled with sand and about 500 sticks of burning incense. As people walked through the entrance, as if stepping over a threshold, they would pass through the cloud of cleansing smoke. The smoke seemed to wash them as they entered the temple.

Water rituals are part of many religions. Catholics cross themselves with holy water as they enter a church. Baptists dunk themselves in rivers. Muslims wash their feet before entering a mosque.

Making Offerings

Indigenous traditions also often make offerings as part of spiritual preparation. My teacher's family regularly make offerings of flowers, candles, copal resin, and cocoa beans. Many objects are placed on the altar as offerings to the divine and to the spirit of the mushroom.

In Mexico, before we do any ceremony, we climb to the top of the local mountain called Chikon Nindo, the most sacred spot in the region. People hike up to make offerings to the *dueño*, the guardian spirit of the area, who resides in the mountain and oversees all the spiritual and energetic affairs of the region. Young parents walk the hour-long trail to present their newborn child to Chikon Nindo and make offerings for their child's protection. The local people are devoted to this spiritual presence of the mountain.

Native Americans often offer tobacco or sacred herbs such as sweetgrass, juniper, or cedar to the spirits. Prior to entering sweat lodges, participants sit together and make prayer ties with specific colors representative of each cardinal direction: east, west, north, and south. They place a small amount of an herb, often tobacco, in the center of a square of cloth. (To Native Americans, like the Lakota or Cree, tobacco is a sacred medicine, to be used in rituals and ceremonies.) Then, while praying, the participants fold up the cloth. They tie the little bundle with a piece of string or thin cloth and connect it with other such bundles. Then, they hang the prayer tie garlands inside the lodge. It is also customary in the Native American tradition to make a circle of cornmeal around the place where one will do a vision quest.

In Bali, people make elaborate constructions with bamboo and palms, weaving the leaves into tiny baskets, which they fill with rice and incense. They make these offerings throughout the day and place them around the house and temples to feed the local spirits.

Some years ago, my teacher Julieta came to stay at our house and asked, "Where will we offer the cocoa beans?" I responded, "You mean on the ground?" and she said, "Yes, where is your place of ritual? Where do the offerings go?" And I told her, "Well, I have this tree out there. . . ." And she said, *"Bueno, vamos!"* Then she asked, "So, do you use cocoa beans or you use something else?" I told her, "Sometimes I use rice, sometimes cornmeal, and sometimes cocoa beans." And she said, "Okay, whatever you want. It does not matter what you have in your hand. As long as you have a sacred place on your land and you ask permission for your work, it is good." It was inconceivable to her not to have a sacred place on my land to make offerings.

In the offering ritual, as Julieta pointed out, we give something symbolic or valuable to the land and spirits to ask for permission to conduct ceremony or to request support or healing. It is an act of recognizing the generous abundance we receive from the earth and offering something back. It is about saying please and thank you, offering what you have with humility and generosity.

Silence and Contemplation

Another way people in indigenous cultures prepare for ceremonies is through observing a period of silence. This listening into the inner self requires quieting the mind through practices such as meditating, watching the breath, meditating with a candle or effigy, or focusing the senses on one object.

A quiet mind can also be attained through reciting prayers, mantras, or sutras. My teacher Julieta was Catholic and prayer was one of her regular practices. She would recite the rosary in front of her altar as she prepared for every ceremony. Woven into her recitation, she would speak directly to the mushroom and name the people present. She would also call on the strength of the earth and the sky, the spirit of the rain, the wind, and the local spirits of her region. She was always in conversation with the saints and spirits, nurturing and affirming her alliances.

A powerful way of nurturing spiritual alliances is the act of remembering one's ancestors. Many cultures maintain bonds with their deceased family members by holding extensive rituals to honor them. As I mentioned earlier, the Mazatec people, similar to some other indigenous cultures, consider the realm of the dead and their ancestors to be accessible through ritual. In the specific case of the Mazatec tradition, the experience of being close to their ancestors offers support for challenging ceremonies. Every year, on the Day of the Dead, they go to the cemetery as a family and decorate the tombs of those who have died as they tell stories about them.[2]

Many of us are so disconnected from our ancestors that we do not even know the names of our great-grandparents. Nonetheless, it is valuable to make a connection with our ancestors, not only because they can support us in our healing work, but also because, in a sense, we are doing this work for them.

In our modern industrialized world, which has such a different cultural context, how can we prepare spiritually before we enter an expanded state of consciousness? There are many practices and rituals for us to be inspired by. We do not have to drink from one spiritual fountain. Those of us from other lands can tap into the pre-Abrahamic spiritual traditions of our ancestors and history.[3] In pre-Christian Europe, traditional healers, sages, priestesses, and oracles flourished for thousands of years before they were decried as pagan, and repressed.[4] If we feel called to certain rituals and traditions practiced thousands of miles away, then we can explore them. We can develop relationships with deities, devas, gods, local spirits, angels, archangels, the Great Spirit, God, or the Goddess. Some of us feel profoundly connected to the sacredness of the natural world, and through the land, perceive the divinity all around and within us.

When we go to a beautiful spot in nature, enter a church, or witness a significant ritual, this experience itself can bring us into an expanded state. We want to find practices that take us to this level so that we can begin to open to the divine.

If we incorporate practices from other cultures, it is important to do so respectfully. We do not want to dilute or disrespect any tradition but rather be inspired by and humbly borrow aspects of their ways. We can incorporate and we can adapt, always with respect. Even though I have been going to Mexico for many years, I still do not understand many things. Their rituals marking the first corn of the year and the coming of spring are beyond my comprehension, but there are many aspects of these rituals that I can understand, am inspired by, and weave into my own life in my own way.

The point of spiritual preparation is to engage with practices and customs that resonate with us. We want to create a foundation and nurture our relationship to spirit through practices that connect us to the sacred.

Personal Preparation

In order to specifically prepare on the level of the spirit, refer to the inventory from chapter 3 to get clear on your spiritual strengths and weaknesses. Reflect on your relationship with these aspects of your life and choose practices for preparation that will encourage balance and strengthening where you need it most. You can prepare on the level of spirit by creating an altar in your home with special objects, flowers, crystals, and statues. If you already have an altar, undo it and make a new one. It is refreshing to remake an altar once in a while. You take everything off and put everything back intentionally. Spend time with each object, touch it, hold it, and place it back down again. Even if you replace the same object in the same location, your attention refreshes the energy of your altar. Or make a new altar with objects that are more current and meaningful to you. The ritual of making an altar begins to relax our inner state as the intentional act of creation itself opens our psyche into a vaster state of consciousness.

As for the purification process, cleanse your home and altar by burning palo santo, incense, or sage. You can use tobacco, resins, woods, herbs, or find substances that resonate more closely with you. Some people sprinkle saltwater, ring bells around their body, or pray to the spirit of water while bathing. Some people spray themselves with rosewater or lavender water or anoint themselves with oil. It is a matter of setting an intention to be purified and having a physical practice to follow it through with.

You can also create your own ritual of making offerings. Find a spot near your home or a local park that feels special or sacred and make offerings to certain trees and plants, the creek, or the local mountain. You can make offerings of rice, cocoa beans, coins, flowers, tobacco, water, or anything that feels significant. It is honorable that before you take something from the earth, before you pick an apple or harvest greens from your garden, to make this gesture of offering. It is customary in the Native American tradition to offer tobacco, but rice, cornmeal, or cocoa beans—these all work as long as they mean something to you.

Sit alone in nature, in silence, and focus on your inner experience or begin a practice of contemplation or meditation for five to ten minutes a day. Go to a church, temple, or mosque; or partake in different types of rituals and ceremonies that appeal to you. Read books on prayer and contemplation from different traditions. Make prayers of gratitude for your loved ones and community, or for your personal aspirations.

Research your ancestors. If you can, talk to family members to find out their names and listen to or record their stories. Perhaps you can get photos to place on your altar. If you do not have photos, you can write their names on a card and place that upon your altar. If you have no living relatives, you might at least know the countries where your ancestors lived. Read up on the history of those countries, listen to their traditional music, explore the food, and reconnect with the culture that is in your blood and bones. In this way, you can strengthen the bond between yourself and those who came before you. Then, when you enter into rituals and ceremonies, you can call on your ancestors and their generations of wisdom that continue to live on through you. Studies on transgenerational trauma have shown that events that occurred up to three generations back have an effect on the living. If you do not relate with your blood ancestors as a source of wisdom, you can call upon other elders or wise people throughout history whose teachings or writings inspire you. If you have a spiritual heritage by birth, by practice, or by mentorship that you identify with, then by all means incorporate it into your preparation process.

It does not matter if we sit beside an elaborate altar or a stream. It is the intention and the remembrance of making an alliance with the sacred that matters. As we prepare on the level of spirit, we experience something larger than ourselves and discover how we are in relationship with the unseen realm. Eventually, as we open ourselves to this realm, we begin to feel how it nourishes us. Like all relationships, our connection with the spiritual dimension takes time and commitment.

8

TENDING THE WEB

Community Preparation

*Wealth (among the Dagara) is determined not by
how many things you have, but by how many people
you have around you.*

MALIDOMA PATRICE SOMÉ[1]

I am with the Mosetén people in the Bolivian Amazon. The village is quiet. In the huts, the women are choosing which necklace they will wear over their white dresses. Each river shell, animal tooth, and seed is symbolic. The men place masks on their faces and begin preparing their drums and flutes. The children watch the preparation silently as they follow each word and action. The flutes sound and families emerge from each hut dancing, hopping from foot to foot, and singing a high pitched song resembling animal sounds.

The children stare quietly, and the adults appear to be in a trance. I am carried into a strange space, both inside myself and out into the forest surrounding me. I don't understand what this ritual means, yet I feel swept into an ancient time. I experience the marriage of humans and nature in the sacred web of tribal life.

* * *

An expanded state of consciousness can bring us to a place of clarity where basic truths are felt profoundly. One of these truths is the interdependence that exists between us and all of the people in our lives—our family, friends, teachers, neighbors, coworkers, and all the others that surround us. Humans have lived in groups and clans throughout history. Hermits living alone are the rare exception; they often live deep in nature and cultivate a sense of community with animals and plants. For the rest of us, living together, cooking and eating together, working together, sharing rituals together, and taking care of one another is the way of life. It is through our relationships with the many people of our lives that we do much of our healing.

In indigenous cultures, rituals that bring people into expanded states of consciousness are often at the core of community life. The elders supervise solitary vision quests and rites of initiation. These rituals are prepared for as a community, experienced together as a community, and integrated as a community back into the fabric of day-to-day life.

A friend of mine went on a four-day solitary vision quest in the mountains of Montana. In preparation for it, all of the vision questers participated in a sweat lodge ceremony. They then received instructions on how to best approach the quest. On the third day, my friend experienced a few hours of intense panic and isolation. He realized he was all alone in an extreme environment surrounded by wild animals and began to spiral into fear for his well-being and safety. He said it was only because he remembered his fellow questers out on their respective quests, sharing a similar experience, and knowing they would all reunite soon, that he was able to be with his fear. He remembered there was a larger container of safety and was able to relax into it.

Once, I asked Julieta if I could journey alone with the mushrooms. She agreed and said I was ready and that it would help me create an alliance with the *Chikones,* the land spirits, and the ancient ways of her tradition. I was taken to the nearby mountain to be picked up in the morning. I was told to create an altar and during my journey to stay sitting in front of it. I was told to sing and pray and listen. I connected with the magic of the land and perceived teachings I have never even tried to articulate. Although I was alone in the mountains, I could feel the prayers and support of Julieta and her family. It was an empowering initiation, spending the night in a profound state of listening.

As previously mentioned, in the Mazatec tradition a mushroom ceremony is often conducted as a family. The group prepares together, praying and singing. They then ingest the mushrooms together. During the ceremony, they share their concerns, fears, and insights with one another. In the case of physical illness or injury, the whole family is engaged in supporting a member's healing, which is considered an issue to be dealt with collectively.

In the Amazon, rituals of healing with psychotropic plants have evolved alongside community life. The native people and plants coexist intimately and the plants are used within group rituals. Their preparation often includes certain diets, specific activities, the way they dress, and how they decorate their bodies. Whatever the preparation, it will often be done as a group. The men and women might prepare differently or have different roles, but they will still be in community in their respective groups.

I have some dear friends who travel regularly to Gabon, Africa, to partake in the trance dance ritual. Coming together and dancing brings them into a unified resonance in which they are able to bond as one organism. The community is the container where people can dance together, inhabited by the healing force of spirit.

In my experience of sweat lodge rituals, all the onsite preparatory steps are done as a community: the building of the lodge, the making of the fire, and the creation of the prayer ties. I have been part of such rituals for many years, and I have come to see how these various group activities strongly contribute to everyone's connectedness and safety during the experience in the lodge.

Many years ago, my friend Oscar was diagnosed with Lou Gehrig's disease. He knew there was no cure for his illness and that he would soon die.

He wanted to say goodbye to his friends before that happened, so I gathered his closest friends in my living room.

He expressed his love and gratitude to each of us and recalled funny stories from our shared past. He lay down in the center, and we made a circle around him, each placing a hand on his body. We hummed songs, making wishes for his soft transition to the other side, as he called it. We felt honored to celebrate his life and to share in his preparation for death. Being together with him profoundly impacted everyone present. At that moment, it was Oscar who offered our community a gift.

Importance of Community

While we in the modern industrialized world live differently from those in the Amazon jungle, on a reservation, or in a village in Mexico, we all have the same human need for connection. One of the most detrimental effects of industrialization is isolation. People's lives are disconnected from one another. Small families or individuals live by themselves in houses or apartments, and the elderly often live alone in nursing homes. Because the modern industrialized world does not foster community, it is up to its inhabitants to create and tend it. As we attempt to explore, recreate, and reclaim rituals as best we can, we can learn from the ways indigenous people incorporate their community into their rituals. We can create community through time spent with the people in our lives by sharing our vulnerability and seeking guidance and support.

Engagement with community begins with the contact that is established between a guide and a journeyer. The guide forges the bond with the journeyer or between the members of the group by creating a safe environment and establishing compassionate support. Even if you are going out to do a solo journey or quest, you will still meet with the guide beforehand to discuss the journey and what is sought from it. Simply sharing one's emotional state with the guide, the leader, or the group creates community on the most basic level.

When I used to work with my teacher Pablo, he would guide us through four hours of preparation before a journey. We would do ritual art and writing processes, spending time together as a group, interacting in different ways.

Each member would share what was going on in their lives, what they were feeling, and their intentions for the upcoming ritual. We would offer one another foot and neck massages. We would sit together in a circle, singing gently, and one by one go into the middle of the group and share painful experiences from our lives. By the time we entered the medicine journey, we felt cohesive as a group, each person surrounded by the compassion and support of the others. We felt safe and we shared a feeling of kinship with one another. In my opinion, this is the optimal way to enter any group work, and I have adopted this method with remarkable success.

One way to incorporate community in the phase of preparation is to take the time to envision what we may need after a journey. We involve our community by being vulnerable enough to ask for their support. If it is appropriate, we can include a friend in our plans and invite them to join and support us afterward. If we are embarking on a solo journey, we can tell a friend what we are planning to do in our upcoming ritual and ask for their prayers. Perhaps we can ask them to drop us off at the ritual and pick us up at the end. They can light a candle for us and send us positive thoughts.

Before entering a journey space, we can reach out to people who possess a certain level of sensitivity and compassion. We recognize the preciousness of certain relationships and the richness that they can offer to our process, especially if they are friends who have gone through a similar experience. Their perspective can offer us support and encouragement, reminding us of the importance of community.

A guide should pay attention beforehand to what someone might need in order to tend to this aspect, before the journey experience. If someone is isolated, it can be valuable to begin the process of reaching out beforehand, and the guide can encourage a journeyer to connect with a community or a group with shared interests. On the other hand, if someone is overly committed and highly social, it is wise to suggest alone time beforehand.

Personal Preparation

In order to prepare for a journey, I encourage you to look over your inventory and see how you stand in relation to your community. You can examine the state of the relationships in your life. In summary, if you feel you lack community, seek out activities, classes, and events where you will meet like-minded people. Find a local meditation group, hiking group, dance community, cooking class, choir, painting group, or book club. Reach out and create an affiliation with groups that you feel solidarity with, such as local nonprofits and charitable organizations.

Spend time with your partner, friends, or family beforehand, sharing your intention and plan. Ask your friends or family to light a candle for you and to send you supportive thoughts. If you are attending a group ritual, ask the facilitator if you can arrive early and help set up. Try to connect with another participant through carpooling or make contact with another person who is more experienced in the tradition or modality. Make sure that you will have support afterward from a friend, a partner, or family. At the same time, ensure that you have a calm, quiet environment to go home to if needed. Human contact might feel overwhelming, and solitary rest may be necessary.

If, on the other hand, you have too much community contact in your day-to-day life, take more time for yourself as part of your preparation.

For thousands of years, indigenous cultures have prepared for rituals that bring people into expanded states of consciousness. These experiences would then in turn fortify the bonds between community members. As we reclaim these rituals, our journey of self-discovery and healing does not need to be an isolating or lonely one. If we do not have a healthy community, we can nurture and tend this part of our life. It is through cultivating strong bonds with others and including them in the vulnerable parts of our lives that we can receive the human connection we all crave. It is a gift to ask for support and a gift to offer it. I encourage every journeyer to involve their community in their preparation process, as it will greatly enrich their experience. Our healing is the healing of all those with whom we are in relationship.

9

NOURISHING OUR ROOTS

Environmental Preparation

*Keep close to nature's heart ... and break clear away,
once in awhile, and climb a mountain or spend a
week in the woods. Wash your spirit clean.*

—JOHN MUIR[1]

Ming, a longtime client of mine, decided to go on a solitary meditation retreat and asked for guidance as to how she might prepare the space for her arrival. She had rented a small cabin in the woods where she would be spending most of her days and wanted her environment to be supportive of her intention to deepen into her practices. I suggested that cleansing the space would be an integral part of preparation. I suggested she air out the cabin, sweep the floors, clean the windows, sage the entire space, and rearrange the furniture to be appropriate for her practices. She could then make sure that her sleeping area felt adequate and comfortable.

I then suggested she make herself familiar with the local environment by visiting the nearby creek, looking for an outdoor place to practice, and familiarizing herself with any trees with which she felt a connection. I added that she could say specific prayers when she built her first fire in the woodstove. I also suggested that she could offer small bowls of grain and incense in each of the four directions around the house as a protection offering.

Ming returned from her retreat with a renewed sense of spiritual connection and reported that the attention she brought to creating a supportive environment was critical. She realized how little attention she usually brought to her own home. She said just the act of caring for the space brought her inner healing and nourishment and that every day she had looked forward to gathering a bouquet for her shrine. She said that she now had a clear intention of tending her own home as mindfully as she had tended her meditation space. In turn, her "home tending," as she called it, became an ongoing practice of mindfulness that soothed her in ways she had not expected.

When we enter expanded states of consciousness, we become more sensitive to our surroundings. This pertains to the people we are with and the physical space we are in: the room, building, or natural environment, as well as the animals and plants that are nearby. Perhaps because of this increased sensitivity, we commonly experience a deeper connection with the natural world. We often perceive the complex beauty of nature as well as our pain in response to the current ecological imbalance.

In chapter 3, we discussed set and setting and the need to prepare the immediate environment. This is the actual building or location where a ritual takes place. But we also want to prepare in regard to the larger environment: all the animals, plants, minerals, and elements of nature.

In indigenous settings, preparing the location for a ritual is a practice in and of itself. For example, in preparation for a sweat lodge ritual, each gesture is symbolic and is considered a prayer. Much attention is brought to the building of the lodge. Long branches of willow are arched and positioned to form the dome of the lodge. Then, the earthen floor is cleaned and carefully covered with blankets, while the fire pit is prepared. This is where the stones are to be heated. My teacher Marilyn Youngbird, a superb lodge leader, makes sure there are no folds in the blankets anywhere in the lodge. As she says, "A folded blanket flap is a prayer unfinished." The door of the sweat lodge faces east to line up with an altar outside the lodge: a small earth mound where people place personal objects. Specific stones are carefully placed into the pit, marking the four cardinal directions. While the fire heats the stones, the participants make prayer ties with organic tobacco and cotton fabric in different colors, each symbolizing a different direction. The ties are then hung along the inside of the lodge in their respective directions.

In the Mazatec tradition, to step into the designated room where the mushroom ceremony takes place is to enter a place of worship. It is a sacred space that has been prepared to welcome spirit. An impressive amount of attention is devoted to the cleaning, the purification, and the decoration of the room. Once the guide has prepared the room, the spaces for each participant are provided with pillows and blankets. Fresh flowers are placed in front of the altar. Even though it is not remade every time, the altar is tended carefully. The guide lights new candles made from local beeswax. Branches of a specific plant have been gathered and are ready to be used for the limpias (cleansing) of the participants. The copalero, a ritual vessel made from clay, is waiting to be used for the burning of the copal tree resin.

In indigenous cultures, nature is central to any ritual that involves expanded states of consciousness because it is nature that brings forth these states. Sprouting forth from the body of the earth itself are the plants and fungi used in ritual to bring vision and deeper understandings. Julieta has explained that nature—the soil, the mountains, the paths, the waterfalls, the caves, the rain, and specific locations—are the sources of earth's sacred healing power.

Depending on the location of an indigenous culture, the elements most present in their lives are likely to be woven into their myths and practices. The rare ones will be the focus of their prayers and wishes. South African Sān people who live in a desert region place a high value on rituals that call in the water element, which is a sparse and valuable resource for them. The rituals of the Yupik Eskimo people, whose survival depends on fishing, revolve around the ocean's abundance.[2] Native people commonly work with the elements—earth, water, fire, air, and space or spirit—in their rituals. In many cultures, purification ceremonies using water have been practiced for millennia: in full-body immersions, in the washing of feet and hands, or by pouring water over the head. The burning of sage or resins goes back beyond biblical times and holds a significance of purification and protection, whether for the Lakota of the sacred Black Hills or the wise women of ancient Europe. In the African Bwiti ritual that involves the ingestion of iboga, the use of body painting is at the core of the preparation process: it symbolizes a communion with the earth and a gateway to entering the realm of the ancestors.

Calling in or physically representing earth, water, fire, air, and space helps us to acknowledge their presence in our physical body as well as in our outer environment. Even if we do not have a scientific way to measure how these practices influence us, we feel a growing connection between us and what we invoke. We can familiarize ourselves with the local spirits of a place.

Alongside the elements, indigenous rituals often begin with an invocation of the cardinal directions. This calling is conducted differently by each culture, but its consistent presence is noteworthy. It is a ritual of recognizing one's physical orientation. Through calling that which anchors each direction (landmarks, energies, and spirits), the center is defined and known. Hawaiian natives call their directions differently than the Sān people of South Africa. I once led a ritual on a Hawaiian island that began by calling the directions. I quickly realized that all four cardinal points were oriented toward the ocean, and that water was obviously the dominant element I would be working with.

What stands at the east might be a desert, an ocean, or a mountain. The ritual of calling the directions is a tangible practice that can help us establish a relationship between the outer environment and ourselves. It is a way to connect with the natural world and to receive the strength and support of each direction and what it represents. As in indigenous cultures, we should adapt our ritual to our geographical location. While there are consistencies between some traditions, every direction correlates to something different for each person. For one person, the east may represent birth and new life. For another, the east may be associated with a certain animal or season. Reclaiming this simple practice, which belongs to all humans, means following one's inspiration and deciding what feels most authentic. Rather than blindly copying a specific tradition, the exercise of paying attention to what is present in each direction opens one up to the grounding the ritual provides.

Those of us living disconnected from the natural world need to find ways to prepare on the level of the environment. How can we draw inspiration and guidance from an earth-based way of life?

Personal Preparation

Look back over your responses to this inventory and reflect on how you stand in relationship with your immediate and larger environment. Be real with yourself. How can you come into a stronger alliance with your environment before you enter a ritual of consciousness expansion?

If you are going to conduct or participate in a ceremony, you can bring your attention and care to where it will take place. What is the room like? How can you best set up the space? If the ritual will happen outside, is it far enough away from the road that you will not be disturbed by anyone? If you do something out in the woods, is it flat enough? Will you be comfortable and warm enough? It is best to keep track of what is going on around you and how you relate to it. How does it impact your experience or mood? The spaciousness, the construction materials, the sounds, and the light all affect how you feel in a space.

You can clean and purify your space before a ritual, and the intention you bring to this clearing is important. You can use cleansing smoke, sound, or fire to cleanse the energy of a space. You can decorate the space with candles, flowers, fabrics, pictures, or things that help you feel safe and connected. You want to feel safe after a ritual as well, so it is good practice to clean and prepare your home for your return. You want your home to be a welcoming and nurturing environment to receive you after you have done your healing work.

As we prepare for our journey, we also want to consider our environment on a larger level. We are intimately connected with our environment. It is not something detached and "out there." What is going on around us impacts what is happening inside of us before, during, and after a journey.

How do we care for the planetary environment around us? How do we protect it? What actions do we take? How are we involved?

To prepare on the level of the outer environment, you can invoke the elements—fire, water, earth, air, and space. You can invoke the directions—east, west, north, south, above, below, and within. Go to a wild place for a walk to connect with nature. Sit alone in nature and listen or make an earth altar on the beach or in the forest out of natural materials. Bathe in a river. Tend the plants around your house. Watch the sunrise or sunset for a few days in a row and pay attention to the phases of the moon. Visit mountains, rivers, and, if appropriate, places local native people consider sacred. Ask nature to support your journey. Decorate and beautify your space of ritual.

Preparing on the level of the environment is a practical act as well as a spiritual one. Bringing awareness to our place of ritual, our environment, and the planet at large strengthens our relationship with all of life. Our awareness not only informs how we locate ourselves in our environment but to what degree we feel connected or disconnected from it.

✳ ✳ ✳

This comprehensive survey of preparatory practices may feel overwhelming at this point for some readers. It is a lot of information to take in. How could you possibly prepare in so many ways, meticulously tending all the aspects of your life, let alone guide the process for another? This may seem like an impossible mission. In reality, these suggestions are just that—suggestions. They are an invitation to know yourself better and to look with gentleness into areas of your life that might benefit from loving attention as you prepare for a dive into an expanded state of consciousness.

The truth is, nobody prepares perfectly. Life ebbs and flows, with new waves every day: emotional events, bodily stressors and illness, and our ongoing dance of relationship with others. It is all constantly changing and keeps us on our toes. The practice of tending the aspects of our life with compassionate attention is a glorious work in progress. An intention to prepare is a path of its own, with no eventual goal besides continuing to strengthen our capacity to honestly relate with our self, others, and all of life.

10
ENTERING THE UNKNOWN

Journey into an Expanded State

The way I must enter
Leads through darkness to darkness—
O moon above the mountain's rim,
Please shine a little further
On my path

—IZUMI SHIKIBU[1]

After the preparation is complete, a journeyer is ready to embark upon the actual journey experience. Whether we are walking into the woods for a weeklong vision quest, crawling in through the flaps of a sweat lodge, or taking a plant medicine into our body, we are leaving the ordinary world behind and entering an intentional space of healing and transformation.

The two qualities of faith and surrender, which I explained in chapter 1, are key as guide and journeyer approach expanded space. Opening the channels that are not flowing requires this faith and surrender. The external and internal experience of a journey will likely be unfamiliar and extraordinary. Entering an expanded state of consciousness requires courage, agility, awareness, and confidence. The journey has the potential to create harmony between the layers of one's being: the physical, emotional, spiritual, energetic, and cosmic. It is like an expedition into a dark abyss filled with old boxes, some filled with dust, some filled with gold. The unconscious is filled with shadowy corners, unimaginable collective resonances, cosmic oneness, unfelt vibrations, forgotten emotional knots, and even terror. However, with a thorough preparation, a clear intention, and a masterful guide, a journeyer should rest assured that as challenging and strange as the experience may be, it will be held as safely as possible.

Arriving at the place where one's journey will occur marks the beginning of an active process. The journeyer is stepping over the threshold from the normal day-to-day life into a time and space designated for a ritual of inner exploration. They might be walking from their car to the location where they will camp for a weeklong vision quest. They might be stepping into the room where they will participate in an evening dance ceremony. They might be finding their seat in a sweat lodge, anticipating the arrival of the hot stones.

The psyche recognizes this moment as the point of no return, akin to slowly ascending the incline of a roller coaster. The journeyer will likely feel anxious or excited. They may feel intense fear or regret as they think to themselves, "What was I thinking to do this?" On the other hand, they might feel eager and ready to go, noticing an unfamiliar yet thrilling courage arising from within.

Different techniques take a journeyer to different depths. For people beginning to explore this path, it is wonderful to have access to gentle techniques that are less intimidating or overwhelming, such as breathwork, painting, or dancing. For journeyers who have more experience, they may be ready to dive into deeper realms of their psyches with a vision quest, a sweat lodge, or a consciousness-expanding substance. One's anticipation is often related to how extreme the chosen technique will be and the expected level of challenge. However, a technique that seems mild may take someone to an extremely profound place. This realm of exploration is mysterious. The guide will already be tracking the journeyer's state, whether eager, weepy, or afraid. As the journeyer steps into the space of the ritual, the process has already begun.

The Four Phases of a Journey

Even though each person's inner experience is unique as well as nonlinear and will not necessarily adhere to this map, most journeys tend to follow a basic arc that can be roughly divided into four phases: the entry, the immersion, the reflection, and the return. The descriptions of the four phases offer a broad map, while the specific types of experience that can occur are examined in detail in the following chapter. Each of these phases consists of their unique intensity, characteristics, and insights.

The Entry

Once the guide and journeyer are settled in their location with everything in place, they are ready to begin the journey. The first phase of the entry begins as soon as the technique is engaged. If it is a plant medicine ceremony, the journeyer takes the sacrament and the guide may begin to sing. If it is a sweat lodge, the flaps are now closed. If it is a dance retreat, the music is beginning. If it is a vision quest, the journeyer sets up camp in the wilderness and speaks their intention. It is now time to surrender to the experience, however it may unfold.

The journeyer will begin to observe changes as they become accustomed to new internal conditions within their physical and emotional experience. If they are in a sweat lodge, this phase consists of acclimating to the darkness, the heat, the crowded conditions, and one's breath. Hearing other people's prayers begins to create a sense of community, trust, and bonding in the shared moment. If they are on a vision quest, this is the first day. They may feel their solitude as it triggers old wounds or basic fears around survival. Alternatively, they may experience a feeling of liberation. If the journeyer has taken a psychoactive sacrament, they may begin to feel unusual physical sensations: tingling, buzzing, warmth, relaxation, or waves of emotion.

As unknown physical and psychological effects occur, fear often arises. Facing an unknown situation may call forth a habitual coping mechanism. One's ego defenses may be mobilized and activated. It is normal to be concerned for one's well-being as perception changes and expands. Especially during this phase, it is the job of the guide to help the journeyer feel safe.

This is the time for the journeyer to breathe deeply, relax, and trust the process and their guide. In the case of a ceremony with a psychoactive sacrament, the journeyer can now focus on relaxing the body and recall their intention for the experience. They can surrender to the reassuring presence of the guide as the guide begins to sing, pray, or silently tend the space while the substance begins to take effect. Feelings and emotions, memories, and thoughts will begin to rise to the surface. This moment can feel overwhelming and frightening or familiar and enjoyable, or all of the above. Consciousness has begun to expand.

The flap of the lodge is closed now. We sit in total darkness. A pile of stones sits in the middle of the lodge emitting an incredible heat. My body warms up quickly, and I begin to sweat. I pace my breathing and relax my body. I duck my head down to catch some cooler air. My neighbor is breathing heavily and making grunting sounds. She is new to this ritual, and I sense her apprehension. Marilyn's chants fill the small space, and somehow it makes me feel safe.

People begin to share their prayers. I listen to each of them, sensing the sincerity of their words. My neighbor tells of her mother, who is preparing for surgery. My friend across the lodge cries when she shares about her youngest daughter. I sense how the heat is softening each of us, both physically and emotionally. As the heat begins to penetrate into my bones, I feel myself surrendering as my emotions rise to the surface of my awareness. I speak my prayer, words for my sister and her cancer treatment. I feel my wish for her healing and my love for her life.

Immersion

The second phase of a journey is the immersion, which includes the journey's greatest intensity. At this point a journeyer may feel they are being flooded; they may feel carried by the experience rather than being in control. Deeper dimensions of psychological and energetic content may begin to churn, and the journeyer might feel afraid as they enter a space that can feel chaotic. The ego may grip even tighter to avoid disintegration. The journeyer may feel stuck and confused or overwhelmed and panic-stricken. Alternatively, perhaps the journeyer's ego defenses are now beginning to relax.

Aspects of the psyche and unconscious reveal themselves in mysterious and unpredictable ways. The journeyer can feel intense emotions, see vivid images, hear voices, or have memories emerge as the material of their deep, inner world is accessed. Journeyers may open the wounds of their past. They may experience cathartic struggle, anger, or frustration. Emotional contractions may release as consciousness shines onto specific aspects of their lives. At times, prenatal or birth memories surface. Journeyers can also experience synesthesia, as their sensory inputs flow into one another and overlap. The dissolution of the ego structure opens us up into an experience of a transpersonal nature.

Journeyers might find themselves in cosmic contemplation, seeing the matrix of creation as an ongoing wheel of eternity. There can be a sense of majestic liberation, infinite beauty, or authentic belonging. Shape-shifting into animals or connecting with material from past lives can take place. Experiences of collective or cosmic consciousness become available. They may even experience a sense of the divine through visions or through their body. Some people tune into a sense of celebration, dynamic vitality, and passion. Others might find themselves exhausted by the complexity of the human predicament.

During this phase, many people feel they finally understand their place in the universe as they realize love as the force of creation incarnating their life. They may experience a profound clarity of mind or settle into inner stillness. Sometimes a sense of overwhelming acceptance and compassion arises as a journeyer contemplates the ephemeral preciousness of their life. This can be a time of floating and resting in this sense of ultimate wellness. The varieties of possible experiences in this phase are infinite.

> *I am in the Amazon jungle in the middle of an ayahuasca ceremony and my visions are slowly intensifying. Neon green and pink insects are vibrating as they multiply across my awareness. The eyes of an emerging jaguar glint black and gold. I feel dizzy, unable to breathe as fear for my survival overwhelms me. It is almost more than I can handle. But I recognize this place and begin to breathe into my belly, feeling for the floor of the maloca below me. Suddenly my visions shift and soften. My body relaxes, and I feel my breath grounding me on the earth. I am okay.*

Reflection

The third phase of a journey is that of reflection. This phase emerges when the intensity of the experience begins to subside and the journeyer's inner witness reappears. The journeyer is now on the other side of the cathartic immersion and may begin to regain awareness of the other people in the space. This is a time when insights are revealed and one begins to reflect upon the richness of what has taken place. There may be visceral realizations or cognitive understandings as the content of the previous phase begins to fit together like the pieces of a puzzle. These realizations are often felt as embodied truths, without any need for them to be logical or rational. A journeyer may reflect on people, situations, and other aspects of their life from a larger perspective. They may realize how teachers, friends, and other influential people in their lives mirror their state back to them. Complex situations can be understood in their intricacy and for their value toward growth. As we reflect on the myriad connections in our lives, we may experience overflowing gratitude. Alternatively, we may perceive the absence of meaningful connections and recognize a sincere need for community.

My dance teacher enters my awareness. She is such a challenging woman sometimes. At this moment, I feel her passion and love acutely. She encourages me toward gifts I didn't know I had. I now understand why I brought this challenging woman into my life: to push me to excel and experience my capacities to their fullest extent. My familiar irritation toward her transforms into heartfelt gratitude as I recognize her role in my life, a role I was evidently ready for, as I sought her out myself. I did not know, consciously at least, how her presence would become paramount to my own empowerment. I appreciate my own unconscious intelligence. I smile at my inner resolve to grow and the mysterious way it all takes place.

Emergence

The fourth phase of a journey is that of emergence. The emergence consists of the return back to normal reality. If the journey included medicine, the journeyer begins to return to normal perception. The journeyer begins to hear the music, the silence, the songs, or the prayers with greater appreciation. The journeyer's sensations will return to normal though they may feel tender or even quite raw. If this is the last day of a vision quest or the last couple days of a meditation retreat, one instinctively begins to reorient oneself toward completion. Some people have a difficult time returning to normal reality, while others simply feel relief. A journeyer may have experienced a wide range of insights and realizations in regard to their relationships or their life's purpose. There can be a feeling of renewed clarity and inner purity. If they have connected with challenging emotions, they often feel too fragile to interact, challenged in their capacity to communicate, and somewhat disoriented. At this point, perception is still enhanced and it is normal to feel highly sensitive. They will need a compassionate guide to help them through this phase and gently support their delicate state. This is an appropriate time for rest. This last phase keeps unfolding into the following days and weeks, as the experience begins to inform one's day-to-day life.

This is a time to be comfortable and cozy as one slowly reorients to the external world. Even if the experience has been positive, the journeyer may feel anxious or sad at this time. It is crucial to simply remain open to what is, as consciousness returns to a more familiar state. At the end of a silent meditation retreat, there is often a ritual signaling a return to talking. At the completion of a vision quest, people may gather around the fire and share their visions with the guide. At the end of a sweat lodge, people may rinse themselves off with cool water and lie on the ground. As a medicine journey comes to its end, people may gaze at the altar and reflect on their experience or enjoy a state of open awareness. Immediately after an individual journey is not necessarily the time to discuss the content of the experience. This is a time to eat some food and drink some tea, to rest quietly, or to gently connect with others.

> I am at the end of a group Holotropic Breathwork session. After an hour of intense movement and visions, my breath has now returned to normal. The music is soft, spacious, and melodic. My body relaxes, sinking into the support of the floor and the pillows surrounding me. I hear people nearby sighing, quietly crying, and taking long, deep breaths. I am coming back to my awareness of everything around me. I feel exhausted yet fulfilled. Tenderness fills my heart.

✻ ✻ ✻

After a journey, self-rejuvenation is as crucial for the guide as for the journeyer. The guide should keep their body nourished and strong as supporting someone's expansion of consciousness can be exhausting and depleting.

A journey can bring a bounty of insights, healings, aha moments, magnificent visions, cosmic consciousness, and emotional resolutions. May my account of a group journey in Mexico transport you to an expanded space.

It is 6 PM and Julieta is in the ceremony room on the bottom floor of her house. The walls are white, and the windows are covered with thick green velvet curtains. Foam mattresses covered in white cotton sheets line the wooden floor. I can already smell the copal smoke as it wafts up the stairs into the courtyard. I go down to find Julieta bent over a bundle of leafy, green branches. Upstairs, a group of ten men and women who have made the long pilgrimage to Huautla de Jiménez begin filing toward the top of the stairs, silently readying themselves to descend into the ceremony room. In the days leading up to this midsummer evening's ceremony, we walked the local mountain paths, bathed in the waterfalls, and spent time in the vibrant marketplace. The participants, eager to partake in tonight's ritual, have spent the day in introspection, reflecting on their intentions and requests for support and healing.

One by one, they pause at the entrance where Julieta stands, leafy bundle in hand. She passes the leaves through the smoke before sweeping each person's body with the branches. All along, she prays aloud in Mazatec, words of protection and cleansing. Julieta asks me to place the participants needing extra care close to the altar for spiritual support. I direct each person to their place on the floor, upon mats arranged to face the gigantic altar. The altar reaches from floor to ceiling in three gigantic tiers, covered in a vast array of photos, icons, statues, crosses, and power objects. There are giant statues of saints and religious figures, and the entire altar is framed by tall vases of overflowing white tuberoses. Everyone is silent now and in their place.

Julieta begins the ceremony by placing slender beeswax candles on a wooden board on the floor and lighting them one by one. She sits on her pillow, and I sit beside her on mine. We prepare a small plate of fresh mushrooms for each person. She exclaims at the size of some of the mushrooms, giggling like a child. She says, "These will open the doors of their minds and hearts for sure. This is a clean work that I do, and these are gifts from our Mother Earth, for our health." I translate her words to everyone, and she nods her head in approval. I place a spoonful of honey and three cocoa beans on each plate, as the tradition instructs.

Julieta jokes and says that the honey will give people a sweet journey. Our plates are now in front of us, and Julieta begins to pray, reading from her large prayer book, weaving her rosary in with Mazatec prayers, asking God and the earth to open their mysteries to us, to shine their light upon us, to help us see the truth. Her prayers are punctuated by the names of the people present. She signals that people can begin eating their plates of small golden-brown mushrooms in silence as she finishes her rosary.

People lie down and cover themselves with woven blankets. We turn off the light and blow out the candles. It is pitch dark now. Within a short time, the quality of the space changes. Everyone's breathing calms and the silence deepens. People yawn, a sign of physical opening into the journey as the brain chemistry begins to shift in response to the psilocybin of the mushrooms. Julieta and I now nibble a couple of mushrooms ourselves, to sharpen our perception and connect with the group.

We take less than the participants to remain able to guide the work and respond to the needs of the group. For the next five hours, Julieta and I will pray, sing, hold silence, support people when they become frightened or feel sick, and work on their bodies when they feel pain.

There is an eerie quiet in the room. As I begin to feel the effects of the small amount of the mushrooms Julieta gave me, the collective energy becomes palpable. Julieta's syncopated prayers begin to take shape as images and patterns in the air, visible to my mind's eye. I am transported deeper into myself. It is a familiar place of light and form, yet new in its texture. The room becomes wide and spacious as if the walls have vanished and the nearby mountain is breathing with us all. As the ceremony proceeds, the air becomes more still, as if suspended in awe.

A dog barks on the other side of the valley; the mountain in its entirety becomes alive with ripples of sounds, echoes, and wind.

The rustling of life is everywhere.

Moisture and air, ancient mountains, pyramids, and walls of rocks appear, dripping droplets of light infused with the knowledge of humanity.

The soul of the mountain emerges.

Its spirits are clothed in dark green capes and are dancing old dances of benevolence and protection.

A mysteriously familiar voice asks, "Have you paid your dues to the spirits? I am the mountain. I speak words of solidity and patience. Are you my messenger to others?"

A resonance now embraces us all through space and time as a translucent membrane stretches out, encompassing all civilization, here and everywhere.

Knowledge, instincts, insights, mind, and heart all blend now into pure intelligence.

Julieta's words cut through, "This is the light of understanding. This is the light of truth." Each person absorbs her prayers as they become forever branded in the core of our psyches.

Truth feels like water now—or is it the rain falling in a steady flow outside, distilling, purifying, and washing confusion away? This truth will forever remind us of what to stand for and what to believe in.

All is one, merging into consciousness, spiraling throughout the universe. We are an eternal nebula of souls united in the flow of one spirit, floating and blessing all that we touch.

Everything stands in its essence and glory.

Time condenses into a tiny point, then becomes irrelevant and disappears. All is suspended now, folded into eternity, vanishing from this reality into a realm of light, depth, mystery, and divine union. Everything evaporates into the eternal void where even spirits do not dwell.

Somber shadows appear from behind a sound.

It is the familiar face of fear and the taste of shame.

Old monsters, tightness, and sweat.

An ancient bird flutters its wings beside a lizard crawling close to the ground, quiet but alert.

There will be a battle, a violent struggle for survival.

When the fight abruptly starts, sheer fierceness takes form.

Silent screams, teeth, beak, talons, and claws.

Heartbeats. Fear.

I kneel beside someone and place my hand on their back to signal, yes, you can go there. You have what it takes to face, once and for all, the past that haunts you. I am here, and I will stay and support whatever is next. A soul sitting beside another soul. A simple gesture in a human's search for freedom and love.

Suddenly, it all changes.

Droplets of bright red blood appear on the battlefield.

The bird loses feathers, and the lizard loses its tail.

No one has won. It is simply about the fight.

Sadness and sorrow fill the space.

Haunting images of dead bodies, blood, tears, and old ghosts appear.

Julieta's voice emerges, filling the room with words of survival, courage, faith, and redemption.

We hear tears and panting as the battle for the heart rages on in the night's darkness.

She keeps singing—an eternal presence through it all.

There is a force here, in this quick decision to survive; there is a glimpse of tenacity. It overshadows any doubt of the strength of the human spirit. These tears can drown the soul or help it float. Which will it be?

It will be redemption.

The budding flower of hope is too precious to be destroyed as it appears from underneath the rubble.

Another breath. And another.

I sing.

A tender melody unfurls its wings of soft, white petals, as an ancient mother's voice sings a song for all aching hearts. New tears flow. Tears of gratitude for the loving embrace of the sacred mushrooms, doctoring soul and flesh, and for the sacred feminine, folding all lives into her great blue cloak.

Outside, the rain falls, washing away the residue of tensions lodged in our bodies, now stretching and shifting positions. The moisture bathes everyone in a cloud of earth and sky, unified by the water descending in fat drops onto the land. Mycelium consciousness lives in this sacred meeting of elements. Niños Santos are fruiting everywhere. One can almost hear them now, erupting from the underworld to meet the sky and air, emerging from the earth to remind us of what is essential.

Julieta asks me to light a fresh candle near the altar; the ceremony is nearing its end. People are beginning to sit up now. They lean against the wall, resting, and watching the shadows of flowers as they dance along the ceiling. Some gaze at the large image of the Virgin of Guadalupe on the altar, gently bridging their inner world with outer reality. Moment by moment, song by song, we all emerge from the mystery and slowly enter the familiar realm of human tenderness.

I light another candle and sing another song. The atmosphere in the room is subdued. Everyone is silent and contemplative. I light the copalero for the last cleansing with the copal, a blessing of burning tree sap, the blood of the earth made visible to us. Smoke fills the room as I move from person to person, signaling the completion of the ritual.

Julieta looks around the room and, with a chuckle, asks, "So, is everybody happy?" Everyone laughs. What a question to be asked by the woman who has just guided us into the deepest, most horrid corners of ourselves. She is quite the trickster, my dear friend, and she knows perfectly well where everyone has been, how difficult it was to navigate the mazes of memories and grief. She also knows perfectly well how lifted everyone was by the spirit of the divine, made tangible by the flesh of the mushroom. She knows how each person has reconnected with the faith in their heart. All the participants are asked to stay and rest in their place. It is a time for personal reflection and stillness.

I accompany Julieta as we leave the room arm in arm. There is no need to speak.

11

TEACHINGS AND HEALINGS

Categories of Transformative Experience

Always remember that you are absolutely unique.
Just like everyone else.

—AUTHOR UNKNOWN

One of the primary teachings we receive from expanded states of consciousness is the visceral understanding of how the aspects of our being are connected. We receive significant healing from experiencing ourselves as unified and holistic organisms. For example, we can understand how our physical body affects our emotions and how our emotions affect our relationships. Or we may see how our relationship with nature nurtures our sense of spirit, which in turn influences our emotional well-being. We can understand the delicate ecosystem of our life and how these various aspects are in a continuous relationship with one another. It is not an intellectual process, but it *is* an intelligent process.

Though the whole is greater than the sum of its parts, we will examine each of these aspects separately, using the Holistic Model for a Balanced Life. We will define the different types of experiences that can occur and give suggestions as to how a guide can best support each as it happens. This exploration is by no means exhaustive as the possibilities of experience are truly infinite. However, having explored and facilitated this work over many years, I have identified broad themes and commonalities.

Each type of experience has its place and is useful in its own right with its richness and distinct purpose to guide the journeyer toward equilibrium. There are difficult experiences, but there are no bad experiences. A guide's ultimate job is to have faith in the process. Surrendering to the process of healing means trusting the inner wisdom and intelligence of the journeyer as a self-organizing organism. During states of expansion, experiences often shift and evolve into others, and a guide must know how to engage with a journeyer. Transformation, much like birth, is a cocreative process and the healing process is often hands-on. The guide does not always wait for things to unfold on their own. The guide might choose to actively move energy and shape the direction of the experience. For instance, the guide might offer some gentle touch, put on evocative music, open the door to let in a breeze, burn incense, or sing a song or chant. There is an organic timeline to all things, and the process can be supported in the physical realm, passively or actively.

Body-Centered Experiences

My body feels immobile as if my entire being was made of frozen, metallic pipes. I feel held in compression and fear and see no escape. I find my breath. It is still here. I can breathe. I am still human. Air comes in, air goes out, and the pipes begin to melt away. I expand, and I feel alive as my flesh begins to warm up. My body cracks a small smile on the inside, slowly thawing the fear from its core. I feel blood circulating, rivers of liquid streaming throughout my veins. I rest in the support that is my structure, my bones, in my body.

—Françoise's Journey Journal, March 2001

As the vehicle of our life and experience, our bodies store the memories, impressions, and emotions that sometimes become frozen in our tissues and musculature. As in my experience above, journeys can bring awareness to these frozen patterns and make it possible to induce the thawing process. The alkaloids and molecular compounds in certain plant and synthetic medicines such as psilocybin, DMT, LSD, and MDMA affect hormones and neurotransmitters in the brain, which instigate a cascade of effects within our body. These chemical changes direct our psyche to open. As I mentioned, research has shown that through certain meditation techniques, we can slow our heart rate and bring the brain into theta waves. In deep meditative states, people can reach a point of barely breathing. In Holotropic Breathwork, the rate of the breath and the amount of oxygen inhaled is dramatically increased. If we are listening to rhythmic drumming, our heart rate syncs up to the beat of the drum. Through dancing, our bodies release oxytocin and dopamine.

During expanded states of consciousness the following types of body-centered experience can occur.

1) Contraction and Pain

2) Numbness and Physical Disconnection

3) Cathartic Release

4) Vital Embodiment

5) Calm, Stillness, and Ease

1) Contraction and Pain

Contraction refers to rigidity and tension in the body. There is little to no movement or breath, and the journeyer will be physically uncomfortable. Pain can appear as cramps, throbbing, pulsing, burning, or tension. The journeyer may be trembling quietly or curled into a fetal position. Sometimes there is no obvious transformation or resolution during the journey.

Whether the guide engages and offers support will depend on the journeyer's story, history, and intention. The guide's job is to know the journeyer's context and discern what can best support healing. It is the guide's job to determine whether it is more skillful to help move the tension and encourage the energy to flow or let the journeyer experience their pain. Do they need nurturing or do they need to learn something important from the pain? Do they have enough psychological strength to sustain this confrontation and grow from it?

If the journeyer has a history of developmental or chronic trauma due to an unsafe or unpredictable childhood environment, it is crucial to provide steady, soothing emotional support. Be gentle and offer physical contact, such as hand-holding or caressing their head. You can guide them into micro-movements or bring attention to their breath in order to encourage a flow of movement in the body. Give them words of encouragement toward relaxation and reassure them of your presence. The guide should tread lightly around the journeyer's defenses and respect any fear that is present; creating and reassuring safety are primary.

Sometimes it is best to let a journeyer remain in their stuckness. This requires that a guide be comfortable with their own discomfort. There is value in, as a friend of mine calls it, "doing *nothing* carefully." The purpose is not to create pain or hurt but to trust a journeyer's capacity to learn from their experience, just as it is, without attempting to save them from their own state. In this case, a guide can be a "sacred witness" and simply be with the journeyer, trusting that he or she will experience discomfort for as long as is needed. It is often by staying with one's pain long enough that one can discover what is happening on a deeper level. What patterns of tension are contributing to this pain? What impact do these patterns of tension have on the rest of one's body and entire life? How were these patterns of tension created in the first place? Even if, as a guide, I do not immediately understand the benefit of someone being stuck for a few hours, I can respect the mystery of their unfolding process.

2) Numbness and Physical Disconnection

This is an occurrence of feeling disconnected from one's senses. The journeyer will feel disembodied, dissociated, and devoid of energy. There is little breath and no movement.

The guide needs to discern: is the journeyer a compulsively overactive person who needs to turn off and unplug? If so, during a journey the guide can sit there silently with the journeyer. There is not much to do but keep faith in the power of the experience. The guide can play soothing music, whistle, hum, or play simple instruments. The intention is to support the immersion of the journeyer into a state of relaxation.

However, the guide might discern that the numbness seems more like a state of frozenness. Does the journeyer have a history of unprocessed trauma or dissociation? In this case, the guide can support the journeyer with breath and micro-movement. Breathe beside them, remind them of their inhale and exhale. Initiate slow movement by gently encouraging them to move a limb or move their head side to side. Or the guide can gently touch the journeyer's feet or stroke the back and shoulders. The guide can make a low hum and invite the journeyer to join, using sound as a way to call breath and movement back into the body.

3) Cathartic Release

> *I hear a voice emerging from the center of my being, afraid of its own power. I breathe delicately to manage it. But it grows and grows, amplifying slowly from within my flesh. Finally, I hear the loud scream liberate itself from inside me, a scream that has waited for its freedom. With it comes strength, possibility, and celebration. It speaks of the raw animal power that is my true nature, unleashing beauty and the flow of my life.*
>
> —*Françoise's Journey Journal, January 1995*

Reclaiming my connection to my breath and power was a crucial moment in my healing. When this level of expansion and release takes place, old, stagnant, or frozen energy is liberated from the physical system through sweating, burping, yawning, coughing, vomiting, spitting mucus, or using the bathroom. It can also come out as crying, yelling, shivering, shaking, or rocking. There can be heavy breathing and forceful exhales. Stagnant energy is being purged from the physical body in a cathartic manner.

This type of release can happen at any point in a journey and can last for a while. If a journeyer has a static lifestyle and is now experiencing a dynamic flow of energy through this potentially explosive tension release, it is best that the guide let this activity happen. The guide can also support the externalization of the process, as this deepens the release. Encourage the journeyer to spit or make sounds or movements. While keeping them safe, make sure to create enough physical space around them so they will not be limited in their movements.

If a journeyer has a history of trauma, this can be a release of long-held energy that has been frozen in the body. In this case, the guide should support the process while reminding the journeyer that they can let go and are in a safe environment. This helps them avoid feeling overwhelmed by the intensity of this experience. Encouragement should be gentle, yet remain steady.

4) Vital Embodiment

This is an experience of aliveness. There is energy flowing through the body. The breath is robust and sensations are alive. There can be a sensual, perceptual openness, and the journeyer may be in contact with their voice and movement. There is a feeling of embodied receptivity. There might be an experience of channeling energy or synesthesia. There may be laughter, crying, or awe as energy moves through their body. The body can become aroused, with the journeyer experiencing mild pleasure to full-body orgasms. This vital erotic energy rises from the sacrum and powerful vibrations move through the physical body. There can be warmth or tingling, and the journeyer often wants to twist and writhe. This is a time when experiences of shape-shifting into animals can take place, such as the sensation of wings opening or antennae growing.

The guide can encourage the journeyer to understand that the experience is perfect for them, even if it appears wild and unbounded. Perhaps the journeyer will want to take off his or her clothes, feeling the need to be witnessed in their physical energy and sensual openness. The guide's job is to stay nonjudgmental and keep the journeyer safe. Of course, the guide should stay in integrity with their own clearly defined personal boundaries.

5) Calm, Stillness, and Ease

This is an experience of spaciousness and stillness. There is little to no movement or thought. This type of experience looks and feels pleasant.

The journeyer is breathing gently and there is a sense of relaxation and regeneration.

The guide can support the quietness through soft music or chanting and refrain from creating too much movement in the room. The guide should stay intentionally quiet and peaceful to align the container to the journeyer's experience.

Mind-Centered Experiences

As the physical body opens up, emotions soon follow. For example, in a sweat lodge, the intense heat and darkness, along with the physical proximity to others, result in the body literally entering a different state as oxytocin and other bonding hormones are released. As the journeyer surrenders to the intensity and opens to the group prayers and intentions, the physical body relaxes and the emotional layers begin to open. The physical opening heralds a deeper emotional experience.

During expanded states of consciousness, waves of emotion often travel through us. We can experience everything from terror to ecstasy. Fear is often the first layer encountered. The unknown inner space is unfamiliar and can sometimes be disorienting or frightening. With the appropriate support and reassurance as we enter this unknown space, we can relax. We can tap into unresolved fear that has become calcified in our body. This fear is often connected with psychological material that is only now revealing itself. Since our usual defense strategies have been disarmed, we can now directly experience the ways fear is held in our psyche and body.

We may be able to access and articulate repressed trauma. There can be insights and aha moments as sudden realizations emerge. We can grasp the mystery of our instinctive intelligence, which leads to clearly perceiving the reality of our unresolved psychological issues. Sometimes we feel judgment toward ourselves about this state of non-resolution, and sometimes we feel self-compassion and love; love for the way we have endured, the way we have survived, and the way we now give ourselves the possibility of wellness. We can experience a cleansing that dissolves layers of fear into a sense of wholeness.

Various techniques that bring us into expanded states of consciousness also allow access to our unconscious. Induced visualizations, shamanic drumming, dancing, or a journey with a psychedelic substance allow us to connect with the intimate contents of our unconscious. After experimenting with many of these techniques over the years, I have found that all methods can be valuable for different stages of exploration. Yet, due to the intensity and depth of experience they activate, it is my opinion that sacred plant medicines, facilitated in a highly supportive context, open the door to the deepest caverns of unconscious material.

As the collective unconscious becomes available to us, we sometimes find we are able to have the experience of someone far away in place and time. It becomes possible to access different realities and connect with ancient creation myths, rituals, languages, and histories we may not know anything about. I have observed, after witnessing many experiences in expanded states of consciousness, including my own, that the content that emerges is coherent with Jung's maps of the unconscious. Experiencing life as a mythic journey complete with various archetypes, the presence of the anima and animus, masculine and feminine forces, as well as the theme of shadow, are powerful experiences to draw self-knowledge from.

The following categories include the most common mind-centered experiences that occur in expanded states of consciousness:

COGNITIVE/INTELLECTUAL PROCESSES

1) Resistance

2) Insights and Guidance

EMOTIONAL PROCESSES

3) Fear and Panic

4) Personal Confrontation

5) Emotional Opening and Release

6) Self-Love and Nourishment

ACCESSING THE UNCONSCIOUS

7) Childhood Memories

8) Visions

Cognitive/Intellectual Processes

1) Resistance

Juan came to me to work through his feelings of repression after years of strict Catholic boarding school education in his home country. Throughout our weekly sessions together, he began to revive his relationship to spirituality by exploring a few practices that he was curious about. When he eventually joined me for a trip to Mexico, he was excited to join the mushroom ceremony. During the first night's ritual, he experienced strong resistance to the Catholic themes, although we had discussed them beforehand. I sat by him, reassuring him of his safety, taking care not to stifle the defiance he was expressing. I knew it was the power of his inner child that had never had a voice to resist. He began to nod and slowly relaxed back into his space. Soon he began to shake and cry, expressing old anger, grief, and hurt. He later shared that he had never had an experience of firm boundaries accompanied by love in a ceremonial setting.

Like Juan, despite their interest in expanded consciousness, some journeyers resist the process. During a journey or ceremony they will often keep their eyes open, sit up, and act normal by arranging their space, looking around, or attempting to engage the guide or others in rational conversation. If they have taken a plant medicine, they may report that they are not feeling anything. If in a group, they may begin disturbing the overall environment, making sounds or distracting others. They can become angry or belligerent. They may want to leave the space or complain that the framework is not working for them, become highly critical, or announce they have changed their minds. It is the guide's role to discern between "intentional" resistance and resistance due to a history of trauma.

If a journeyer is intentionally resisting the experience, there is value in letting it happen, trusting that this is their teaching. Sometimes journeyers need to exhaust their energy of resistance. This can be a powerful process of liberation, although it may not look pleasant during the journey itself. It is difficult to subdue a journeyer who is determined to resist. At a certain point, it can be useful to suggest breathing and stretching to encourage energy to flow through the body. However, it is not certain that the journeyer will be willing to follow directions. The guide might have to take the journeyer out of the group to a more secluded space with an assistant present in order to allow the journeyer to explore this challenging space. Again, a guide's main job is to trust that whatever is taking place is perfect for the journeyer's unfolding.

If a journeyer has a history of trauma and their physical resistance is simply a fear-based response to avoid overwhelming psychic or physical sensations, it is useful to gently coach the journeyer to breathe. The guide can offer touch, reassuring the frightened child within that there is a safe and supportive container within which to feel and release the fear. Gentle words of encouragement are helpful to remind the journeyer of the guide's compassionate presence.

2) Insights and Guidance

During the journey, creative insights, ideas, inspirations, and visions can arrive in abundance. These can include practical insights about finances, scheduling, energy management, or diet. There is often a sense of empowerment and emotional strength when a journeyer gains awareness into the purpose of their life or insight in their vocation or relationship. The experience sometimes includes scientific insights into the nature of reality. If the journeyer voices insights, and it is appropriate, the guide can take notes. Otherwise, the guide should take mental notes and remember them for later. The guide can mirror the vitality and clarity that is being expressed in order to encourage the process.

Emotional Processes

3) Fear and Panic

Here the journeyer may feel flooded by frightening images, sensations, or thoughts or begin to cry, shake, roll around, whimper, or yell. At times, they might reach out for help, seeking contact or wanting to escape the experience. I have seen breathwork sessions activate fear as people relive their birth and reconnect with frightening moments that took place early in their life.

Sometimes the right thing for a guide to do is to simply offer to help. If it is a journey with a sacrament, a change of music or environment may lower the panic and help to calm the journeyer down. It is best to stay in contact; there is no merit in leaving someone struggling with this kind of panic and fear. The guide can direct the journeyer's breathing or offer them co-regulation through shared slow, rhythmic sounding. They can offer to put a cool washcloth on the journeyer's head or use aromatherapy, such as lavender essential oil for calming and soothing, or vetiver oil to help with grounding.

During an experience of fear, a guide should stay present, gently contacting the person physically, offering verbal reassurance, and inviting the journeyer to breathe and focus on their breath or the music. The centeredness of the guide is crucial to being able to help regulate a client's agitation, as the frightened journeyer will be relying on the guide's presence during this challenging phase. If the experience includes the use of a psychedelic substance, the guide can simply (though not necessarily easily) help the journeyer wait it out until the effects subside. Meanwhile, the guide can provide the most peaceful environment possible. They can remind the journeyer that they are in a safe location and that they are protecting them from harm.

4) Personal Confrontation

Sometimes in an expanded state of consciousness, one has the experience of confronting themselves and realizing the impact of their negative patterns of behavior. This insight offers a moment of honest realization as to the damage one has done to oneself or others.

A journeyer may experience genuine emotional pain as they perceive the extent of their toxic behavior and self-destructive actions. This might include self-deceit, lies, avoidances, denial, self-wounding, substance abuse, addictions, or the destabilization of health or relationships. This can be a painful experience and the journeyer may express anger, sadness, or regret as they confront their shadow. This is a precious moment of accountability.

If a journeyer is confronting the destructive effects of an addictive pattern or the absence of self-care, it is best that the guide does *not* rescue them. Let it be a confrontation and allow awareness to increase. The guide can remain a compassionate witness. Compassion does not mean making the pain go away.

There is almost always some degree of shame in a personal confrontation, and it can be beneficial to let a journeyer simply sit with it. It is best that they acknowledge the consequences of the decisions they have made, as well as their level of accountability. There is benefit in letting the process endure for as long as it needs to: it is not a guide's job to make everything better. Rather, journeyers must process their material at their own particular pace.

5) Emotional Opening and Release

Clark had spent most of his time alone as a child. His dad was often away on military deployments, and his mom would go out drinking to numb her anxiety and loneliness. He had immersed himself in school, which garnered him praise from his teachers and occasional attention from his mom. He had grown up to become a sharp business lawyer. He was successful, but he complained: "I feel empty inside. My success is okay, but it does not make me happy. I am bored in my life." I sensed a depressive state, the kind of state born out of repressed feelings. I suggested he participate in a sweat lodge so he could be close with others in a healing environment. I explained some of the rituals and practices he would be asked to join and described the darkness and the heat.

Clark returned to share how the lodge had gone for him, and the first thing he reported was how he fell apart. "It was so good. I mean, it was tough, but I went for it." It turned out that when the heat was becoming too oppressive for him, the lodge leader had placed him beside her. She told him to lie down with his head on her lap. She placed her hand on his cheek and continued singing her chants. Her attentive care cracked his heart wide open, and he wept like a small child. She kept on singing, gently stroking him from time to time. When his turn to offer a prayer came, he prayed for all the children who did not have present parents, asking that they each find their way to love and support someday.

An emotional opening, such as Clark's, can initiate repressed or unexpressed emotions to come to the surface. It can be anger, resentment, sadness, or grief, or it can be acceptance, forgiveness, joy, gratitude, or unconditional love. Painful memories that have not been fully processed or have been unconscious can reside in us like heavy stones at the bottom of a pond. These can include repressed memories such as sexual abuse, as the details of an event can surface after many years.

A journeyer may feel overwhelmed as they realize the physical impact an original event had on their life. Some people experience intense anger toward a perpetrator or feel sorry for what they endured as a child. Sometimes an emotional opening brings forth compassion as to why an abuser or one's abusive parents behaved the way that they did.

If, in the beginning, an emotional release feels embarrassing to a journeyer, the guide can encourage sound and movement. The guide can join them by initiating sound and support them if the release is one of power and strength. If the emotion is primarily anger, words of encouragement and validation are useful to keep the process flowing. If the expression is one of grief or sorrow, the guide can stay physically close to the person, not to soothe or comfort necessarily, but to remain present. It is best to allow this process of grief to express itself without interrupting it with spoken words or searching for meaning.

When memories are still present in the tissues of the body, which is often the case with sexual abuse survivors, it can take significant energy to release them from the body. Trembling, shaking, or a syncopated breathing pattern can signify the release of trauma on the level of cellular memory. When people deal with sexual abuse, they can tend to disassociate. The guide should support the journeyer to stay in their body via eye contact, gentle physical contact, and verbal encouragement. This supports the process being an embodied, conscious purging of energy and memories rather than the downward spiral that can result from reactivating an original trauma.

6) Self-Love and Nourishment

This is an experience of emotional well-being and tenderness toward one's self. The journeyer is often relaxed and smiling, feeling ease and joy. The body is open, perhaps even blissful as the journeyer viscerally experiences the healing balm of love. The journeyer is connecting with a sense of comfort, safety, reassurance, self-nourishment, and connection. From an empowered sense of autonomy, as one relaxes into love and sweetness, they may have insight into what it is that nourishes their being.

The best way for a guide to support this experience is to acknowledge and validate it. The guide can immerse the journeyer into the experience through guided imagery or encouragement. The guide can lead them to feel it in their body and help anchor it in. Or the guide can let it happen and mirror back the awe and wonderment of the experience, as a way to support the healing.

Accessing the Unconscious

7) Childhood Memories

I am seven. My father has made a net for catching shrimp. We walk down to the beach at low tide. The water is far from the dry sand. The colors of the sunset surround us as I walk by his side, water up to my ankles. He lowers the net into the water, then lifts it up. We bend over it, watching dozens of shrimps jump around. I gather them into my little bucket. This is the silent dance of my father and me, out in nature. There is a felt intimacy. No words, just water, sand, animals, and the net he built for us. There is a simple tenderness that anchors itself in my young bones.

—*Françoise's Journey Journal, December 1997*

This type of experience includes memories of key childhood experiences similar to mine and oftentimes includes psychological insights about their significance. A journeyer may reflect on previously forgotten memories and experiences, positive or negative. A memory such as my catching shrimp with my father can be profoundly nourishing and significant. Challenging memories can be held with an open heart and mind as we realize what we endured as a child and how we attempted to cope. It is difficult to be angry with a young child who was simply doing their best to survive. We do not want to repress the experience of the inner child, but rather to embrace and integrate it. Compassion naturally arises as the adult self is now able to grasp the understanding that the child struggled for, but could not achieve.

There is not much for a guide to do to support this type of experience beyond holding the container with faith. If the experience appears to be challenging, and the journeyer seems fragile, the guide can stay close by. The guide can offer appropriate physical contact holding their hand or putting a hand on their back. But most of the time, reflecting on the story of one's life is an experience of personal empowerment. It is best to allow a journeyer to reclaim their own strength and understanding within their life story.

8) Visions

In this experience, the journeyer projects the imagery of their inner world outward onto their experience. The journeyer may see shapes, colors, or patterns. Depending on the technique, the intensity of the visions will vary. Breathwork is known to induce visions, while a long meditation retreat can also open up a visionary world. Many plant medicines induce visions of melting and twisting; in some states the external world appears as if through a kaleidoscope. The journeyer can sometimes see fractal patterns as they perceive visions of subatomic structures.

There may be visions of distant lands and times. With plant medicines, it is common to have visions of a plant's original environment. A journeyer might see a jaguar or even feel like they are shape-shifting into one. They may feel mycelium radiating out from their body. The music, the space, the posture of the guide, the journeyer's intention, the state of mind, and the mood all affect a journeyer's visions. The guide can encourage the journeyer to engage with their visions and stay curious about what appears to be challenging or frightening.

If the visions are difficult, the guide can hold the journeyer's hand or stay close. It can also be helpful to suggest to the journeyer to move a little bit, offer a bit of touch or massage to help move the process. Remind the journeyer to breathe deeply while encountering difficult visions. The guide should stay present, steady, and soothing so the journeyer feels safe engaging with the visions. The guide can encourage them to stay curious with whatever is being shown.

Spirit-Centered Experiences

During expanded states of consciousness, we can also have visions of religious and spiritual imagery that we may or may not recognize. Sometimes it is reminiscent of our childhood religious upbringing, and sometimes it is completely new. We connect with ancestors, spirits, angels, devas, or the spirit in inanimate objects. We understand profound spiritual teachings we have received or read in books. Sometimes we connect with the local spirits of the place where a ritual is held, which were previously unknown to us. These are experienced more as visceral understandings rather than intellectual insights.

Realizing the impact of every action and event in our personal history leads us to perceive the possibility of karmic cause and effect. As we view these experiences from the perspective of an objective witness, we see how they fit into the perfection of our life's unfolding. By accepting what is, we can know greater forgiveness, tenderness, and embrace compassion toward our self and all of life.

Beyond our human capacity to accept and forgive, we can also experience the divine and the profane as one and the same. All things become unified in the divine matrix of creation where we are the players. We can perceive the paradox of how our destiny interacts with our free will.

When we tap into our capacity to see the sacred in everything and everyone, we have the opportunity to perceive our own divinity. The following five categories include the most common types of spiritual experiences people have in expanded states of consciousness.

1) Meaninglessness

2) Reclaiming Our Spiritual Life

3) Messianic and Spiritual Archetypes

4) The Underlying Perfection of All Things

5) Ego Dissolution

1) Meaninglessness

This is an experience of realizing the absence of meaning and spirit in one's life. However, this is a spiritual experience by virtue of perceiving the emptiness of a life devoid of spirit. This can be felt as a state of emptiness or shown through visions that are mechanical, barren, or stark. There can be metallic worlds or desolate landscapes, or an overall feeling of hollow meaninglessness.

The guide can simply stay present and stand witness. This is generally an internal process, and few signs are visible from the outside. Do not rescue or save a journeyer from this experience of hitting rock bottom, spiritually speaking. A loud wake-up call is valuable and not to be avoided. Trust that this experience is the bottom from which the journeyer will spring up. As a guide, it is crucial to discern when to intervene. Does the journeyer have enough resources to remain in this challenging state or are they spinning into a black hole?

2) Reclaiming Our Spiritual Life

This is an experience of realizing or grieving a lack of spiritual belief in childhood, reconciling childhood religious structures, or reflecting on one's spiritual history. Sometimes a journeyer reconnects with the spiritual framework of their childhood that was rejected or abandoned at some point. At other times, a spiritual world opens up that was previously unknown. This can be an experience of encountering a spiritual deity, such as a god, Jesus, or Buddha. A Christian might have an awakening of a Buddhist nature. A Jew might encounter Christ Consciousness and feel Jesus's teaching in their core. An agnostic may have an unexpected faith-based experience. There can be a deeper appreciation of ritual and prayers, or one might see specific religious symbols, visions, or images, or hear mantras. One can experience a sense of pure grace or feel fully awakened in the presence of the divine.

At times, this experience also includes a sense of connection with our spiritual teachers or our ancestors, as we acknowledge our spiritual or birth lineage—or possibly connect with a lineage previously unknown.

The best thing for the guide to do here is to listen and encourage the process. The guide can take notes on what is being shared to aid further exploration during the integration phase.

3) Messianic and Spiritual Archetypes

I am made of fire, curled up in the center of the earth. I swirl and I boil. I am love and destruction. I am sexual power and heat that will warm your cold heart. Feel me under your feet, always there, present and ready to appear, in explosive bursts that flow and scorch everything in my path. I have always been right here, warming you from deep below, throbbing with power and grace. I am fierce and gentle. I am Pele, Goddess of Fire, made of the blood of the Mother.

—*Françoise's Journey Journal, September 1986*

Like my experience of becoming Pele, a journeyer may have the embodied or spiritual experience of being an entity or a god or goddess blending with pure creative force. They may truly feel that they are the Great Spirit, Buddha, the Goddess, or another deity. For some journeyers, becoming an archetype such as the Lover, the Warrior, or Kali, or connecting with great teachers such as Gandhi, Nelson Mandela, or Mother Teresa might occur. These experiences can leave a lasting impression of power, courage, and love.

These potent visions, when experienced internally, are rarely visible to an external observer. If the journeyer shares what they are encountering, the guide can listen, reflect, take notes, and play appropriate music to support the encounter. The guide can simply remain a respectful witness to this experience as it unfolds.

4) The Underlying Perfection of All Things

This is an experience of a journeyer gaining understanding into the circumstances that contributed to his or her core beliefs. What are we here to learn in this life? This is an experience of taking ownership and understanding the reasons why certain things have happened and how they have served our evolution. We may realize the importance of the exact circumstances that have supported our soul to evolve in the way it has. This can be a process of resentment transforming into self-compassion, acceptance, and love. This experience may reveal that all things are connected and nothing is separate. There can be an understanding of the impermanent nature of all things and the perfection of the unfolding. People report a felt experience of love and benevolent energy at the center of all creation. The journeyer perceives love as the force that holds all and is felt and translated in all they do. Such insight can lead to tenderness, forgiveness, reaffirmed values, and loving actions based on solidarity and sharing.

Again, an internal realization of the underlying perfection of all things is so profound and intimate that a guide can only stay present with it. The guide can support this experience by accessing a calm space within himself or herself, so the client and guide can resonate, even if only subliminally. If a journeyer shares their experience through words or gestures, the guide ought to remain a quiet witness of such a deep opening. The guide should take care to not disturb this spiritual state by physically moving, making sounds, or talking too much to the person. It is best to support the delicate vibration of such a sublime state.

5) Ego Dissolution

I see the ancestors as smoky undulating forms in underground caves. It is dark, and the flight of the bat is the only breeze there is. The ancestors beckon me, and I approach. They surround me, enveloping me with their shapeless cloak of gray and brown. I am not afraid. I say yes to their certainty, and I die. I sense my will dissolve like a line erased on a paper, nothing more. I cease to exist. I have been taken away from myself and all I know myself to be. I merge with the nothingness that is vibrating around me and within me. My shape disappears, and I am the gray and brown ancestors of the past and future. I exist only in essence, swirling through million-year-old caves. There is no fear here as I vanish into eternity. There is no more "I."

—Françoise's Journey Journal, March 2005

Many modalities can bring forth an experience of ego dissolution, which is also called ego death. Ego dissolution can occur on many levels; the first level being a journeyer's surrender of their capacity to make decisions on a conscious level. The second level is the surrender of their identity while still maintaining a sense of witness. The deepest level is the loss of any witness, perhaps maintaining a vast open awareness or losing even that. The experience of complete dissolution echoes the shamanic process of dismemberment and death. This can be terrifying yet transformative. This last level of dissolution is not always remembered but can leave a taste of liberation, which can lead to significant growth after a journeyer returns to normal consciousness.

If someone is supported through the process and can surrender, they can enter states of breathtaking bliss, well-being, and love. This can lead to an experience of oneness with everything. It can reconnect a journeyer to a central axis of spirit. The journeyer can have the experience of transcending all states and resting as pure, vast awareness. Someone in this state is beyond words and will communicate very little. Their normal self has completely dissolved. Their identity has temporarily "died." This is the ultimate experience of going beyond fear into the unknown.

This level of dissolution necessitates a solid trust in the guide and the setting. For someone entering this state, there can be initial resistance. It is natural to fight against the dissolution of what one holds to be their identity. The guide can support the journeyer by offering reassurance and reminding them to let go. The guide can encourage slow breathing and offer physical contact.

Some people enter this state gracefully and it can appear uneventful, with a feeling of floating in peace and serenity. Sometimes a journeyer's breath can appear to stop as they are suspended in awe and amazement. A guide can offer simple presence and support for an experience like this. Continuing to create safety during the experience allows a journeyer to let go, knowing that the guide is holding the container for this experience to unfold. The integration phase will be significant, but the experience happens by itself and needs no assistance beyond keeping the journeyer physically safe.

Community-Centered Experiences

The aspect of community is intimately related to the emotional dimension of our life. In expanded states of consciousness, it is common to reflect on the relationships in one's life. Many emotions can arise as we perceive the types of relationships that are present or absent in our life. We can perceive how past relationships have impacted our present capacity to connect with others.

A journeyer can have insight into their connections with the people in their life: partners, children, teachers, friends, family, or even casual acquaintances. They might perceive the role they play in their partnership, family, or larger community, or realize how deep or shallow the connections they have truly are. They might realize how they do or do not show up for the people in their life. For some of us, this exploration might lead us to acknowledge a level of isolation and the fear of not belonging or being seen and accepted for who we truly are. While this experience can be painful, it can also lead us to connect with the events in our past that have contributed to our current situation.

We may experience an enhanced awareness of others, their mystery, and importance in our lives. We might gain insight into past traumas and our capacity to connect, or for the first time, we might feel truly seen by our guide or our community.

Some of us might be confronted with our fear of the other, in whatever form the other takes for us: race, religion, sexual identification, lifestyle, or whatever else feels unfamiliar and challenging to accept. This can lead to facing old fears learned from unfortunate experiences or taught to us in childhood and open us to wider acceptance. We may feel a sense of belonging to the human family and reaffirm our choice to live an incarnated life. We might feel gratitude and a sense of honor for all things human and nonhuman as our sense of belonging can extend to the whole planet and the entire cosmos.

At the beginning of a ritual with other people, some journeyers might feel uneasy with the role of the leader and be suspicious or frightened by the leader's power. Feeling angry and disturbed by a leader's voice or words might be due to a past experience of power having been abused or resistance to receiving support. A journeyer may feel invisible or depressed by the people around them because it reflects what they are working on internally in their personal process. Other people will go into the same ritual and appreciate the care and support of the facilitator and will surrender into the structure and form of the ritual, feeling nourished by it. Whatever shows up around this topic in a journey is reflective of how a person is in relationship to safety, authority, and intimacy in their life.

We humans are social creatures. We are not born in a vacuum. We are connected with other people and community, whether it is our family of origin or our family of friends or our school or our workmates. We all want to belong; we all crave connection. Community is something that we are born into. It is unavoidable that at some point we need to deal with our relational dynamics. Whatever technique we use for inner exploration, we will likely encounter other people. When we go into a ritual, unless we are completely alone, we will be with at least one person and often more. We will be interfacing with a guide or a group leader or fellow participants. We will likely be in the care of someone, which will embody our general sense of ease—or lack of ease—with being under someone else's care. This dynamic often recapitulates our experience with our parents and how they did or did not nourish us, showing us not only how we relate in one-on-one relationships, but with our larger community.

Sharing expanded states of consciousness in a communal setting can highlight the importance of what it is to be in community, as the journeyers can experience connectedness, mutual support, and passion together. A communal setting can also bring out insecurities, self-consciousness, and judgments. However it is that we feel in community and in our lives in general will be amplified in a journey.

The following categories include most of the community-centered experiences that occur in expanded states of consciousness:

1) Perceiving the Impact of Isolation

2) Healing Our Relationships

3) Celebration of Belonging

4) Global Human Family

1) Perceiving the Impact of Isolation

Renee refused to connect romantically with anyone, despite the encouragement of her friends. She was stubborn, which led her to contract and avoid contact even though she was aware it would be healthy to reach out. In our work together, we explored her self-consciousness, her shyness, and her stories. Now, it was up to her to try new ways of relating and expressing herself.

During her mushroom journey in Mexico, she felt isolated. She saw how she hurt herself by not giving herself a chance to repair her past. She saw that she had a habit of self-punishment. She saw her body shriveling from the lack of human presence and touch. She heard her inner voice locked inside her throat. Her heart seemed like a lonely piece of herself, unable to receive love, shielded by fear and stubbornness. She realized she couldn't continue anymore. It was slow suicide. Her loneliness was painful; she knew she deserved better now. She wanted life.

Renee's experience of isolation and perceiving the internal barrenness of her emotional landscape is an example of insight on the level of community that someone can receive during a journey. There can be memories of loneliness as a child, and an acknowledgment of the painful aspects in one's biography. There can be feelings of emptiness and disorientation. The journeyer may feel sad, disconnected, or abandoned. The journeyer might appear fragile and shiver or whimper. The journeyer may experience an empty silence or a cold, dark void. This can be a nonverbal experience.

If an experience regresses back to childhood, the guide should stay physically present and offer nurture and connection. By providing soothing attention, the guide can help create new pathways in the brain around connection and feeling cared for, providing healing from isolation.

2) Healing Our Relationships

This is an experience of contemplating and reflecting upon relationships with our partners, parents, children, friends, pets, community, and ancestors. There may be memories of various people from childhood, such as teachers, mentors, or people who have been hurtful. The journeyer may have insights into the character, personality, attachment patterns, or conditioning of people they know well. The journeyer may contemplate predicaments and wounds and gain an understanding of specific relational dynamics. The journeyer may understand his or her own patterns and tendencies in relationships.

This may (or may not) lead to increased compassion or acceptance. A journeyer may connect with raw emotions and acknowledge hurt, betrayal, anger, or grief. Final resolution is not necessarily completed during a journey experience itself.

Journeyers may for the first time allow certain feelings, memories, or reflections to be fully present. Realizing the richness and the rightness of all the people who have crossed their path in life, they may reflect on the significant players and realize the perfection of the cast of characters in the play of their life. This often leads to an acceptance of the relational dynamics through which we all grow and evolve.

During this psychological and emotional experience, the guide should allow the journeyer to go into an internal process of reflection. If the journeyer shares this experience verbally, the guide can validate insights and ask skillful questions to deepen the experience. The guide can gently lead the journeyer toward compassion and encourage the expression of the emotional process, while taking notes of the realizations or intended actions to be taken in the future.

3) Celebration of Belonging

This is a positive experience in which a journeyer realizes the essential nourishment of belonging in community. One feels the rich presence of others, the love and support that are present, as well as one's own impulse to support others. It is recognition of one's personal value and gifts as they are reflected back by a group. One may perceive the essence of their connection to their community and their unique contribution. There can be unexpected joy in the celebration of communal belonging by virtue of similar interests or activities. This experience of belonging deepens one's sense of safety in the world because once connected with others, bonded through a common interest, the healing that can take place can alleviate a sense of emptiness from early on in life. For people who were only children, orphaned, or isolated in a family where there was neglect, a renewal of communal life and shared joy offers an entirely new reality.

If this communal affiliation is an internal experience, the guide will not see the depth of the insight. But if the person is talking about it, then the guide can validate, affirm, and reflect the beauty of communal bonds. Hold and encourage the unfolding in its mystery. The guide can support whatever is being expressed and trust that what is unfolding will be fruitful.

4) Global Human Family

I am a child of the world. My heart is one with others. I am the child in Tibet, the African grandmother, and the English businessman. My family is the human race. I have chosen this vast, colorful, and diverse family to teach me about myself in this lifetime. I am the sister of the man who plants trees in the deforested jungle. I am the father of the boy who picks through a pile of garbage, looking for food in India. I am the confused, corporate man who sees money as proof of his success. I am all of them. My family is complex and multidimensional. Sweet and horrible. My parents are all the people who came before me. My children have yet to be born. I am a hologram of the whole. The whole is me.

—*Françoise's Journey Journal, July 1986*

This experience of directly sensing my belonging to the global family came in the early stages of my own explorations. As a child, I was very curious about other cultures and places. As a young woman I related to people in other countries and other cultures with ease. This journey experience reminded me of my early sentiment toward others.

This type of experience brings forth an embodied sense of oneness, solidarity, and empathy toward the joy and suffering of others. The journeyer may explore the collective unconscious and even experience a new cultural identity during a journey. There is an emotional acknowledgment that we all share the same basic instincts for love and connection, regardless of our culture or our location. Attention to these basic instincts allows us to feel the interconnection of all beings. There is a sense of belonging beyond personal interest, based on human values and our shared planetary consciousness.

The guide can validate this experience of belonging and the empowerment it brings by looking for ways to unfold the insights and explore them further. They can listen and reflect, validate, and help the journeyer go deeper into the experience and translate insights into actions. What is it like emotionally and physically to have this realization? Connect the dots.

Environment-Centered Experiences

In expanded states of consciousness, journeyers often find themselves deeply contemplating their environment. The first level of this exploration is looking at one's home as a reflection of one's inner world. Is it tended, neglected, messy, or organized? Noticing one's tendency to pile things up in a corner can reflect what remains untended in one's psyche. Trash left on the kitchen counter can guide one to inquire if there might be shadow material festering in their psyche. Many people report being inspired to clean up and organize their living space in an expanded state. Others may come to realize the importance of a pleasurable environment and how the beauty that surrounds their everyday life nourishes them. One can see the impact of how attention or neglect toward their living space reflects their relationship with themselves.

The next level addresses one relationship with the natural world. This level of insight is quick to emerge, especially if the ritual being conducted includes the elements, is rooted in ancient shamanic practices, or is held outdoors. The journeyer may feel a connection with the planet and all of its inhabitants. They may perceive the profound reality of planetary interdependence, realizing for the first time how their survival depends entirely on the well-being of the earth's delicate ecosystem. They may even experience themselves as an extension of the planet; a walking, talking sprout of this earth.

In the traditions that include plant medicine, a journeyer ingests a portion of a plant or fungi. A journeyer literally takes the living environment into their body as a sacrament. What does it mean to ingest nature and commune with it in such an intimate way? How does one invite nature in as a teacher?

The following categories include some environment-centered experiences that can occur in expanded states of consciousness:

1) The Pain of Living in a Toxic Environment

2) Realizing Our Responsibility for Nature

3) Merging with the Elements

4) Perceiving the Intelligence of Nature

1) The Pain of Living in a Toxic Environment

This experience brings awareness to our home as the immediate container influencing our moods and mental state. One can realize the impact on our well-being of a messy, dirty, uncared-for living space. Being expanded in a beautiful, well-tended space can awaken one's awareness of the state of one's own home.

In an expanded state, one may also feel depressed by the state of pollution and destruction of our planet. There may be visions of ecological devastation—oil spills, water pollution, or dead wildlife. The journeyer may feel despair, helplessness, fear, or rage. This is a meaningful, raw experience, as it is a confrontation with the reality that most of us normally avoid.

This reality can be simply allowed and reflected back by the guide. Yes, it is awful. Yes, it is appropriate to feel terrible and tormented by planetary destruction. It is best to let the journeyer get in touch and express these feelings fully rather than soothing them.

2) Realizing Our Responsibility for Nature

As I sat in the woods that day on my vision quest, I listened. It was easy to hear the wind whispering through the trees, and the dew on the leaves speaking of thirst and water. I heard the flies buzzing around me, humming out a symphony of sounds. Then, as if it had traveled far to reach my ears, I heard another call, one of pain and illness. This one was spoken by the earth herself. Every time garbage is dumped into her rivers, when pollution prevents the butterflies from finding their home, or when the oil is extracted from deep down in her body, she cries. What pain! What sadness she feels, and at this moment I feel it with her. She trusted her children, but they did not take care of her. She has become a resource to exploit. What do I do with this? What CAN I do with this? I am such a small character in this nightmare of destruction. As I feel the breeze moving through the trees and kissing my face, I sense the purity of her heart and of my own. I will do what I can. I will not abandon her. I will stay and listen and do the little things that I can.

—Françoise's Journey Journal, June 1999

This vision quest increased my awareness about the ways I was out of integrity with my environment and how I could change. This insight and my experience of empathy with the earth supported my desire to stay engaged, creating harmony and balance where I was living and working. In my immediate environment it translated to removing clutter, adding beauty to my living space, and cultivating more mindfulness toward what I was consuming and how it had been packaged.

A journeyer may feel the emotional distress of what the human species is doing to planet Earth and a deepening commitment to do more to care for her. This remembrance of right relationship with Earth leads us to feel responsible for what is happening to the planet as a whole and make decisions that will have a beneficial effect. These insight-based decisions create a link between thoughts, feelings, and action as one realizes that it is only through right action that one can nurture the health and survival of the planet. This personal engagement supports a journeyer's sense of belonging to Earth as an intelligent living organism. This is a potent experience of compassion and empowerment.

Depending on the context of the ritual, these insights can be shared with a guide or a group. Feelings can be expressed and decisions can be made in these powerful moments of clarity. The guide can offer support by validating this increasing awareness and inviting the journeyer into deeper engagement with their enhanced clarity and determination.

3) Merging with the Elements

Blending with nature can be an experience of shape-shifting and relating intimately with the natural world. These experiences can take a person toward a profound understanding of the power of natural elements, such as the rain, the ocean, plants, rocks, or animals. Accessing such intelligence is a life-changing experience, as it allows someone to feel a visceral communion with the natural world.

Having a direct experience of the natural world can be life-changing on many levels; the power of the elements can be a touchstone during integration work. For example, someone may have insights into how—like water—they can be more in the flow, or how—like the mountain—they can learn to be patient with change. The journeyer may realize the many similarities that humans share with all the manifestations of nature. This can encourage surrender to the cycles and seasons and, again, enhance one's sense of belonging. This experience has the power to mend feelings of isolation and heal the pain of disconnection.

Once again, depending on how internal the experience is, this intimate communion can be difficult to perceive from the outside. A guide may have an intuition that the person is accessing a state of rapture and vast opening, yet it may remain impossible to identify the source of this joy. The guide should remain present with the mystery of what is taking place within the journeyer. If the person can communicate the depth of his or her communion with nature, the guide can offer validation and encouragement for the journeyer to move, breathe, sing, or dance, to express what is being discovered.

4) Perceiving the Intelligence of Nature

A journeyer may find herself connecting with the intrinsic intelligence of nature, her rhythms and healing powers, and how she regenerates and heals herself. A journeyer may perceive how a cloud can affect a continent far away, how nature balances out herself through her droughts and floods, even in a state of imbalance due to global warming. A journeyer may perceive the intelligence of the massive organism that is our earth, all of her networks of relationship and communication, and her power as a matrix for creation. There can be insight into the ebb and flow of the natural world as a metaphor for the ebb and flow of life. This is a direct experience of nature's intelligence, her seasons, her weather, her landscapes, her flora and fauna, and how her underground world informs life on the surface. This can engender humility and respect. It can also be direct teaching as to how we, as humans, can learn how to apply these rhythms to our lives.

Realizing the magnitude of nature's intelligence, power, and creative force can evoke awe in some and anxiety in others; the guide should be prepared to support the possible feeling of overwhelming humility without blocking its course. Physical support and steady presence are beneficial. Holding space for an experience as large as this requires that a guide be centered.

✱ ✱ ✱

Whether we are the journeyer or the guide, with time, we come to understand that the experiences had in expanded states are an organic response to what needs to unfold. A journeyer will experience what his or her psyche is ready to reveal. Once a type of experience begins to manifest itself, a guide goes with it. An experienced guide will see quickly how a particular experience that arises is right and timely. A journeyer might feel confused about why a certain experience took place. The guide is there to help make sense of an experience in relation to the initial intention. Sometimes it is only in retrospect that the guide can see how the material connects back to the intention. This is the art of the guide.

I have observed many journeys of expanded consciousness followed by spectacular transformation. Time and again, I have witnessed the healing and growth that each experience provides. No one has an absolute understanding of what takes place in these spaces. At times, the experience is visible, verbalized, and expressed, while at other times, especially with the use of entheogens, this unfolding takes place within the journeyer's inner world and is not seen or perceived by the guide during the experience itself. Nonetheless, there is a perfection to the unfolding. Expanded states of consciousness direct a journeyer toward wholeness. Whatever aspect of life needs to be tended or pruned in service to one's movement toward evolution is going to surface. This process is not about finding instant gratification or happiness. Every experience has a specific purpose; none is random. Fundamentally, a journeyer's core wisdom guides the process.

12

RETURNING HOME

The Art of Integration

In the long run, we shape our own lives, and we shape ourselves. The process never ends until we die. And, the choices we make are ultimately our own responsibility.

ELEANOR ROOSEVELT[1]

My client Joel came for an integration session after three weeks alone in a cabin in total silence. He reported that it had been challenging. He had felt fidgety at times, and peaceful and still at other times. By the end of the retreat, he had connected with a gentle sense of equanimity, toward himself and the external world. He had revisited many relationships in his life, which revealed insights. He came to see me to receive support for the integration phase following his retreat. It was important to him to somehow express the many insights he had received, the emotions he had felt, and his renewed feeling of serenity.

> *As we explored the ways he could express himself, he came up with the idea of writing a song, recording it, and sending it out to the people who had "visited" him during his retreat. He was a guitar player, but singing was new to him. This felt like a sweet way to honor his connection with them, as well as a creative endeavor. He came back the following week with his guitar and sang his song to me; it was a delightful distillation of his heartfelt feelings. He sent his song out and surprised his family members and friends who got to see a part of Joel they had not seen before.*

Expanded state experiences such as Joel's have the power to initiate growth in our lives and expose us to new possibilities. While a journey can shift internal patterns and belief systems, this does not necessarily mean one's external reality is transformed. More lasting effects appear during and by virtue of the integration process.

In indigenous cultures, because ritual is woven in with day-to-day life, there is less of a need for intentional integration practices. The community often engages in ritual as a group, and each person is likely to receive support from friends and family. The person facilitating the ritual, the local curandera or shaman, often lives in the village and can keep an eye on those who were present. In our modern industrialized world, while rituals and ceremonies are gaining popularity in many communities and cultures, many journeyers return to their family, work, or school after an extraordinary experience and find there is minimal appreciation or understanding from others. This leaves many journeyers with few people to connect with and a potential sense of isolation. Thus, the integration process is something we must intentionally create in order to honor these experiences in the best way.

An extraordinary experience, whether through a ritual with a psychedelic sacrament, a ceremony, a vision quest, or a retreat, can stand alone as a treasured event. There is something inherently valuable in surrendering to spirit, being one with the cosmos, and understanding the patterns of the universe. But the real question is, what does it contribute to our daily life? How does it make us more whole, balanced, and awake? What is the use of seeing God if you cannot be kind to your partner? What is the value of relating to the earth as a living organism if you still choose to bleach your laundry? What is the point of realizing that all beings are connected if you are unable to look a homeless person in the eye?

My background as a somatic counselor and Hakomi practitioner has taught me the importance of expressing the invisible dimensions in tangible ways. I believe that the gifts of our consciousness exploration can add value to our daily life and should be expressed through real-life actions. The healings and teachings received need follow-up and follow-through.

Integration is the process of bringing separate elements together into a whole. For our purposes, it is the art of weaving the extraordinary into the ordinary—interpreting a journey's mythical and symbolic layers, revealing its gifts and treasures, and anchoring them into our lives.

If one's intention is the seed of what they are calling into their life, and a journey is the ritual that opens that seed into a sprout, then integration is the nourishment that helps it grow healthy. If you do not commit to tending the living, evolving process that is your life, no one will. When we commit to the process of integration, we honor the transformation that has occurred.

The phase of integration may last a few days, a few months, or a lifetime, depending on the content of the journey and the magnitude of what has been revealed. Memories, glimpses, or moments can visit us years down the road and finally give us the aha moment of why a certain vision or insight appeared and how it fits into the overall scheme of our lives. But because we are more psychologically adaptable for the days and weeks following a journey into an expanded state, this is the best time to introduce practical changes and anchor new insights into our lives.

What happens without integration? Most of the time, what may have seemed clear during the journey slowly fades like a dream as old habits and tendencies return. Occasionally, the absence of integration can result in disorientation, as expanded states of consciousness can expose previously unknown and possibly painful layers of the psyche. People have come to my office in severe states of disorientation after having powerful expanded state experiences they were not able to process. Their intention to access the transpersonal realm brought them face-to-face with complex parts of themselves. Without the necessary support and integration skills to make sense of these inner states, they were frightened, had nightmares, or found themselves becoming anxious or depressed and unable to function in their everyday lives. What could have been a significant inner transformation instead resulted in a destabilized state.

It is an insult to the potency of this inner work to not take the time to integrate what has been revealed. Without proper follow-through, the journey becomes another fleeting experience and loses its power. It is a tragedy to squander such potential for growth. As the experience fades from a journeyer's immediate memory, it is the commitment to integration that will keep the teachings and insights continuing to inform all aspects of their life.

The Role of the Guide in the Integration Phase

When someone begins to explore expanded states of consciousness as a healing modality, they do not know the personal realms they will encounter, the importance of integration, nor how this entire method works. Thus, the integration process is best facilitated by a guide in close collaboration with the journeyer.

The guide, who presumably has guided the preparation process and ritual experience, should meet with the journeyer within a week of the journey for the initial integration session. Many journeyers will need ongoing support during this phase of integration. The guide can help connect the dots of the various layers of the experience and support the integration process wisely and effectively. If the guide is not a therapist, and the journey addresses psychological layers, the guide should help the journeyer find adequate psychological and emotional support.

During the integration phase, it is the guide's role to notice how the intention relates to the content of an experience, reflect these connections, expand the elements that have emerged, and along with the journeyer, track apparent themes. Of course, material will arise from the journeyer's unconscious that the guide has no understanding of. That is okay. It is more important that the guide knows how to support a journeyer in their own process of understanding than to conjure up possible meanings. Similar to dream interpretation, there are collective archetypes and universal meanings that may be helpful to explore. At the same time, each person has their own dictionary of symbols infused with personal meaning resulting from their life. The guide should encourage the journeyer's self-inquiry while keeping their intuition and objective mind engaged, offering gentle suggestions as is appropriate.

A guide should support whatever is unfolding organically rather than pushing the process to immediately focus on the practical aspects of integration. For example, if someone is in a tender emotional state after a journey, it is the guide's job to remain gently supportive while this tenderness finds its outward expression. Staying present with a tearful moment can be one hundred times more helpful than rushing into a cognitive process of understanding the content of a journey.

I want to emphasize again that the entire process of integration must be infused with wisdom, creativity, and love. A guide needs to be creative and adapt to the individual needs of a journeyer, while also remaining wise and attentive to boundaries and limits. Finally, the guide's core motivation should be to hold the entire process with loving care. The more a guide expresses these qualities, the more they impart them to the journeyer. Over time, the journeyer internalizes the support and guidance offered to them by their guide, and their own inner guide becomes more available.

Caution: If You Have No Guide

If you have an expanded state experience without a guide, at least make sure to confide in a friend afterward so your experience can be shared, witnessed, and supported. Do not isolate yourself if you are processing vague or perplexing content that feels confusing or destabilizing. There are integration groups that offer excellent support. Experienced therapists, psychologists, and mentors can offer the skilled listening you may need to make sense of your journey. These people can help you recognize the gems within your experience and help you set them into your life.

Integration Framework

The integration process is best done as a facilitated three-part progression. The first step is the return. The journeyer shares their narrative, while the guide keeps their initial intention in mind. The second step is to identify the type(s) of experience that have emerged according to the categories of transformative experience. The third step is to devise concrete practices and exercises that will support ongoing integration.

Although there are exceptions, for the most part I do not encourage entering an expanded state of consciousness without a trained guide, teacher, or mentor. However, those who do not have access to a guide and still choose to journey can also use the following framework to create an individualized plan of integration alone or with a friend.

The Return

The return begins when the guide meets with the journeyer a few days after the journey. I always start by first bringing awareness to the present moment. How is the journeyer now feeling physically, emotionally, and psychologically? The guide should compare how the journeyer was before the experience and how they are afterward.

The journeyer can then recall and restate the intention that they crafted and named in advance of the journey, which is the seed of the experience itself. By virtue of recalling the intention, an invisible thread appears. Restating the intention brings context to the content of the experience and invites deeper meaning to emerge.

Then I invite the journeyer to share their narrative of what happened during the ritual. As I listen to the narrative of the journey, I pay close attention to what was felt or seen. When people relate the story of their journey—whether it was a ritual, a retreat, or a vision quest—further levels of insight begin to arise as awareness is brought to the sensations, images, memories, or states that were experienced. The act of verbal expression begins to pull into form that which before may have felt abstract. Like recalling a dream, at first it may feel hazy and far away, but as it is brought to the forefront of attention, the pieces begin to fit together and the narrative gathers coherence.

Identifying the Experience

During the return, the guide listens carefully to the journeyer's narrative while also remembering what they witnessed. They should pay attention to which feelings, sensations, thoughts, insights, or visions were experienced. From this the guide can determine which categories of experience have been accessed. What seems to be the theme of the journey? Some experiences are clearly physical in nature, and other ones are emotional or access deeper unconscious layers. Some experiences touch spiritual understanding, while some experiences are about our relationships, family, or greater humanity. Some experiences have to do with the environment and connection with the earth. If the journey touched several aspects, what seems primary? I ask myself, "What did I witness and what did I feel while supporting the journeyer's process? How do the apparent themes relate to the journeyer's intention?" An expert guide has questions, tools, and a well-honed intuition that help decipher and decode the content of a journey and connect it with the original intention.

It is impossible to make generalizations about the content of journeys and the meaning of anyone's particular experience. The innate wisdom of the psyche guides the process in ways that are often mysterious. Someone with an intention to expand the spiritual dimension of their life can easily end up having an excruciating physical experience, their body confronted with the pain created by unconscious tension. The somatic symptoms can be interpreted as intelligent communication, relaying that the patterns of contraction, possibly due to a lack of safety in childhood and the resulting fear, need to shift before a spiritual expansion will occur.

One of my mentors says, "The thing about journeys is that they are all exceptions." There are no two people who have the same constitution or history. Everyone will have a unique experience. In all my years of guiding and supporting people through a variety of inner explorations, one truth has affirmed itself over and over. There is no such thing as a random experience; all journeys offer the perfect teaching for the moment, even if they are at first confusing. Some experiences will be easy, some will be challenging; all are valuable.

Creation and Application of Integration Practices

Taking the intention and the narrative of the journey into consideration, as well as which categories of experience were accessed, the guide and journeyer can create integration practices that will sustain the development of the themes that have emerged. Although one or a few obvious themes will be revealed in a journeyer's experience, it is most important to remember that a holistic integration requires the involvement of all five aspects of one's life. The guide ought to be mindful to include these other dimensions while creating practices. By overemphasizing one aspect of life in an integration process, the risk is of unintentionally creating an imbalance in the journeyer's life. A new passionate commitment can create a new imbalance. A guide should keep an eye on the whole gestalt of the journeyer during the integration process, spreading the healing intention into all the aspects of their life.

As with this entire approach, the phase of creating integrative practices should engage the qualities of wisdom, creativity, and love as the guide helps the journeyer discern their most potent course of action. This discernment calls forth wisdom. The practices should be designed creatively. But the most fundamental quality to draw upon during the phase of integration is love. By love, I mean a posture of compassion and tenderness. Sometimes the most compassionate way to support someone is to tell the truth in a direct manner. Regardless, love and support should remain at the core of a guide's motivation.

Integration suggestions should be doable and feel good. They should not feel like a burden, or induce intense stress, although they will likely feel new at first. If meditating every day is not something a journeyer is realistically capable of doing or has resistance to, then maybe meditation could be done every other day or once a week. A guide should be realistic so that the journeyer can honor whatever practice is decided upon. Start small. Practices can be increased after a week or two if they are easily incorporated into daily life. A walk in the park once a week, drinking a cup of herbal tea in the afternoon, or writing in a journal every few days is easy to implement. If a journeyer is able to stabilize in their new practices and feel enriched by them, they can take them further.

After a post-journey integration meeting with me, one of my clients flew to Florida to confront her abusive father. During her experience, she had physically felt the body of her father on her small child's body. She had felt physically suffocated and enraged. She had been estranged from him for seven years. He was now dying and she felt that time was of the essence. She reported back to me that once she arrived in Florida, she found him weak and bedridden. She stood at the foot of his bed and told him what she remembered. She told him she was angry and asked him what he had to say. When he said nothing, she stood there, staring at him in silence. She could feel the strength flowing through her veins, the strength she had repressed as a child. She was free of the secret, the "not telling" he had insisted on when she was small and frightened. Facing him now, she felt free from his intimidation. She asked him again if he had anything to say to her. He lowered his eyes and shamefully answered, "No." She walked away. She said that she finally felt complete.

Keep integrative practices intentional and practical. They can be challenging and cathartic—confronting someone like my client did or releasing anger. They can be tender and vulnerable, grieving a loss through a ritual, meditating, reading, or writing a letter to the inner child. They can be fun and enjoyable—running in the waves, or going out dancing with a friend. They can be joyful—painting, singing, or simply spending time with our loved ones.

A guide doesn't need to argue if there is resistance. If there is resistance to suggested changes, then explore the resistance. Work with the journeyer's fear of *what will happen if I change?* The theme of resistance is real. We have all studied something and then dropped it. We thought it was fabulous and then we found ourselves not doing it anymore. We want to establish an engaged dialogue with the journeyer so that they do not feel isolated or discouraged. They might find they dislike the practice or need to be more creative and do something that supports them in a different way. Stay with the aspects touched during the experience, and create integration practices appropriate to the specific content of the journey.

There is a bumper sticker that says, "Do it out of duty until you do it out of love." A guide helps the journeyer commit to the integration practices not out of obligation, but because it is the right thing for them to do. This is not based on any concept of morality, but on the journeyer's personal integrity as someone seeking support on their personal path of transformation. The only relevant duty is the duty toward one's self. Hopefully, through the practices, the journeyer will eventually find greater joy, notice changes, and like how they feel.

The guide can support the journeyer to keep their integration practices ongoing. The journeyer can modify or adjust their practice but should not abandon an inner message or guidance toward healing. A practice may evolve. Something that holds value after a certain experience may shift into another. It is also beneficial to have a variety of practices. Doing yoga is wonderful, but someone may get a different and equally joyful feeling dancing to rhythmic music. Approaching the process nonjudgmentally is important. If a client starts with meditation because it calms their mind, they may find that making art or playing music works even better. As long as the overall purpose is addressed, the practices can vary. It is important to be creative with the integration practices. It is not about cold discipline; it is about tending to one's self in a way that feels authentic and kind.

It is the guide's ongoing job to continue to support the journeyer and to track the transformational effects of the practices. The guide should stay in touch with the journeyer for as long as is necessary to facilitate follow-up sessions and make sure the work has been fully integrated. If a journeyer's integration practice is a one-time action, such as writing a letter to express previously suppressed emotions connected to unresolved experiences, or traveling to a gravesite far away, or fulfilling a dream of seeing Antarctica, the guide should check in on the aftermath of the action. Its effects will ripple outward and could possibly affect many layers of a journeyer's life.

The transformational benefits of an expanded state experience do not end at the completion of a journey: they continue for days, weeks, or months, depending on how much attention is brought to the aftermath. Our attention is part of our commitment to the return. We do not want to overanalyze it: it is more valuable to simply track and notice the aftermath. How do the visions, realizations, and insights continue to create echoes? The most important thing is how the journeyer feels on the other side of the experience—and how its lessons become anchored into daily life.

Our culture teaches us to be consumers of all things, including experiences. However, a journeyer's active involvement in the integration process creates a different kind of relationship to the experience. There is an arc of transformation, which includes all of the journeyer's preparation, the actual journey, and finally, the integration phase, which invites the journeyer to engage with their own transformation. As a client of mine said about this work of personal healing, "There is nobody out there; we are it. It is me with me, facing me, talking to me, healing me."

Expanded states of consciousness can bring insights, teachings, and gifts that become practical as they are integrated into daily life and translated into concrete actions. We are creatures of habit and our habits are often stronger than our insights. If we do not actively commit to ways of dismantling our unhealthy habitual ways of being, our old physical tensions, behaviors, and tendencies will likely reassert themselves. Integration includes supporting and reinforcing new healthy brain pathways and neural networks through these committed intentions and practical actions.

Furthermore, by embodying and grounding these sometimes abstract or obscure experiences into everyday reality, we deepen our experience of the sacred in the everyday, and we bring a different vibration to the world. In this way, we support our intention to place love and wisdom at the center of our reality. Not only will the integration work affect the journeyer, but it will ripple out to touch their family, friends, and community. In the end, the commitment to sustain integration practices is not only to our self, but to all those we love as well.

It is easy to say we want less suffering in our lives and that we aspire to be of service. However, when we are given the gift of awareness and perceive what we can do to lessen our suffering and become more actualized humans, then it is up to us to take the steps—to truly walk our talk. We do not have much control over what happens during a state of expanded consciousness, or most of life for that matter, but we do have control over how we relate to the experiences we have.

In the following five chapters I will go through the categories of experience I defined in chapter 11. I offer ideas, based on my years of fieldwork, as to why a journeyer might have this type of experience, followed by suggestions on how to approach the integration of each type of experience.

13

COMING TO OUR SENSES

Integrating Body-Centered Experiences

If you don't do your dance, who will?

GABRIELLE ROTH

My client Josie had always felt that people did not like her. She had freckles and bright red hair, and kids had made fun of her throughout her childhood. She had lacked protection or reassurance from her parents and, as a result, had shut down and resigned herself to being shy and withdrawn. Yet when Josie sat across from me, I was taken aback by her beauty, her voice, and her graceful movement. She had done a little psychotherapy but said that talking about her childhood had not helped her in any way. She wanted something else that would help her open up: her shyness and constant fear of being mocked made it difficult to make friends, let alone enjoy a romantic relationship. I suggested she attend a weeklong 5Rhythms dance retreat as a way to explore her fears and move through them in a safe and caring container. She was willing to try it.

When Josie returned, she reported that at first she felt meek at the retreat and stood at the edge of the room, watching others so free and uninhibited in their dancing, which only made her feel more intimidated. Then, gradually, she dared a little more and entered into the group. She slowly found the movement in her body and began to breathe through her shyness, accepting it as something that she did not have to fear. Smiling, she told me: "I even danced with a man, and I survived!" She was so ecstatic about her breakthrough. It was like watching a flower blossom into radiance.

I assured Josie throughout her integration phase that this significant experience would lead her to feel embodied on an ongoing basis and more celebratory of her beauty. I encouraged her to let down her gorgeous red curly hair and learn to love it. Additionally, she decided to add more color to her wardrobe. She scheduled a few massages to experience touch in a safe environment. She continued to work with me for another year. Two years later, I received an announcement for her upcoming marriage with a man she had been dating for a year. It included a photo of them together, her hair wild and free.

Our body is a physical expression of who we are and a magnificent vehicle for sensory experience. As I have explained, our bodies store and process everything we experience—fears, sorrows, sadness, and anger. Undigested emotions, thoughts, memories, and experiences stay stored in our tissues and nervous system. Over time this stagnant energy can wreak havoc in our guts, lungs, heart, or skin. Self-exploration through expanded states of consciousness can bring us closer to equilibrium by helping us understand what is blocking our ease and wellness. Body-centered experiences can lead us into understanding parts of our childhood and how particular blockages or habits were formed. There are causal reasons why our body feels the way it does.

In a journey with an entheogenic plant medicine, a meditation, or dance retreat, as we begin to relax and open our bodies, we may find ourselves more able to perceive the link between a physical condition and its psychoemotional source. We begin to inquire into the interdependence of our psychosomatic issues and our biography. Why do we have chronic back pain or digestive problems? Why do we carry tension in our shoulders? We might realize we have been carrying the weight of the world on our shoulders or realize the impact that our mother's depression had on us. We might see how our father's unpredictable anger caused us to hold our breath and develop ongoing anxiety and fear.

As I mentioned, in indigenous cultures, the phase of integration is woven into community life as rituals take place within the collective. Particular attention is given to diet; a journeyer is often given specific meals to restore physical strength and to break the fast that might have been indicated prior to the ritual. In the Mazatec tradition, a person is sometimes rubbed with alcohol to heat the body to the point of sweating, in order to support further release. Special teas may be given to enhance dreams, sweating, or rest. Sexual abstinence is supportive in the integrative process, as it supports a journeyer's return into their own field of energetic integrity, as the experience may linger in the physical body for a few days or weeks.

Detoxification and sweating protocols may be prescribed as a further level of purification if the process was left incomplete after a ritual. Some of these protocols use herbs, chants, or human guidance. In many cultures, rest and sleep are considered the most basic support for integration. The completion of a ritual extends beyond a linear timeline, and the healing process continues through the journeyer's return home, even if they feel back to normal on a basic level. If the ritual has been static or held in an enclosed location, walking in nature can bring movement and deeper breath back into the body.

Often integrating a new understanding regarding the tension or pain in our body initiates the healing process. The simple virtue of awareness alone begins to dismantle tensions. But although we might feel physically better by having insight, we also need to know which practices will best support our well-being. Integration is the follow-through, as we develop new habits of self-care; such as better sleep routines, regular bodywork sessions, hot soaks in a bath, intentional breathing, or movement practices. Small changes in habits can have a huge impact. Removing a toxic influence from our life can give us more years to live. Eating healthy foods can restore our self-esteem. Sleeping more deeply leaves us rested, which brings us more emotional balance and creativity. Wherever we need attention and care will be recognized after the journey, with the diligent interpretation and support of an experienced guide. Let's look again at the various categories of journey experience and how we can best support their integration.

Contraction and Pain

While day-to-day life can keep a person active and preoccupied, contraction and pain stop all distractions and create a confrontation with that which is immediately present on a physical level. Staying present and curious with a sensation of contraction can lead a journeyer to understand the source of the tension or discomfort. In what way does their tension serve them? What is held in the tension? What is their pain communicating? Where is it leading? What are they afraid of or avoiding? What are they refusing to feel? What are they resisting? Pain can be due to old injuries or current psychosomatic blockages. Sometimes a journeyer will feel tightness in their brain and nervous system from too much anxiety, stress, sadness, or grief.

Contraction and pain can indicate different conditions. They can result from unresolved developmental trauma from childhood, which creates chronic tension in the body. Growing up in an unpredictable environment under the threat of violence, abuse, or neglect can create this tension. Someone physically abused during childhood may present as tight, pulled in, and ready to brace themselves against an external threat, in an effort to stay safe—or to fight and protect themselves. Contraction can be the result of an unprocessed traumatic event such as a rape, a car accident, or an injury. Even if we have done extensive psychological and emotional healing, our history can stay etched in our body posture and physical tissues and may appear vividly during a journey.

Chronic tension can also be a response to the ego's fear of entering unknown circumstances. It can be a safety strategy. Experiencing pain can be an opportunity for a journeyer to meet their process head-on and reclaim their personal power. This can also be a lesson about surrender and can lead to compassion for the suffering of others.

If the journeyer has become aware of how tension is affecting their body, but the tension persists, the goal of integration is to guide the body toward releasing the tension that has been brought to awareness. We want to support the opening that has been initiated. That can involve bodywork, visceral massage, or breathwork. We can encourage actions that push the physical body a little further toward its edge. We want to encourage the journeyer to exert their body in safe ways. Once the tension opens up, we then gauge what needs to be stabilized. While offering the following suggestions, make sure to respect the physical condition of the journeyer.

- Engage in stimulating and highly active practices such as bicycling, hiking, kickboxing, Ashtanga yoga, or lifting weights (as long as you don't have a cardiac condition)
- Meet with a breathworker to explore active breathwork
- Carry a bag of stones around for a day
- Practice intense dancing or stomp around
- Hike up a steep hill for a sweeping view

If relief was received during the journey, the integration goal is to continue the process of comforting, soothing, and relaxing the body.

- Practice restorative yoga, *T'ai Chi, Chi Kung,* or Continuum
- Receive soothing bodywork
- Take a hot bath with essential oils or relax in a float tank or pool
- Walk in nature or rest in a hammock
- Explore gentle breathing, guided meditations, or listen to relaxing music or binaural beats
- Eat Ayurvedic foods that soothe the fire or air in the body or take soothing herbal remedies

Numbness and Physical Disconnection

Numbness and disconnection can be a physiological strategy connected to trauma. If a person was in such intense circumstances that they needed to play dead or to freeze to survive, this strategy can remain in the physiological memory. However, during journeys, people sometimes seem to leave their bodies; and although there may be little movement, they are in fact perfectly fine. A guide should learn how to distinguish between the two, intuitively and by checking in with the journeyer.

Numbness can also appear in someone who is primarily outwardly focused and overly active in his or her life. It can be a shutting down of the nervous system, which needs to regenerate and rest. Experiencing the absence of movement allows a person to finally appreciate the presence of movement and energy.

If the journeyer moves through the experience of numbness and physical disconnection into a more embodied state, then they do not need to explore the numbness any further but rather receive support around the experience of embodiment. Gentle movement, singing, sounding, and dancing are effective for this.

If the person feels numb throughout the entire journey and is left feeling deadened, the following guidelines are especially useful, since they encourage a more embodied feeling. These practices will help reawaken the senses and help people recover the kinesthetic, sensory levels of their body functions.

- Explore somatic modalities such as 5Rhythms, Biodanza, Soul Motion, or Authentic Movement
- Receive massages or have a large ball at home to roll on
- Take voice lessons, join a choir, or sing with a friend
- Receive sound healing sessions with tuning forks or Tibetan bowls
- Walk barefoot along the shoreline or lie in the warm sand
- Bring fragrant flowers into the home

If the feeling of deadness is a response to overactivity, then it is useful to encourage the journeyer to recognize the overall pattern and the swing of the pendulum. How can they come to a better balance somewhere in the middle? To help slow down, they can try the following practices:

- Sit down with a daily cup of tea and drink it mindfully
- Practice sitting, walking meditation, or a longer retreat
- Take a weekly hot bath with lavender or seaweed added to the water

- Receive nurturing bodywork treatments, such as craniosacral therapy or a Feldenkrais session

- Read a book for fun and relaxation

- Explore purposeless, impermanent activities: draw in the sand and watch the waves wash it away or make an altar of leaves on a windy day and enjoy watching it blow away

Cathartic Release

This is a release of inner tension or contraction in the physical body. This release can feel overpowering—or exhilarating. It often feels like a deep, thorough cleansing. People who go through a cathartic release may be holding chronic tension due to inactivity or they may need to discharge the physical residue of a past trauma. Sometimes shaking and shivering are a simple indication that someone needs more movement in their daily life and that pent-up energy simply needs to be released.

Journeys with cathartic release can be terrifying but rewarding, as the following account demonstrates.

I was in the journey room in my teacher's house in Mexico, and the mushrooms were taking me. I felt terribly uncomfortable and agitated, coughing and spitting as if something wanted to get out of my body. I kept retching and heaving. I was nauseous but unable to vomit. I was simply miserable, in a kind of physical hell. Unfortunately, this process of purification did NOT come to a satisfactory ending during the journey, and I was left exhausted, with a feeling of inner toxicity.

My teacher took me to my room and applied pure cane alcohol all over my body. She wrapped me in blankets so I could sweat . . . which I did! She then applied cool cloths to my face. She gave me an herbal tea to drink in large quantities as a diuretic. I spent a few hours in an in-between state, seeing colorful patterns and the faces of people from my childhood. Memories of toxic experiences from my past began coming into awareness, and everything started to make sense. I completed the process of sweating and peeing, followed by a night of vivid dreams. The next morning I awoke feeling cleansed.

During integration, the guide needs to discern if the purification is still in process. The goal is to complete and support the process that began during the journey. If the process of release feels incomplete, the guide should encourage the release to continue through strenuous activity, while being mindful not to overstress the body or incur possible injuries. Identify what needs to be eliminated and aim to reduce what is toxic in the journeyer's life, such as unhealthy foods, harsh exercise, demeaning sexual encounters, or smoking and drinking to excess. Some suggestions are:

- Apply appropriate diet restrictions or a food cleanse to detoxify
- Do guided tobacco or herbal purges
- Do sweats or sauna, receive colonic irrigation, or do natural purges with salt water or laxatives
- Do an Ayurvedic *panchakarma* cleanse
- Receive bodywork such as Rolfing or Chi Nei Tsang

If the process feels complete and the journeyer needs to rest after a vigorous purification experience, the goal is to stabilize a sense of calm in the body and to enhance the feeling of purity. Incorporating gentleness accomplishes this and encourages this state to become a solid foundation. It is useful to support the ongoing awareness of movement in the body. Walking, breathing, and fairly active practices will keep the flow of energy moving and prevent an old static state from returning. Pay attention to the content that might have appeared during this release: memories, emotions, or fears. Make sure to highlight the connections. We are not looking for a blind release, but for notable connections between the release and one's emotional life and history. Here are other suggestions to follow:

- Practice pranayama for flow of breath
- Bathe in a lake or river of flowing water
- Explore gentle yoga or massage

Vital Embodiment

A friend of mine had been feeling depressed and disturbed and was seeking spiritual inspiration. She decided to attend a ten-day silent meditation retreat.

During the first two days, she felt agitated by a mix of emotional states, feeling confused and angry about *not* reaching peace and calm. During the next two days, however, she began to surrender to the physical experience of these emotions. She felt energy flowing through particular parts of her body, and it was as if she had become a neutral witness, able to observe her experience. During the remaining days of the retreat, she felt connected to the intensity of her physical experience, even though she was just sitting on her cushion. She was inhabited by a surging life force that mobilized her complete attention. Her body was alive like a river of fire, solid as the earth and as light as the air. She was calm yet in movement, intense yet peaceful.

After the retreat, she supported her opening by committing to going to the beach once a week. She wanted to be in the presence of nature's vitality, to mirror her newly opened energy. She ran in the waves, did cartwheels on the sand, and sang loudly into the ocean wind. She continued to dance and play, alone and with friends. She felt she had unblocked her life force and she wanted to enjoy it.

Vital embodiment is the feeling of the life force returning to the body after a long absence, perhaps after a period of grief, worry, or depression. For example, I have seen people recover their sensual and erotic energies during expanded states including the mushroom ceremony, even those who had been sexually abused.

The integration goal here is to support the grounding and stabilization of an experience of vital embodiment. The guide ought to be aware of the fragility of recovering such self-expression and sensuality. An approach of respectful guidance and support are key in this situation; it is vital for this process to be at once gentle and firm. The integration practices should engage the senses and be a celebration of physical incarnation. Some suggestions are:

- Roll down sand dunes
- Find new art for the home
- Spend time with friends
- Explore sensuality and sexuality with self and other (after sufficient days of integration)
- Eat living, fresh foods (green juice, raw foods, or tropical fruit)
- Write poetry, paint, sing, or dance—express yourself creatively

Calm, Stillness, and Ease

For those who have rarely felt it, an experience of calm, stillness, and ease can be deeply regenerative and evoke the richness of a life without constant productivity. This experience is especially meaningful to people who are constantly in motion, overly active, or agitated. It teaches them the value of receptivity and the healthy benefit of physical relaxation. It helps them appreciate the beauty and significance of meditative states.

The integration goal is to support the ongoing presence of ease in the journeyer's life. The guide can encourage this continued opening in gentle ways and encourage the journeyer to do the following:

- Practice restorative yoga, water floating, or Watsu
- Receive nonsexual cuddling from a friend or partner
- Take heart-opening flower essences such as rose, hawthorn, or beech
- Drink a cup of nourishing herbal tea every evening
- Go to a local temple or zendo for a dharma talk or evening meditation
- Take a daily nap or begin a daily contemplative practice

✳ ✳ ✳

The integration process on the level of the body is crucial, as the body is essential to all other aspects of life. Whatever positive shifts we make to support our physical health will affect our mind and our emotions. We all wish for effortless pleasure in our physical bodies. We long for rest, comfort, exertion, breath, nutrition, and sensual expression.

When in full physical health, we wake up eager to meet the day. We feed ourselves nutritious, vital foods that replenish our minerals, fats, proteins, and sugars. We exercise, increasing our flexibility and strength. We dance and sing for our pleasure. We spend time in nature, receiving her balancing energy, breathing clean air into our lungs. We meet the sensational world with curiosity. We take in tastes, smells, textures, and colors. We climb, we swim, we run, we walk, we jump, and we roll. We feel safe in our body, buffered from, yet attuned to the external world. We are able to receive and give loving, safe touch. We can hug our friends and family, nurtured by their loving embraces. We seek pleasure through soothing contact and comfort, play, arousal, and orgasm. We express our anger and sadness in healthy ways.

We can exist in a state of ease and relaxed attention. We can surrender to a state of nonaction as we lie in a hammock, sit in front of the fire, or lie under a tree. Like a well-tended garden, a well-cared-for body naturally radiates beauty and joy.

Clearly, expanded states allow for a direct and visceral experience of our tissues and bodily tensions. Exploring and opening our physical bodies is the best avenue to open our emotions, our creative expression, and recover our vitality. Maintaining a healthy physical balance is not easy. It might sound simple and the list of things suggested obvious, but I have observed in many clients over the years that tending and nourishing the body are the surest and most direct routes to wellness on all levels.

14

THE TRUTH WITHIN

Integrating Mind-Centered Experiences

*Be proud of your scars. They have everything to
do with your strength, and what you've endured.
They're a treasure map to the deep self.*
—CLARISSA PINKOLA ESTÉS

My client Clara had been involved in meditation practices for years and considered herself very stable and balanced in her life. She had a sense that some deeper place was awaiting her and she came to consult with me, as she wanted to explore what might "add meaning to her life." We started by doing a guided meditation inventory during which she oriented her attention inwardly, witnessing various aspects of herself and observing the developed areas of her life as well as the weaker ones. She shared that she was a serious person, rarely playing or laughing. Even her spiritual practice felt somber. Soon, she was sharing with me how her parents had been highly academic scientists, dedicated to research and immersed in books and charts all the time. She wanted to further explore the effects her childhood had on her, so we decided to do a breathwork session together.

During her experience, she felt tightness in her breath, a lack of movement in her body, and a sort of frozenness. I modeled for her how she could open her breath and invited her to join me. I stretched her arms out, then reached my hands beneath her back and lifted her up from the mattress in an arching position; her breath amplified, and she started to make sounds and sighs. Within two minutes, she was roaring like an animal, laughing, rolling on the floor, throwing pillows and blankets with her legs in the air, her wild hair on her sweaty face. She looked alive, vibrant, and healthy. When this phase wound down, she started to cry a lot. She had accessed an inconsolable sorrow and memories of being left alone and told to be quiet while her parents worked at home. She began shaking from her core. I gently placed one hand on her back and the other on the back of her head. I sat with her, a witness to her release. Silently I reminded her, "I see you, I am here. You can cry. It's okay."

In our meetings that followed this experience, I made sure to acknowledge all the facets of her emotional expression. She described this journey as liberating because she felt she had reclaimed her inner child by making sense of the complexity of emotions she had experienced in her younger years. It was her child who had known loneliness, but who had also known playfulness. As part of her integration phase, she decided to learn to sing a few children's songs. In support of the more tender side of her inner child, I suggested she write a letter to that little girl who had been so lonely. She wrote the letter and additionally created a collage of photos of herself in her younger years that she placed on her altar, which she surrounded with fresh flowers.

Integration of the mind aspect includes emotional and psychological transformation and healing. During expanded states of consciousness, we often explore our past and our present; we become aware of our authentic emotions and transformative resolutions may unfold from within us. Unconscious aspects of our psyche may reveal themselves through images, visions, and archetypes. These shifts and releases can be sustained in a journeyer's everyday life through intentional follow-up.

In some cultures, the ritual is not considered complete until a significant dream has appeared. Thus, solitude and quiet become important. In the Mazatec culture, people pay attention to their emotional state—sadness, joy, grief, or anger—at the end of a ritual. They share their experience with other people involved. They remember their dreams and share them with one another.

Often, in expanded states of consciousness, people experience a sense of connection with the elements of nature, between the human and the divine, and between the planet and the cosmos. These understandings are not merely intellectual; they are visceral, felt sense understandings. Those understandings are concretized through offerings, prayers, art, and celebrations. In many indigenous cultures, the visions seen during a ritual inspire embroidery, painting, carvings, and other artistic expressions. People wear textiles, jewelry, or hats that express these understandings.

I have observed that people of the Mazatec culture have an intimate relationship with the divine, but do not relate very much with psychology; the language of the Western psychotherapeutic model does not seem to apply to their way of speaking of themselves. Their view is that one needs a spiritual connection in order for healing to happen. The Mazatec people have many sources of spiritual nourishment, including nature. Julieta would often say that if one connects with God, the light of God will illuminate their shadow and allow them to see themselves in full truth.

Cognitive/Intellectual Processes

Resistance

Some journeyers are determined to stay set in their ways. They resist opening to an expanded state. People who want to stay in charge resist out of stubbornness, and their resistance may show them the limitations of their mindset. It can show them that they need to change in order for their life to be more flowing and healthy. Resistance can also stem from a fear of the unknown. For those who have experienced trauma, it can be a strategy to avoid becoming overwhelmed. If a guide can encourage the journeyer to let go, he or she may see they have nothing to fear. The recognition of resistance can also be useful for people who have chronic pain due to tension in the body.

The guide should support an ongoing sense of safety so the journeyer can travel beyond their resistance and willingly express what is happening. If someone persists in a resistance pattern or a critical, skeptical state, then the guide should listen to the resistance and work with it. What is the resistance saying? Engage it. Do not blame or condemn it. What is it protecting? What does the journeyer need to feel safe and comfortable?

In the integration phase, the guide might encourage the resistant journeyer to do the following:

- Write daily in a journal
- Read books that are intellectually engaging
- Walk in nature and connect with the elements
- Watch educational media such as Joseph Campbell's *The Power of Myth*

Often after a journey that includes significant resistance, there is an alleviation from the resistance, as it is exhausted and has been expressed. If the journeyer is more relaxed and open afterward, support that process. Encourage the journeyer to explore more heart-opening activities such as the following:

- Take a break from academic or intellectual books to read heartfelt stories or poems
- Explore gentle expression, make a collage, or arrange flowers
- Write a letter to a loved one

It is important to mention that sometimes a journey of resistance does not resolve itself for a long time. A person may need weeks or months before they are able to look at their refusal to open. Sometimes someone decides to cease their internal exploration and it is the guide's job to respect their choice and keep faith in the process. The person's psyche simply may not be ready to move forward.

I once brought a client to Mexico, and during the first evening ceremony he was triggered by every song he heard. Traditional Mazatec songs often speak of the Virgin of Guadalupe or of God. The man could not bear any of it and was furious the entire time. I tried to soothe him by inviting him to connect with the spiritual dimension rather than the literal religious meaning, but he could not. He barely made it through the ceremony and went directly to bed afterward without joining the group for food and herbal tea after the ritual.

The following day his mood was heavy but contained, and he chose to isolate himself. Nothing I would do or say was able to bring him back to the group or inspire him to talk about his process. Once we returned home, he informed me that this type of healing work was not for him, that his religious childhood had been oppressive enough, and he ended his work with me. Regardless of my invitation to remain engaged in his process and view this experience as an opening into his childhood and a possible healing, he never contacted me again. Although I felt some sadness about the way he had been wounded in his childhood, I had faith that his choice was the best one for him in the moment. I understood that he was not yet ready to explore this material, and I assured him that my door was open if he ever chose to return.

Insights and Guidance

During a journey, some people will receive insights that may help guide them in their future actions. If they have felt disconnected from the direction of their life, these insights can be especially valuable. Or they may be on a clear path and receive new information about what to do next. Insights come to reignite creativity and passion in our lives. Sometimes a journeyer realizes how their present experience connects with their past.

It is up to the journeyer to discern whether a decision that becomes clear in a journey should be immediately followed through with or considered for a while. Explore the motivation for change. Sometimes it is best to mobilize the post-journey energy to make the shift. Sometimes it is better to wait and consider a decision for a while. A guide should use discernment when giving support either way.

Encourage the journeyer to engage in small changes that immediately bring health and well-being. If the decision is a life-changing one such as moving, quitting a job, or ending a relationship, validate its clarity, then see if it might be better to advise the journeyer to wait a couple of weeks before making a move. Some further suggestions are:

- Keep track of insights and decisions

- Create a list of what you want in your life; envision a new job, place to live, or lifestyle

- Get organized; create a structure; create order; create a plan, vision, life schedule, or timeline

- Or loosen up the schedule and have more unstructured, creative time

Emotional Processes

Fear and Panic

Fear and panic arising in a journey may signify that a person is disconnected from his or her emotions. If there is a buildup of unexpressed and unfelt emotions, then opening into an expanded state can release the floodgates. This level of intensity can be frightening.

Fear and panic can also arise when there is a melting of the frozen energy of fear in the body. Fear and panic can also arise for someone who is attached to being in control and only feels safe in the familiar. Their control is being challenged by unusual circumstances. They are out of their comfort zone in an unpredictable environment. They may find the silence unfamiliar, the heat in a lodge too hot, their solitary quest too challenging. Being in a new territory can create panic. If they feel they have hit their limit, sometimes people want to escape. Perhaps they have reached the limit of what they can process before taking on more. I always say, there will be other chances to explore.

Assuming that the fear and panic have subsided, the guide can support whatever state the journeyer is in at the end of a journey through a dialogue about the fear. The guide can ask questions such as "What emotions were coming up for you?" "Was that a familiar state?" "Did you have images or physical sensations with the fear?" The point is to validate and explore the fear. Do not reassure it away. Stay in active inquiry with the fear. A guide should never hold negative judgment toward fear. Keep exploring the aftermath of this release, which may result in a more liberated, energetic, or emotional state.

The goal is to support the new state in practical ways. Create a ritual around the fear that was released or validate the experience of fear by writing a letter or speaking with whoever was involved in the original event.

If the journeyer is still afraid afterward, the guide can offer presence and continue to work on building safety through gentle verbal communication. Offer soothing, calming, reassurance, listening, and physical touch. Fear may dissipate through physical release and movement. The guide can suggest soothing physical practices such as the following:

- Take supportive herbal supplements, lavender and chamomile essential oils, or flower essences

- Reach out to friends and community for physical comfort, to share the journey, and to receive compassionate presence

Many years ago, I attended a 5Rhythms dance retreat focused on the theme of sexuality and expression where I met a woman named Laura. She was excited to be working with Gabrielle Roth, the founder of this captivating movement modality. She was curious but inexperienced in the personal work aspect of the retreat. The beginning of the first day was going well as everyone found their place in the group and tuned in to their inner process. But that afternoon, Gabrielle guided us into a challenging exploration in dyads involving the movement of the pelvis. Laura started to become agitated and began to display an obnoxious attitude toward the group and the leader. The rest of that weekend was a disaster for her. Laura later told me that the whole time she had felt angry and uncomfortable.

Since we had shared some movement together, she reached out to me afterward, and we chatted by phone. I encouraged her, "It seems like this seminar offered you an opportunity to explore some places of conflict in yourself. There's nothing wrong with finding this out. There are many ways to keep exploring. Counseling, journal writing, continued movement practices, and telling your story in many ways will lead you to some clarity about your history, your wounds, and your strengths."

We stayed in touch for a few weeks after the seminar. Laura eventually told me that she had started counseling and began to uncover repressed feelings and pent-up expression. It turned out that her pelvic movements had led her to connect with old memories of inappropriate touching by her cousins when she was a child. Even though these moments were more exploratory than abusive, the arousal they had produced in her body had frightened her and made her shut down the sensations in this area of her body. She began to paint and write poetry as ways of supporting her healing. Even though she realized she was at the beginning of her inner explorations, she no longer felt disoriented and confused.

Personal Confrontation

This sort of experience is confrontational, humbling, and often unpleasant. It is not about causes, reasons, or childhood experiences but rather the raw truth of one's behaviors, choices, or addictions. It can bring up overwhelming shame.

It is worth noting that shame can be useful on the healing path. It is a state of feeling badly about how we have or have not acted, or about something we have or have not said. It is an awareness of a way we have been insensitive, transgressed another person, or neglected ourselves.

Some people find they collapse when faced with shame. If someone cannot acknowledge the impact of their actions as an adult, they unwittingly keep themselves in a child state. They will need more resourcing and ego strength before they are ready to look at their situation head-on. Someone cannot turn toward their pain and shame until they have the ability to face it. Leave the topic of shame aside while someone is doing the work of ego-strengthening. What in their life brings them support and strength? Once someone recovers a core sense of self and ego strength, they can return to their past or present situation with a stronger center.

We cannot forgive ourselves until we sit in the fire of our shame and feel the magnitude of our actions. It means that we stop taking refuge in our excuses and acknowledge the impact our actions have had on ourselves and others. This can serve as a catalytic force toward mending, and, ultimately, toward empowerment. Recovering a sense of accountability is necessary before we can step into self-compassion and self-forgiveness.

It is not a guide's job to create a happy experience for anyone, but to support the revealing of truth. It is best not to infantilize an adult. Some journeyers may feel they are ready to make amends; others may want to change things; others still may experience a new positive intention. Confronting one's difficult personal patterns can lead to a deeper understanding of the causes of addictive behavior.

At the end of the day, we are each responsible for our actions. It is often by acting out of our integrity that we discover our integrity. It is by going out into the ocean, without discipline or self-awareness, that we realize our need for an anchor. The integrity and values we cultivate become our anchor.

An experience of personal confrontation offers us a mirror. We need to see what we are doing before we can change. The mirror can motivate us to take action to avoid causing more damage, sickness, or loss. Perhaps we see trauma or insecurities underlying our codependence. This can lead to finally understanding the underlying matrix that results in addictive patterns. Although these confrontational experiences can be unpleasant and leave us challenged, they can also leave us feeling optimistic or even resolved. Once the truth is known, there is often spectacular relief.

When a journey takes us to a place of personal confrontation, integration is crucial. If there is no integration, the experience can increase anxiety rather than diffuse it.

If we are dealing with addiction and its underlying causes, but the content of the experience is not integrated, things can actually get worse. An addiction to a substance, person, or activity such as work is often an attempt to self-soothe and manage painful emotional states connected to unresolved trauma. It is paramount to create a safe environment for the states that can be reexperienced in journeys. If these traumatic events, their physiological impact, and their emotional content are not addressed, the client may simply feel frightened, flooded by overly intense feelings, and possibly shut down or dissociate.

More than once I have had people come to me fresh out of an experience in another context that included an expanded state of consciousness. They show up in my office asking if I could "put them back together." They have been confronted with their own shame and self-destructive habits and they don't know what to do about it.

I inquire about the expectation they entered their experience with. What did they want? What was the content of their experience? In what way were they confronted? What is the story of their life that justifies this type of confrontation? How do they feel about their self-destructive patterns? It is not the guide's job to save anyone from their own self-confrontation. In fact, it is the guide's job to support whatever is most useful to their healing, which confrontation can be part of.

Often, there is a lack of comprehensive intake that includes a physical and psychological history, and the facilitators do not know the background of a participant. I understand that a meditation teacher or a leader of a sweat lodge may not include a thorough intake, scan for the presence of addictions, or do a psychological history with every participant. However, any experience that includes a change in the physiology can uncover intense emotional material such as shame. Someone can be suddenly thrust into relating to the gravity of their previously unconscious psychological and emotional content. Clearly, this type of experience is so confrontational that radical changes are crucial.

If the guide is not a trained therapist, and the content that a journeyer has accessed is beyond their skill level, they should refer them to someone who is trained to work with this material. It is important for any facilitator of expanded states to be prepared to refer their participants as needed.

Assuming the guide is psychologically trained, then depending on the courage and capacity of the journeyer, the guide can start by suggesting change on a small scale, to begin the process of recovering personal integrity. It is always critical to make sure that these changes are doable for someone; the journeyer has to choose what area they want to affect.

Often in the integration phase, the journeyer will say, "I do not want to feel this way anymore." A guide could then ask, "What are you going to do so that you will not feel this way anymore?" As long as a person behaves in destructive ways, the resulting negative feelings are going to be there. Concrete actions are needed to support this type of integration.

For people who are facing addictive patterns or confronting toxic behaviors, there is value in coming to the truth and bringing all of it out from the inside and onto a piece of paper. It is a liberation practice. It is a confession where you write down all that you carry in your heart. Sometimes I tell someone with a drinking problem, "Every time you want a glass of wine, go into your garden and take care of your plants or make yourself a cup of tea." There are skills and practices that can help shift addictive patterns into beneficial actions. They may seem like small steps, but each step in the correct direction requires tremendous courage and energy. Some further suggestions for integration are:

- Change diet, smoking, drinking, or substance use habits
- Go to 12-Step meetings for support
- Read books on shame, addiction, or recovery
- Get honest about affairs, lies, deceits, and the people impacted by writing a list of your actions that have been out of integrity
- Go to therapy for deeper understanding or ask for support from others around this clearing (the fragility of this kind of transformation requires ongoing encouragement)
- Walk in nature for reharmonization on a soul level
- Increase daily physical activity or see a nutritionist for dietary support

Emotional Opening and Release

There is an inherent value in feeling and expressing anger or other powerful emotions that have been repressed. Of course, we want to reach a place of forgiveness, to feel better and take charge of our life. But the reality is that if a childhood wound emerges during an expanded state, this can be a major healing, an opportunity for empowerment where one can feel what they were not safe to feel in the past. The situation might have been so intense that one was only able to survive. An emotional release can also be one of great joy, perhaps a joy that had to be contained in childhood. Release is not limited to sadness or anger; expressing grief, rage, sorrow, joy, awe, or rapture can be deeply restorative. As the quote attributed to Rumi says, "The wound is the place where the Light enters you."

A journeyer who is normally emotionally contained may find an opening and be swept into a flow of emotional expression. People who tend to be shy or who have repressed their emotional life often access these openings of emotional ease.

Even though intense emotions have been felt, explored, understood, and possibly embraced during the journey, it does not necessarily mean they have been fully released or are ready to go away. We need to recognize their value. Then some gentle integration can support the completion of the process. Depending on whether or not the journeyer has found a sense of completion during the journey, the integration will vary. The nature of the release will determine what practices will be most supportive.

Some journeys consist of emotional openings that do not feel complete. The journeyer may feel angry or betrayed or victimized or broken-hearted. Perhaps the journeyer revisited being a helpless young person who was abused or exposed to something inappropriate. Because the journey comes to an end does not mean the internal process is complete. It may be necessary that the journeyer get ongoing care, ideally from a therapist who understands how to work with the inner child.

If someone has uncovered a traumatic memory, it can be helpful to suggest therapies such as Eye Movement Desensitization Reprocessing (EMDR),[1] Emotional Freedom Technique (EFT),[2] Somatic Experiencing (SE), or another technique that aims to release trauma from the body.

Such a person will need a good amount of maintenance in the integration phase. The integration practices should be activating but not too overwhelming.

The guide can have the journeyer paint ugly paintings and write uncensored letters to crank up the charge again.

A journeyer can also write about their emotional experience and how they are feeling on the other side of the voyage. If doing so would be safe, they can communicate with the original perpetrators. They can perform a ritual of release if their tormenter is deceased. Some further suggestions for integration are:

- Explore active breathwork
- Run up hills or stairs
- Take a bat to a dead log and beat it up
- Break used plates against a wall or throw rocks
- Join a drumming group or listen to recordings of drumming
- Dance wildly

I had a client whose father had been a violent alcoholic, abusive and insulting toward him during his childhood. We decided to arrange a sound and breathwork journey. Although we discussed his history beforehand, he had not yet touched this anger in its raw form. In his journey, he got in touch with repressed anger he had toward his father. He made sounds, roared, felt his power, and cried. It was a true physical expression of his rage, sadness, and despair.

After the journey, he knew his expression was not complete. The journey had opened things up, but there was more to release. During the integration phase, I wanted him to continue expressing his feelings while in a normal state of consciousness. After considering what might help him complete his process, I instructed him to go to a park by his house with a baseball bat and find a fallen log to beat. At first, he was hesitant, as the exercise seemed contrived. He did not see how it would bring up the charge he had felt during the journey.

But he decided to do it daily, and after three days he began to look forward to the exercise. He could feel his breath opening and a healthy vitality coming through. On the fifth day, he accessed the intense emotions that had been pent up since childhood. Hitting the log, he was able to move the anger through his body in its raw and visceral form, expressing a primal quality of raw, unrefined emotion. Releasing the child's anger from the past as well as the adult's outrage for what the child had experienced helped him understand the complexity of his feelings. The more he expressed, the more he got in touch with his emotions—and ultimately his power. At the same time, he wrote about his experience and met weekly with me. The physical expression of his anger ultimately allowed him to feel lighter and more in touch with his boundaries and sense of self.

If an emotional process is complete, the rage or sorrow has been experienced and betrayal worked through, then a journeyer may feel complete for the time being. In this case, it is best to offer soothing support. Rest and restorative practices will help comfort and calm someone after such a vast opening and emotional flush. When we undo an emotional knot, there is more space. What does that sense of spaciousness feel like? What is the spaciousness saying? What is it doing? How does it want to be expressed? Some people go hiking in the mountains without a plan. Some people feel they have more space to begin a new endeavor. Perhaps they want to learn an instrument or start writing. When a process like this happens, the energy that is created on the other side is the gift. It is less about the emotional process itself and more about the space that has been created and how the journeyer chooses to fill, enjoy, and celebrate it. Because there is space available, however, does not mean it has to be filled. It can be fantastic to simply have more spaciousness in one's life. Further integrative practices include:

- Write poetry or letters to relevant family members or people
- Listen to gentle music or chanting
- Drink nourishing tea or take a bath
- Get a massage or take a slow walk

Self-Love and Nourishment

This experience is often a direct experience of self-care and self-love. As a person feels the joy and ease available in this state, a new blueprint is suggested to the psyche. Its value lies in its naturalness, as there is a possibility of recovering wellness through self-love. A new tender relationship unfolds that might not have been there before. Someone depleted by childcare, work, or family grief might be restored and healed through such an experience. A person who has not been valued or cared for through parental nourishment might also have this experience as a way of receiving nurture from inside; from one's self toward one's self. There is a vital difference between being nourished and generating self-nourishment.

There is something profoundly touching in witnessing someone recover self-nourishment. It is an intimately private experience and yet being witnessed can offer measurable support. It is like a parent watching her child ride a bicycle for the first time; it is a moment worthy of being witnessed and the inner thrill is unmatched. The goal here is to sustain the experience of self-love through various approaches such as body care, emotional connectedness, spiritual rituals, or time in nature alone or with friends.

Self-nourishment and self-love are possibly the most transformative experiences we can have in an expanded state of consciousness. They can heal our past wounding, celebrate our present potential, and shine a light of care toward our future. The integration of these experiences is crucial and delicate. Help the journeyer determine what it is that nourishes their well-being. Is it a nurturing relationship or solitude? Being out in nature or in civilization? Following steps toward a goal or freeform creativity? Then devise practices or actions that will weave more self-love into everyday life. Further integrative practices on this theme include:

- Write a letter of personal gratitude, acknowledging yourself—*What is loveable about me?*

- Cook yourself nourishing food

- Bring more beauty into your life by having flowers or other natural elements in the home

- Listen to restful or fun music, dance around, run in wildflowers

- Do self-compassion exercises such as *metta* meditation

- Take time to be with yourself—do yoga or make art

- Do what you truly love and what uplifts your spirit

Accessing the Unconscious

Childhood Memories

Lara was rigid, opinionated, and stuck. She complained that therapy did not help her, meditation drove her crazy, and nature bored her. She wanted a deeper approach, and a friend of hers suggested she contact me. I knew that she would not stick with the process if I suggested we take it slow and replay her story over the months to come. We decided that she would join my next trip to Mexico. She felt that this type of journey would open up deeper layers of her psyche and help her access a fuller understanding of her situation. We took the next few weeks to prepare. Lara did tell me much of her life story, what was most challenging for her (her anger), what she liked most about herself (her body), what support she had around her (her friends), and what made her feel so stuck (her anger toward her mother).

Lara's inner journey during the ceremony in Mexico was arduous. She was sad and angry, feeling closed and stuck. I watched her as she struggled with her sub-conscious issues emerging to the surface. I told her she was doing great, although she did not agree with me. I could have moved closer and nurtured her, but I felt that her journey was unfolding appropriately for her. Even though I did connect with her repeatedly during her experience, nothing I did was good enough, and her inner critic voice was very active. She was confronted by her stubbornness and opinion on everything.

Ultimately, Lara accessed her exhaustion and sense of despair as her deep hurt came to the surface. She finally accessed her fear as a child and her need to control her environment at all costs. She was finally seeing where her patterns had stemmed from. She found a core truth in seeing the abuse she had endured as a child, and despite the pain of it, she felt liberated. When the ritual ended, she was relaxed, open, and smiling. She had exhausted the grasp of her anger, which, in the end, did not even involve her story about her mother.

Many people who journey do not understand how their childhood biography connects with their present psychology. Connecting the dots can illuminate the present dynamics in one's relationships. People who anger easily have an opportunity to see the process of projection and re-own it as a reflection of their own mind. Such experiences project the personal theater of one's life onto the screen of the inner eye, illuminating subconscious facets of one's psyche. The anger can then be replaced by a feeling of acceptance and even compassion for one's history.

There is much for the guide to support after insights such as these. After the journeyer reports the narrative of the story they have come to understand, the guide can offer positive reflection and validation of their insights by mirroring, affirming, and celebrating realizations with respect and love.

As memories resurface, depending on their nature, a guide should support them differently. The guide can invoke the "child" and positive memories of childhood. In the case of challenging memories, the guide should tend to the vulnerable emotional experience of the child through ongoing support. The guide can also encourage the journeyer to find ways to express their story and memories, along with the emotional components. Sharing the narrative by telling the story is central to this type of integration.

Additionally, the journeyer can do the following:

- Draw a timeline that includes positive and negative experiences throughout one's entire life
- Participate in a family constellations workshop
- Write a letter to the lonely or suffering inner child or to someone from the past (parent or perpetrator)
- Play, make sandcastles, or go to a playground

Visions

Internal visions illustrate the inner world as it projects itself onto the mind's eye. They can show patterns of energy that can be perceived visually. Every modality or psychoactive sacrament has a unique nature to it, which bring forth specific visual patterns and imagery. Some sounds induce particular images, colors, and patterns.

If an experience is accessed with an entheogenic plant medicine, sometimes the plant can reveal itself. For a few years, I regularly attended ayahuasca retreats. I was astonished how much of the imagery was of snakes, vines encircling tall trees, and thick, moist jungle scenes. I even felt myself as a jaguar. I felt transported into the very landscape where the ayahuasca vine grows. Last year as I was traveling to the Bolivian jungle, my friends pointed out the ayahuasca vine in the midst of a jungle tangle and I had a flashback of those vibrant visions I had seen in my inner journeys.

This experience can also reflect the inner state of a journeyer, exquisite or gruesome as it may be. When there are visions of other people in other times, it seems that the journeyer is accessing a deeper collective unconscious. It is hard to explain how these experiences happen. The journeyer is being invited to understand something about themselves through their connection with another person's life. Visions show up when there is a reason to see and explore them.

The guide can have the journeyer describe and connect the visions back to their intention. What do the visions illustrate about the inner landscape of the journeyer? How might these particular visions be guiding them forward on their life's path? The guide can invite the journeyer to explore his or her personal meanings around what was seen. It is helpful for a guide to have some understanding of symbolism, myth, and archetypes. Pay attention to *how* the vision appeared, not just *what* it was. Was it threatening? Was it kind and reassuring? What emotions or memories did it arouse? The goal is to evoke meaning and expression. Visions can be approached like dreams; we can decode the symbolism and explore the archetypal energies that appear. As one works with their vision, it begins to reveal its deeper significance.

When someone has a vision of a person from another time or space, it is an invitation to interpret and understand what is being offered. It is valuable to honor these visions as teachings. If the journeyer had a vision of someone from a different space and time, the guide can ask: What would it be like to be this person? Whom do they remind you of? What qualities stand out about this person? What questions do you have for this person? What is the felt meaning in your body of this connection?

If the journeyer tapped into suffering occurring somewhere else in the world, perhaps it is an invitation to offer support and love in that direction. Or perhaps they are being reminded to look at the suffering in their life, where they may be acting complacent. How can one's actions match their felt empathy?

If someone has received a powerful vision, sometimes I suggest that they paint it. Sometimes they end up with a fascinating image they want to keep. It is wonderful to make visions tangible and give them form. What we see is who we are. Whether we believe that all the images we see come from our unconscious, our collective unconscious, or that we are perceiving real external dimensions normally unseen, we are making contact with the images here and now for a reason. The visions come with a purpose. The invitation is to enter into a relationship with our visions, stay curious about them, and eventually weave them into our life as teachings.

- Write a narrative, draw, paint, mime, or act out the vision
- Study and explore the visions by reading about the image, animal, or object that appeared

When I was thirty years old and pregnant with my daughter, I did a series of shamanic drumming work sessions. During the drumming process, I had a vision of a land turtle. I would see her sunning herself, walking with her home on her back. My guide told me that the animal came to teach me something on a symbolic level, and I was instructed to invite that animal's presence into my field on various levels. She suggested I read about turtles, visit them, and watch movies about them. The more I learned about land turtles, the more fascinated I became with them.

It began to make more and more sense on the symbolic level why this animal had appeared to me. I went to the zoo and watched them, and I received their teaching. For me, the lesson was about slowing down and taking care of my immediate home. It was time for me to make a nest for my baby. Before the drumming session, I had not felt any special connection with turtles. This animal came as a teacher and remained one for years.

✳ ✳ ✳

Our intellect is in a state of balance when it supports our development and an increasing understanding of ourselves. In this state of balance, we seek a variety of experiences to learn from. We pursue factual information that can give us maps and models. We delight in stories, events, and stimulating activities that can also teach us. We make time to understand and integrate the information we take in. We feed our hunger to know and to make meaning of our experiences. We balance the intellectual information we receive with direct experience. As we stay intellectually curious with our felt experiences, we cultivate wisdom.

When we are in a state of balance, we can cultivate calm and stillness in our minds. We rest our thinking processes and avoid unnecessary distractions. We keep our minds sharp, cultivating concentration and focus. We cultivate presence through meditation and awareness practices. We feed our curiosities in healthy ways. We follow our intuition and learn how to trust it.

We feel that all our emotions can be felt and expressed in appropriate ways. We find we are able to reflect on our emotional state. We can harness the courage to be sincere about our human frailties. We commit to being authentic in acknowledging and expressing our love, disappointment, and anger. We are determined to uncover our inner truths and create vows to uphold them. We stay open, bringing attention to our places of rigidity and contraction and our intention to heal them. We strive to maintain equanimity within ourselves and are able to accept our complexity.

We create space to explore and express our unconscious through painting, writing, dancing, singing, and ritual. We are in a relationship with our dream world and attuned to the magical guidance around us. We pay attention to the images and signs that reveal themselves to us. We feed our creativity and allow ourselves to explore new ideas, visions, and theories. We stay curious about our unknown inner dimensions. Happiness does not depend on complete self-knowledge. A sense of peace comes with accepting what we do not know. We face our shadow material, unpleasant projections, fears, and anxiety with open eyes and compassion. We accept the mystery of our unfolding. We expand our knowledge of healing modalities and ways of self-exploration through reading and direct experience. We commit to the path of self-discovery and personal expression.

15

THE FARTHEST SHORE

Integrating Spirit-Centered Experiences

I am the joining and the dissolving.

I am what lasts and what goes.

I am the one going down,

And the one toward whom they ascend.
—GNOSTIC NAG HAMMADI[1]

Expanded states of consciousness lead us beyond the physical realm, beyond our ego and human constructs, into the unseen and what some of us may call the realm of spirit. Even though we often have to travel through complex layers of psychological and physical blockages, encountering the spiritual dimension is a magical experience that can change our perception of life forever. I have seen scientific, nonspiritual people go into journeys and open to a spiritual dimension. Experiencing something so vast can awaken or reaffirm one's faith in something greater than their separate human identity. This spiritual resource offers the possibility of deeper meaning in one's life.

Integrating a spiritual experience into one's life may seem elusive, yet it can be tremendously valuable. Like any aspect of life that we focus on, the spiritual dimension can grow. People can continue to nurture whatever opening they experience through reading books by spiritual teachers. They can begin singing or praying. They can start a meditation practice or one of inner listening and stillness. They can create an altar with spiritual images. They can practice *kirtan* or devotional singing from the Hindu traditions, or sing hymns. They can visit a church or temple or explore additional earth-based rituals and ceremonies. If they have a specific vision of a deity, it is useful to find a book and study the mythology of the deity. It is wonderful to read books by people who have devoted their lives to spirit.

A spiritual practice does not have to mean meditating or going to church or associating with a special deity. There are many different ways to be in relationship with spirit. Some might prefer individual practices to community practices. For others, it might be better to join a group and be carried along by the group energy rather than trying to create something new on their own. Spirit does not have to be something you sit down and commune with. For people who have a busy social life, it might be most constructive to create a space of solitude, to carve out the time and do a practice alone.

I once had a client who decided to serve at the local soup kitchen, after deciding that service would be his spiritual practice. He soon realized that he was not only nourishing his soul through the act of giving; he was also connecting with people he would never have met in his regular life. His definition of friendship broadened and he let go of the stigma he had carried around regarding poverty, lack of education, and addiction. His integration practice had started by deepening his spiritual service, and he found himself actually becoming a more compassionate person.

Spirituality and community overlap when spirituality gets translated into service and simple actions. In this way, someone embodies the qualities of the deities and saints through their actions.

In my own spiritual journeys, I have encountered pure creation energy, Jesus, and Gaia. These were all unforgettable experiences. Yet, after all of these, it has been the practices of sitting by a tree, meditating, reading divine poetry, and visiting sacred places that have been most important to my spiritual life. These embodied actions, which bring the dimension of the spiritual into one's daily life, are the best way to anchor the journey's clarity, power, and love. The way to integrate a spiritual experience is to create an ongoing practice involving whatever has been connected with.

Meaninglessness

Sometimes our inner world is disappointing. Encountering a flat and colorless inner world during a journey can illustrate a disconnection from spirit in one's life. This flatness might be a holdover from a cynical attitude toward the world of spirit that was present in one's childhood. A desolate inner world can also appear as a warning, pointing toward the outcome of a life oriented around extreme materialism, surface appearances, and attachment to maintaining a false self.

This barren inner landscape can be reinvigorated by spirit through the introduction of various practices. It can be useful to guide the journeyer toward reflecting on the events or situations in their life that may have contributed to this inner desolation. In the case of an adult who is living a life attached to greed, power, and materialism, some choices and changes are necessary to thaw this frozen inner state. For people who perceive the absence of spirit in their lives and want to change that, they need to receive support as to how to nurture this part of their life. I have had many clients who come with no knowledge or history of spiritual practice, yet seek to develop this dimension of their life. Depending on where they are coming from and what piques their interest, I give these clients books to read, such as the Gospels, poems by the Persian poet Rumi, or books on Tibetan Buddhism or the Kabbalah.

A guide should respect the background of a journeyer and any request to avoid certain things. Some people have intense resistance to organized religion, which results in them avoiding all aspects of spirituality. This might have started as the healthy defiance of individuation, but then they end up with nothing. The guide can gently reintroduce simple meditation practices or suggest they spend time in nature listening to the world around them. Further integration practices include:

- Listen to spiritual music or study a spiritual lineage
- Participate in a ritual or begin a meditation practice

Reclaiming Our Spiritual Life

Finding meaning in a new or previous spiritual framework is a pivotal moment. It reconnects someone to a felt sense of spirit not previously accessible. If it is a matter of reconnecting with a religious or spiritual framework from childhood, this can lead a person to acknowledge the formative values and positive aspects that were present, regardless of the religious constraints that may have led the person to reject or dismiss the whole template.

If it is a matter of encountering something previously unknown, it can unfold into a self-defined spiritual cosmology. This experience may engage the journeyer's interest and offer encouragement toward further exploration. The capacity to open oneself to unfamiliar practices alone offers a lesson on flexibility and increased tolerance. It can be fascinating for someone who has never read a book on meditation to have a personal experience of the inner stillness the Buddha spoke of.

If there is a reappearance of a past framework, the guide should first ask what practices the journeyer feels would be best, as it is not the time to impose or even suggest anything. The earlier rejection might have been caused by an authoritarian approach to practicing religion. However, depending on the receptivity of the person, a guide may offer more acceptable practices, always leaving the final decision to the journeyer.

The goal of this integration is to support the reintroduction of the values and perhaps some of the practices that embody the spiritual lineage that was rejected or dismissed. If the emergence was of an unfamiliar tradition, the guide can encourage the journeyer to explore and study the tradition in practical ways. For instance, if the journeyer connected with their ancestors, they can continue to explore traditions in which connecting with ancestors is of immense importance. In the Native American, Taoist, Mexican, and other traditions, there are practices of feeding the ancestors. In the Christian tradition one prays for the deceased in order to continue one's relationship with them. The journeyer could build a spirit house or shrine for their ancestors, where they can offer them incense, flowers, candles, food, or drink. Further integration practices for this type of experience include:

- Create an altar

- Visit a place of worship or kneel before an icon such as a cross, the Virgin of Guadalupe, or on the earth
- Attend a sweat lodge and create prayer ties
- Listen to podcasts or audiobooks by spiritual teachers
- Attend a dharma talk or open meditation
- Try devotional movement such as Sufi dancing

When I did my first ceremony with my teacher in Mexico, I was ready for (and expecting) an ancient transmission of wisdom from the mushrooms. As I entered the journey, I heard my teacher pray to Jesus and Mother Mary, and I immediately felt resistant to being brainwashed. As an adolescent, I had to step away from what had felt like the terrible constriction of oppressive Catholic beliefs. I was not about to be brainwashed now while being on mushrooms!

Yet here I was, in this sacred indigenous ceremony, with these ancient songs, and my teacher's faith and devotion to her God. Within an hour I was transported back to my own early devotion to Mary and her benevolence for earthly humans and to Jesus as a messenger of love and generosity. I reconnected with the deepest values of my childhood, without the oppressive teachings on virginity, obedience, and the subordinate role of women.

I brought home images of the Mother Mary, lit candles for her, talked with her, and sang songs to her. I reminisced about moments of my childhood filled with the Christian values of solidarity, charity, and compassion. I told my mother how grateful I was for the spiritual structure of my early life, how as a child I had felt the beauty of this, though in my adolescence I had rejected it. I reconciled with a key part of my spiritual identity, which had been inside me the whole time, waiting to emerge.

Messianic and Spiritual Archetypes

This experience of seeing or embodying a spiritual archetype can come as a blessing to people who have thriving spiritual lives. The archetype can come through one's body or be seen in considerable detail. This can be a transmission of power, compassion, clarity, love, or any spiritual quality that the archetype radiates. It can be understood as a symbol or believed to be literal.

Sometimes people become grandiose and messianic after a journey. "I have seen God!" Okay, so you see God, and yes, you are the divine, but there can be a false sense of having it all figured out, of having *arrived* in a final sense. It is wonderful you had an experience of arriving into the light of the Great Spirit, and now you are saved forever. I am thrilled for you, but let's see how it is going to pan out. Regardless of the depth or significance of a spiritual experience, it needs to be integrated via concrete actions.

Making contact with archetypes can also take place when someone is so disconnected from the spiritual dimension that the only way to reestablish contact is through a massive reminder, such as seeing or having the experience of becoming a powerful archetype. The intensity of this experience is often in proportion to the person's original rigidity around spiritual matters.

The goal here is to integrate the vitality of a spiritual experience into the journeyer's life in practical and enriching ways. The guide can affirm and support the truth and legitimacy of such an experience, since after the experience it might seem unbelievable. Archetypes are symbols of spiritual dimensions and act as messengers or portals between the human form and the invisible dimension. Why do people have this experience in the overall spectrum of their life? What does it offer?

The guide can orient the journeyer toward a continuing embodiment and concrete expression of how the archetype was seen or felt. This can be explored through movement, ritual, art, devotional chanting, participation in group worship, or reading about the specific archetype. If someone has a vision of Gaia as the essential creative feminine force, they could cultivate the relationship by making altars on the land or spending time alone in nature doing pagan rituals. If the experience was of being Kwan Yin, then they may find a statue of her, read about her, and get to know her. If the vision was one of being Jesus, then they could read the gospels, explore what Christ Consciousness is, and explore the image of Jesus and how it touches their life. If the visionary experience was of a respected teacher like Gandhi or Mother Teresa, again, it is useful to cultivate a relationship with the teaching of that person. We can study their humanity, the words they spoke, the issues they stood up for, and the way they lived their lives.

Any vision of a spiritual archetype that arrives in an expanded state is coming to us as a teacher and a guide, and it is our responsibility to follow up with the relationship. The vision needs to be addressed, honored, and sustained. The most straight forward integration practices here are:

- Surround oneself with images of the archetype that was encountered
- Create an altar or ritual to celebrate and honor the archetype

The Underlying Perfection of All Things

A dear friend of mine endured terrible sexual abuse by her father in her childhood. She had worked with a diligent commitment to her healing through counseling and other methods of self-expression. It all helped her tremendously. Eventually, she decided to travel to South America to experience ayahuasca with a group of friends at a center that would support her healing on a spiritual and psychological level. She told me that during one journey she came to understand how the horrific abuse was what had led her to seek transformation and personal growth. Even though she knew what had happened was inexcusable, she felt grateful for the path she was now on. It was a huge relief for her to realize, from within her heart and mind, that there was a strange but perfect order to her destiny.

This type of insight delivers us into the spiritual perfection of our soul's path as it evolves throughout the cycles of life and death. It might be that someone needs this kind of opening and support in the face of emotional agitation, blockage, or fear of death. It might also be that a person has done enormous work on the emotional aspect of their life and is now coming into a broader view of life.

The goal of integrating an insight into this level of perfection is to keep the broad understanding alive while also making it concrete. The guide can support this integration by encouraging the journeyer to cultivate an ongoing relationship between this compassionate understanding and the emotionally intense parts of their life. If the experience touched on the person's relationship with death, it can be followed up with gentle relaxation, and if desired, a deeper reading into various cultural views of death, such as afterlife and reincarnation. The understanding that life unfolds in mysterious ways and brings each soul toward wholeness and healing is a perspective that a guide should personally explore. Further integration suggestions include:

- Listen to music that was played during the ritual as a reminder
- Write one's own eulogy
- Explore serving in hospice care or being present at someone's death

Ego Dissolution

Ego dissolution teaches the journeyer that control over their reality is an illusion. It shows them that much more is at play on the subtle and mysterious levels, which is beyond cognitive understanding. This experience illuminates the term "expansion of consciousness," as it brings consciousness to dimensions beyond normal perception.

Having an authentic near-death experience or a journey experience of ego dissolution shows one how to let go and dissolve. Once they surrender, people report experiences of fearlessness, bliss, white light, and liberation. This experience offers teachings on acceptance, embracing death, and letting go into stillness. It is the ultimate experience of surrendering into the unknown.

The magnitude of letting go depends on the modality. Regardless of the person's emotional or psychological maturity, such experiences can occur as moments of grace. Total ego surrender can also serve as a much needed support in times of despair, grief, and loss. It can also appear as a springboard from which one can dive into the difficult task of sorting out a challenging past. Such an experience can teach us about unity and the depth of universal soul connections. It can often lead to tenderness, forgiveness, loving actions, and values based on solidarity and sharing.

Someone facing a life-threatening illness may find reassurance through an experience of connecting with an expansive space of belonging, in which the ego structure of the self dissolves. In this type of experience people report knowing peace, gratitude, and the ultimate importance of love.[2] This type of experience may come to someone who is facing grief around the death of someone in their family or community. It can also come to someone who has a fear of change and impermanence. Ego dissolution can appear when someone has a compulsive need to control his or her environment and relationships. This experience serves to teach us that death and letting go are a natural part of human life.

The guide can invite the journeyer to notice any difference in their feelings that the journey may have caused. Often, the journeyer will become more available to love and tenderness. Usually, encouraging a posture of curiosity in the face of old patterns of *knowing* is the best way to offer support in the aftermath of such a vast expansion. Inviting the journeyer to ask for dreams is also useful, as the dreams might echo this opening.

We are all wired with survival instincts and an innate fear of death, and an experience of ego dissolution can become a real resource, a stroke of grace that comes unbidden. Surrendering to the dissolution of our ego structure moves us through fear, and this type of experience is rarely forgotten. The guide can support the journeyer's experience by suggesting practices that remind them of their opening and surrender. This experience can be the beginning of a potent awakening. A guide can suggest the journeyer explore a daily practice of connecting with the aspect of their being beyond ego. Additional integration practices include:

- Explore spiritual or non-dual traditions such as Zen, Dzogchen, Mahamudra, Kashmiri Shaivism, Advaita Vedanta, Kabbalah, or the mystical branches of any religion[3]

- Explore kirtan, devotional singing, or prayer

- Spend one day per week or one weekend per month in silence and stillness

- Explore sensory deprivation in a flotation tank

- Pay respect to the dead: offer flowers at a grave

- Cultivate an appreciation for the loss of youth in one's self; pay attention to the wrinkles, gray hair, or the changing face in the mirror

✳ ✳ ✳

Within expanded states of consciousness, we can have experiences that transcend the laws of our individual physical form. The paradox is that when we open to the spiritual dimension of our being, we move beyond our identity as a separate self. Yet it is through our individual, visceral experience that we can experience the spiritual. Whatever we experience is known through the flesh, remembered in the flesh, and integrated into the flesh.

The body is not a vehicle to be transcended. It is the vehicle within which we are embodied while we are here on Earth. And yet, perhaps it is simply the radiance of the spiritual dimension. The exploration of expanded states brings us to paradox. Everything that is, is not, and everything that is not, is. Fortunately, we can turn to spiritual teachings that have been pointing this out for thousands of years. We are not alone in this heroic journey. Many have come before us, and many will come after us.

Tending our relationship with the spiritual means being connected to inner and outer dimensions that are larger than our body and mind. We might have been born into a spiritual tradition that taught us how to do this from a young age, or later in life we may find our way to a tradition that speaks to our heart. We may find we are touched by grace or an unexpected spiritual experience, with our interest piqued to explore further. However it is that we make our way to the spiritual, we find it is a relationship that we nurture through our actions, words, and way of life.

The essential idea of a spiritual practice means . . . *practice.* It means we train in the activities that cultivate the qualities we aspire to emanate. It means taking the time to create new habits and actions aligned with our highest intent. One way to create discipline in our lives is by creating routines, structures, and rhythms that support our daily practices. We can also explore what it is we love that brings us closer to spirit. Then, we can let that love guide us.

Spiritual practice is often referred to as a path. We start where we are and choose a tradition or teacher or set of teachings that will guide us forward. We may pick from different traditions or choose to fully invest ourselves in one. Some traditions hold that we are already inherently perfect and liberated and should conduct our lives accordingly. Whichever path calls to us, finding a resonant spiritual tradition offers us the nourishment that we all hunger for. Hopefully, through our devotion and practice, our path takes us all the way home.

A healthy relationship with one's spiritual self offers support and strength to the psyche, as well as the emotional and physical body. The more we are attentive to the mysterious unfolding of life, the more we develop a capacity to meet life's challenges with acceptance and care. We can cultivate a stable equanimity that can meet whatever problems life brings us. We can develop a perspective of loving nonattachment. We are fully present but not solely identified with our human predicament. We are not consumed by the need for happiness or certain states or particular material possessions to feel complete. We do not create unnecessary drama, nor are we controlled by fear or hope. We dance gracefully with movement and change.

A healthy spiritual life is anchored in the qualities of discernment, generosity, compassion, patience, presence, and gratitude. These are the qualities that increase as all the outer aspects of life fade away. When we cultivate these qualities, we become initiated members of our community: leaders, teachers, and elders—humans that the world deeply needs.

16

THE BEAUTY OF INTERDEPENDENCE

Integrating Community–Centered Experiences

Each experience of love nudges us toward the Story of Interbeing, because it only fits into that story and defies the logic of Separation.
—CHARLES EISENSTEIN[1]

Lisa was a woman in her forties, a mother of two, and a physician with a professional practice. Her relationship with her husband was stable, but she regularly felt angry with him for no apparent "logical" reasons. She explained that she felt an uncontrollable sense of irritation at the slightest mishap on his part. Lisa knew that it had nothing to do with him and wished to explore inwardly, to see what was going on. She had undergone some psychotherapy and felt she had worked through her father issues over the years. After careful preparation and resourcing, she was ready to enter the deeper regions of her subconscious. She came to Mexico with me determined to "get to the bottom of this."

Lying on her mat on the floor of the ceremony room, Lisa began to feel the effects of the mushrooms, and a strange nausea arose in her that she could not soothe. I invited her to follow its tracks and listen deeply, to stay curious with where it was leading her. After about thirty minutes, she curled up in a ball and began to whimper. I stayed close to her so she could feel my supportive presence. This continued for about two hours. Eventually, her whimpering ceased, and she asked me to take her to vomit. When we returned to the room, she was peaceful and calm.

Later on, Lisa reported that she had accessed memories of her grandfather abusing her sexually during the summer vacations when her parents would leave her with her grandparents. She had been confused for years around this tangle of memories and emotions. She had loved her grandfather, yet these sickening memories remained buried in her subconscious. As an integration practice, I suggested she write a letter to her deceased grandfather, expressing her anger and disbelief. It also felt important to me that her integration include her family of origin, starting with her siblings. Fortunately, they became allies in her healing process and supported her when she decided to tell her mother. Lisa knew the news would rock the boat, but she found the courage to disrupt the family status quo. Her mother was horrified by her news, but not entirely surprised. The family dialogue allowed Lisa to find more empowerment with herself and connection with her husband, who no longer needed to carry the projected burden of her unresolved trauma.

Lisa's courageous story shows us the value of sharing an insight, gained in a journey via the light of awareness, to one's family and surrounding community. In earth-based cultures, rituals and ceremonies often take place in groups. The container is created by the ways people relate to each other during the time of the ritual. This communally shared ceremony is often followed by sharing food, visions, and experiences. People may talk about the way they saw the divine presence, the way they felt about one another during the ritual, or the way their emotions were released.

A journeyer might find a way to bring peace and resolution to family tensions. They might find clarity on how they want to raise their children.

They might feel inspired to honor their ancestors by spending time adorning their gravesites, staying connected to the roots of their lineage, and recognizing certain people as ongoing influences.

Sometimes, integration is best supported by solitary and contemplative time. Even though our industrialized society is more individualistically oriented than indigenous cultures, individual reflection is a cross-cultural practice. People have always gone into nature to sit in reflective space, contemplating how they are in relationship with themselves. They may reflect on the way they behave poorly toward a family member and decide they need clarity about it before speaking it aloud to them. In meditative communities in the East, after a long meditation retreat, people reenter communal space after being alone for a while and may share a meal together in silence before resuming their ordinary lives.

Because most of us in the industrialized world do not live in a small village, we need to intentionally reach out to our friends and family to create a communal level of support during our integration phase. It is a human impulse to want to share about a journey with our partner or friends or a group of close friends. That being said, after a complex experience, there is also value in keeping one's experience to one's self and not diluting it too quickly into words. This way, a journey keeps unfolding and unraveling undisturbed. Because a ritual is complete does not mean the inner process is complete. When the time is right, it can be of benefit to verbalize and share the insights or challenges one has felt. Sharing is an opportunity to integrate and affirm our experience through our narrative. Finding clarity through our words can be empowering and stabilizing.

The main point of integration on the level of community is that any insights about how one relates to the outside world and one's community be woven into daily life.

Perceiving the Impact of Isolation

Feeling the depth of one's loneliness and how they have avoided relationship shows a journeyer how this lack of connection is a source of emotional and physical suffering. This can result from either a lack of trust, a fear of vulnerability, or a lack of confidence in the ability to forge and nurture connection. It can show how other priorities have taken precedence over connection. Because human beings are by nature tribal creatures and because we thrive in close contact with others, the absence of connectedness is painful and can deprive us of a rich facet of human life.

There are generally two types of people who perceive their own isolated state during a journey. One is the shy, introverted type who does not understand why they are socially uncomfortable because it manifests from an unconscious, wounded place. Perhaps this derives from a childhood with parents who did not sufficiently mirror, acknowledge, or include them. The young child knew he was missing something crucial, but did not know what. This can lead to a life of feeling puzzled about why he does not feel safe forming social connections. In a journey of felt isolation, an adult may finally be able to empathize with the impact their family environment had on them as a child.

The other type of person has developed psychological strategies to defend the shy child within. The fear and uncertainty around connection are the same, but they express themselves differently in their life. This is the person who is often busy with work projects, sports activities, or social life. When there are defensive strategies in place, the adult faces a different level of accountability—they may realize how they actively contribute to their own experience of isolation.

Of course there are people who consciously choose to isolate themselves for spiritual or medical reasons. Traditionally, yogis enter long meditation retreats in solitude, sacrificing human contact for relationship with other aspects of the living world. They might cultivate intimate relationships with the land they are on, the local elements, or beings in the spirit realm. In these cases there are specific practices to support that choice, transmuting the physical need for others.

For the rest of us, it is unnatural and even harmful to starve ourselves of our innate need for social contact. Yet, we already live in a culture of isolation, with everyone in their separate homes and cars, staring at their computers, TVs, and cell phones. Feeling the pain of isolation can be an excellent motivator toward healing. An experience like this can lead us to create human connection or explore our difficulty with intimacy.

This realization of one's isolation can often be an impetus to engage, open emotionally, share, and grow. A guide can encourage the journeyer to reach out to friends, initiate connection with family members, join a hobby group, hiking group, or support group. The client can make lunch dates, join clubs or spiritual groups, or take classes. The aspiration is to reach out gradually, to come out of isolation, and cultivate greater connection. One does not want to dive too quickly into complex situations. Simply reaching out and making real-life contact in person are a start. The goal is to go beyond mere texting, emails, or social media, all of which appear to offer intimacy but do not. The journeyer can ask themselves: Am I keeping busy as a way to avoid connection with others? How is the pain of my unmet need for connection being compensated by other activities? What are the unhealthy things I do to avoid feeling lonely? What kind of intimacy do I long for? What kind of community do I aspire to belong to? A few further integration suggestions are:

- In therapy, continue to explore the roots of isolation in one's family of origin

- Explore slow and gradual connecting: talking with one person or reaching out to deepen a relationship with an acquaintance

- Join a therapy group, hiking group, or take a local cooking class

Healing Our Relationships

This experience is about taking ownership and responsibility for one's part in relational dynamics. A journeyer may realize the impact their communication and social style has on their relationships.

This experience comes to people who are either having challenges in relationships and need insight or who need to know themselves better through the path of relationship. It can show a journeyer his or her innate longing for harmony, mutuality, and clarity in a specific relationship or in their many relationships. It may be teaching someone how to see others with the compassion and empathy needed for authentic relating.

Relationship is a path of self-discovery: External dynamics mirror one's internal dynamics. I recall a client who was constantly finding faults in her partners. One was not emotionally engaged, the other was too rigid, and the next one was lethargic and dull. Her constant, critical opinions left no room for anyone to get close to her. She was always better; they were never good enough. During one particular journey, she became so submerged in this constant stream of negative commentaries that she became nauseated. She soon realized that *she* was the target of her negative mind and that, in fact, she did not like herself one bit. The barrage of her inner critic was overwhelming. Everything she projected onto others had first been received and internalized by her. Originally these had been the voices of her critical teachers and parents who had never let her feel "good enough" as a child.

A guide can support the journeyer in tracing their relationship with themselves back to childhood and their family of origin, including the self-protective strategies they developed. We can use the content of our relationships as grist for the mill in our self-work.

The goal is to express the feelings that were evoked during the journey and to give words and actions to insights and realizations. The guide can encourage the journeyer to write letters, initiate dialogue, or seek mediation or support for specific relationships. The guide can help with the inquiry into what is sought in a specific relationship: does it need healing or does it need resolution? In the case of a situation that feels resolved, the guide can suggest a ritual that symbolizes this sense of completion. It is helpful to support the journeyer in connecting with authenticity, vulnerability, and courage as they start healing their relationships. Further integration practices include:

- Look at and address unresolved issues with people in one's life and find ways to come to peace and completion with these
- Write letters to people who are deceased to express or create completion
- Explore Gestalt therapy,[2] Family Constellation work,[3] or Voice Dialogue[4] work—all different schools of psychological thought that explore the ways we internalize our early childhood or ancestral relationship dynamics
- Read a book or join a workshop on Nonviolent Communication[5]

Celebration of Belonging

This experience expresses our need to feel connected with our fellow human beings. It also highlights the talents and unique style that we bring to our community. There is value in self-reflection and acknowledgment around how one participates in creating community. This experience expresses the joy, passion, and safety that result from belonging to a community or the pain of its absence. There is a deep sense of relief in knowing we are part of something larger.

This experience highlights the exchange between the journeyer and his or her community. There is a transformation to be had through the act of receiving and giving support and energy within one's community. Belonging in a community brings useful teachings around being vulnerable, asking for help, and receiving the support that is offered. What is it like to give and be generous, even if anonymously? What does it feel like to sacrifice self for the benefit of others?

Someone who lives an isolated life can feel that this type of experience offers an invitation into communal connectedness. Someone who is a part of a community could have this experience as a celebration and appreciation of what they have cultivated and are a part of. The community becomes the greater organism. Surrendering to a larger entity helps us drop our ego defenses in service to the vision of the whole. Each person has a role to play, and each role is indispensable. This experience forges equality and mutual respect.

This experience can also help us achieve a balance between belonging to a community and honoring the personal. Sometimes communal activity can be used to avoid being with one's self. Being in a community can offer a sense of connection and belonging that we cannot give ourself. We might have a moment of insight and realize that we are not able to be alone with ourself. Paradoxically, sometimes having a big social network can result not in connecting more, but in connecting less. It can be useful to unhook oneself from one's community in order to re-own one's individuated self and the capacity to exist on one's own.

A guide can support the journeyer in following up this type of experience with a creative expression or project that celebrates the joy of belonging in community. The journeyer can also be guided to ask for or offer help. The goal is to act on the particular insight that has arisen, whether that is offering something to their community or asking for something from their community. The overall goal is to encourage balance in the journeyer's communal engagement: Balance between community time and personal time and balance between giving and receiving.

A guide can encourage the journeyer to reflect on their role in their communities and their impact on others. Have the journeyer ask him or herself: what role do they hold in their communities? Are they there to rock the boat? Are they a leader or a slacker? How are they expressing their nature and talents? How do they participate? How do they show up? How do they nurture and create community? Additional integration practices include:

- Call a friend to ask for support
- Support friends who are going through surgery or illness, or reach out to someone in the community who is struggling
- Bring flowers or homemade presents to friends or cook for someone
- Initiate an event, activity, gathering, celebration, donation, or a fundraiser
- Practice saying "no" to unwanted invitations and carve out personal time

Global Human Family

In an experience of being a part of the global human family, one feels the fundamental bond that connects all human beings. It can provide profound reassurance and can take someone out of their loneliness. It can also teach about generosity, solidarity, and service. It can suggest how to bring compassion into action and manifest concrete acts of giving. This experience can occur for people who live in isolation, disconnected from others, or who are selfish or stingy. This experience encourages someone to open themselves to the human beings around them and, in doing so, heal their tendency toward isolation that has crippled their life. Other people have this experience because their heart is genuinely already open and generous. In this case, this experience is affirming the nature of who they are. Often in a ritual we remember that our purpose is to serve one another. We can connect with an inner compassion in our hearts, which longs to be of service.

The goal of integration here is to express the experience of equality and unity among human beings, through acts of service and generosity toward other people. If we have an abundance of money, time, or energy, we have a responsibility to share it. An abundance that is kept for oneself can become toxic. An abundance that is shared continues to flow. Does the journeyer feel called to do something? How can the journeyer honor the felt sense of connection? How can this feeling be developed into concrete action? Further integration practices include:

- Mentor an underprivileged child or volunteer in a homeless shelter, soup kitchen, or hospice, or write letters to an inmate

- Become active politically, or participate in Restorative Justice circles working for a better world[6]

- Learn and teach Nonviolent Communication

- Explore being generous with people without any expectation or desire for reciprocity

- Adopt a child somewhere in the world and support them financially or send money to refugees in disaster areas

---

Amy had grown up entitled and wealthy. When she came to see me, she complained that she had felt isolated most of her life, different, and disconnected from the rest of the human family. During a women's retreat with me, she connected with her feeling of intense isolation and realized what a handicap her privilege had turned out to be for her. Her pain was intense, and she was determined to create a different situation.

I suggested she find somewhere to volunteer locally around the holidays when she would usually get together with her wealthy friends and "splurge out on the town." Amy agreed to do this, and when she came back to tell me about it, she said she had been moved to tears of gratitude. She had decided to spend a few Saturdays volunteering at a homeless shelter and said she felt more human than she had in a long time. She decided to make a monthly donation to the shelter and volunteer once per month. She knew she couldn't change the situation of everyone who stayed in the shelter, but she could slowly change herself and reach out from the sense of separation that had plagued her throughout her life.

The spectrum of community goes from an isolated person who does not have any friends all the way to the person who belongs to many communities and is incapable of being alone. Then, of course, there is everything in between. There can be a healthy relationship with one's community, and on the other hand, there can be a tendency to avoid relationship with one's self, using community as a distraction.

When we are balanced on the level of community, we are in an honest relationship with our self. We relate from a place of clarity, accountability, and vulnerability, and we are able to express our gifts and wounds. We can speak our truth and remain vulnerable with those around us. We consider the exploration of relationship as a path toward self-discovery and self-compassion. We keep an attentive eye on the balance between giving and receiving. The act of service is nourishment for the soul, and we aim to cultivate a sense of global connection. At the same time we understand the need for solitude and alone time. We share our love and support with others.

From the organs in our body to the organism of our planet, all things work in cooperation and through a symbiotic relationship. When we go into expanded states of consciousness, we can truly perceive this oneness. There is no separation between ourselves and the other; we are different facets of the organism that is our shared planet. At the same time we are distinct beings. Honoring our uniqueness and the truth of who we are as individuals is paramount to healing. It is through the realization of this paradox—our uniqueness and our interdependence—that we grow stronger and more connected to those around us and ourselves.

Our survival as a species in the twenty-first century depends on our capacity to establish functioning communities. We see more and more evidence of this: we seem to be engaging in a renewal of human connectedness in the face of poverty and climate change. All of us have witnessed or experienced coming together around a cause and the impact it can have on the world. While personal actions toward change are valuable, a community in action is incredibly powerful.

17

NATURE'S MIRROR

Integrating Environment-Centered Experiences

*Hello, sun in my face. Hello you who made the
morning and spread it over the fields…. Watch, now,
how I start the day in happiness, in kindness.*

—MARY OLIVER[1]

My client Jen was a single mother of three and nearing sixty. Her relationship
with her mother had been filled with frustration, abandonment, and betrayal.
As a child, Jen had been tormented by her mentally disturbed older brother and
had felt unprotected by her mother. As she struggled to process the recent death
of her mother and the complexity of her grieving process, she realized she was
becoming obsessed with her mistakes as a parent, simultaneously experiencing
herself as a neglected child and an inadequate mother toward her kids.

> *I led her in a drumming ritual in the forest by my home to explore the various aspects of her role as a parent and her relationship with her mother. She was immediately drawn to lie on the earth. She began crying, laughing, smelling the soil, and rubbing leaves on her face. She later told me she felt safe and reassured there. She knew the earth could absorb her sorrow and restore her vitality. The archetype of motherhood resonated in "the cells of her body," as she later said. She was able to forgive herself, realizing how competent a mother she was and how deeply committed to her children she felt. She was able to come to a sense of peace with the kind of woman her mother had been able to be with her. She also felt strengthened in her capacity for love and presence with her children.*
>
> *To continue her newfound relationship with the natural world, she decided to spend more intentional time in the wilderness where she could explore her sense of connection with the joy of lying on boulders, on the banks of rivers, and in meadows. She later chose to further her integration by sponsoring the planting of hundreds of trees in a place that needed reforesting.*

Jen's experience was not only healing for herself as a mother, and for her relationship with her own mother, but it also opened her relationship with the earth as the archetypal Great Mother. In modern life, the poignancy of an encounter like this can bring forth an immediate sense of connection with nature and the greater environment that would more commonly occur in a more earth-based lifestyle.

Earth-based cultures exist in villages or small towns surrounded by nature, where the inhabitants cultivate the land for sustenance, and their entire lives follow the rhythms of the crops and the seasons. Indigenous groups consider the land to be the home of local spirits, powers, and energies, which they believe to have profound influence on their well-being. The natural world is part of their psyche, their cosmology, and their spirituality.

When a ritual is conducted in a natural environment, and there is a felt connection with the land, the earth continues to hold the participants even after a ritual is complete. The people will return to their fields, eat the food they have grown, drink from their well, and make teas from herbs they know will restore and purify their bodies. They may make offerings to the spirit of the river, burn sage to the sky, or if they are of the San Pedro tradition of South America, they might open their sacred bundle—which is their altar made up of stones, carvings, sticks, amulets, and herbs—to the stars.

Julieta taught me that after a journey, people are considered very permeable. Hence, for a few days they are advised not to deal with trash and are told to stay in their home to shield themselves from unpredictable interactions in the streets. The home becomes a safe container for the residual effects of the journey on the physical level. Again, Julieta would repeat that it is nature that does the healing. She who births the sacred mushrooms as medicine for humans is the true healer. The wisdom of the earth and the mushrooms can return people to a healthy state, on all the levels of their being.

We may have lost this deeper level of connection, but we are aware of the environment in different ways. We are usually aware of where we live and our neighborhood. It is common during an expanded state of consciousness to reflect on the greater environment, our local rivers and watershed, mountains and lakes, our city, nation, and the state of the planet and its ecological crisis.

Sometimes we realize that where we live is chaotic or boring, in need of color, art, and beauty. Our perception of our environment can be a reflection of our inner state. Is it in harmony or chaos? Sometimes by realizing how dull, drab, and empty our home space is, we are led to perceive our inner emptiness.

As a guide, I find this level of integration especially fascinating; our state of permeability after a journey allows us to be more receptive to the healing and rebalancing power of nature. As I listen to someone's recollection of a journey, I listen to the ways nature appeared and I follow my intuition toward imagining what would support the integration process. I know through my years of experience how healing reconnecting with nature can be, how it can nurture beauty in someone's psyche, body, and heart.

In indigenous cultures, healing is intrinsically connected with nature. The guide should support the integration of nature-based rituals into a journeyer's life, whether the experience has been one of communion or a revelation of personal disconnection from nature.

The Pain of Living in a Toxic Environment

During a journey, someone who does not pay attention to the way they decorate or maintain their living space, office, or yard may realize the importance of their personal space. The person may understand the impact of a poorly cared-for home and how the immediate environment can engender depression, confusion, or anxiety. Someone who is a hoarder or who never cleans their home and leaves piles of papers or laundry everywhere may see how their external and internal environments reflect each other. If the home is messy, confused, or untended, this is direct information about how one is neglecting their environment. They may see that they are capable of applying simple changes to their external situation to shift their inner world. They can learn to bring awareness and care to their living and working environments. Conversely, those who are engaged in tending their living space may feel validated in their attention to beauty and harmony.

A guide can suggest concrete actions toward organizing and cleaning one's home, office, or yard. The goal is to apply changes that reflect the understanding of the impact of such external chaos, while supporting the journeyer to acknowledge how the changes in their environment affect them energetically and emotionally.

The guide can suggest certain actions and commitments the client may want to make, especially concerning their home. The guide can encourage them to bring a sense of beauty and balance into their personal environment. Living in a balanced environment, even if it is simple, nourishes a person's soul. Someone could explore the following:

- Walk through the rooms of your home and see how they feel

- Remove items or products that feel toxic

- Bring beauty into the home by hanging art on the wall and making or buying colorful pillows

- Keep fresh flowers on the table or a basket of fresh fruit on the counter

- Bring natural elements into the home such as shells, rocks, or branches

- Choose a small area such as a drawer or a closet to sort through and organize
- Dedicate time weekly to cleaning and beautifying
- Consider buying local and organic products

My client Ann told me her life was "beige." I found that to be a strange word for her to use to describe her life. She said that colors were too daring for her, so she dressed in pale taupe, and her apartment was painted and decorated in monochrome beige. Beige was elegant, she said. During a sound journey, in which she participated with the intention to bring more vitality into her life, she recognized how flat the world around her felt and how affected she was by this flatness. She felt boring and dull. She longed for something wilder and bolder but was afraid of this unknown territory. As part of her integration phase, on my suggestion, she decided to buy one red shawl she would drape on her beige sofa, and she decided to try to wear one piece of color every day. The results were startling; she loved how the red shawl made her feel as soon as she came home, and her indigo blue sweater gave her a "lift." She ended up repainting her living room light lavender and reported discovering her enjoyment of the colors around her.

Realizing Our Responsibility for Nature

As humans, it is natural to feel devastated as we witness the deterioration of our natural world. A journey may allow us to access the pain of the earth herself, a living organism going through a toxic illness. One may have this experience as a heart-opening reminder to move out of individual narcissistic complacence. The journey can invite us to open our eyes and reestablish our relationship with the natural world.

If a journey has brought insight into the agony of ecological destruction, it is helpful to encourage the person to stay with the pain, as it increases their capacity to feel. The guide can help them find ways to express anguish at the planet's toxic state through ritual, poetry, painting, or expressive arts. It is healing to outwardly express the pain that is felt inside, to offer it out as expression. Indeed, this is the impetus for many artistic masterpieces. It is unwise to suppress our grief for the state of the planet, as it stagnates into toxicity or depression. It is healthy to feel the fullness of one's heart, even if it is full of grief or pain. This can inspire the journeyer to change their personal relationship with the natural world and to act in higher integrity.

The integration goal after a journey like this is to bring form and action to the ideas born from the experience. The guide should encourage the person to take greater personal responsibility for the equilibrium of the planet. Someone can make an active contribution to their well-being this way. It is about mobilizing one's personal engagement and life force to honor the environment. Individual choices toward sustainability contribute to the balance of the whole. Every person doing their part creates change. Further suggestions to support integration are:

- Read, study, and participate in the work of leaders in this movement in your country and region such as Joanna Macy's *The Work That Reconnects*[2]

- Explore the work of Charles Eisenstein[3] or Naomi Klein[4]

- Connect with the Pachamama Alliance[5]

- Attend national and international gatherings such as the Bioneers Conference to gain a sense of solidarity, support, and inspiration, or look at their websites and actions[6]

- Participate in local events, lectures, or rituals that mobilize awareness about ecological issues

- Get involved in political actions that support local environmental protection

- Pick up litter while out walking or hiking in nature

- Consider using biodegradable, nontoxic cleaning products

- Minimize use of packaging (plastic bags) and get involved in recycling

A client of mine, Orion, decided to do a vision quest. He sat for four days beside a tree. At first, he felt alone. It took a day for the tree and the meadow to feel familiar as if he were in the presence of friends. After two days, Orion started to "hear" the earth, and what he heard was her pain. As marvelous as she looked from under his tree, he also felt her fragility and how she was polluted. He started to feel sick himself as if this toxicity were becoming his own. The rest of his time in this vision quest oscillated between incredible ecstasy and visceral pain. Afterward, it took Orion a few days to return to his normal state. His integration was focused on his personal choices, as far as the pollutants he was using. He rethought detergents, recycling, and carpooling. He even joined a political campaign for sustainable fishing techniques. These actions were directly connected to his vision quest experience. He felt that his vision quest journey had reoriented his life toward a higher level of ecological accountability.

Merging with the Elements

During a journey, it is common to feel as if one is merging with nature. This indicates one's need for the visceral teaching of nature and their need to deepen their connection with the natural world. They may understand how nature acts as a mirror of unseen human qualities. Perceiving the similarities between one's human life and the natural world (her cycles, seasons, expansions, and contractions) can bring someone an embodied sense of connection. There is wisdom to be gained through observing the natural ebb and flow of day and night, our time of activity, and our time of calm and rest. The way things grow is the way humans grow. The ways things decay can teach us about death. Recognizing the impermanence of nature teaches us about the impermanence of our lives.

A journey may also offer teachings on how the elements of earth, water, fire, air, and space are present in one's body. It can reveal a personal resonance with aspects of nature such as mountains, lakes, trees, and rocks. By resonating with or having the experience of merging with these elements of nature, one can find support for specific emotional situations, connecting with the qualities of solidity, flow, patience, and resilience.

The guide can support the journeyer to deepen their exploration into the specific aspect of nature that was evoked. If someone felt a resonance with trees—their stability, strength, or vitality—the guide could suggest they go spend time with a tree, touch the tree, draw the tree, and gaze at the tree from up close and afar. Have them feel the roots of the tree below the ground and understand how the tree absorbs light from the sun and makes its own food and nutrients from the soil to nourish its roots.

The idea is to stay curious about, explore, and deepen whatever has been illuminated in the journey by weaving its content into everyday life. This is how experience becomes embodied wisdom. Further suggestions for the integration of this type of experience are:

- Go to the woods, a river, or a beach, and listen silently to nature's sounds

- Journal on the themes of nature that are reflected in you

- Watch nature documentaries or read books on wilderness life

- Sit in the moonlight under the stars

Perceiving the Intelligence of Nature

This type of experience appears as a reminder as to how one can learn from nature and remember their own inner wild and intelligent nature. This is an experience of connecting with the whole that is our living planet and understanding how this organism regulates herself. As an entire organism, she is regulating herself through both cataclysms and peaceful transitions. During a journey one can find themselves tapping into volcanoes, raging waters, fires, floods, or into more peaceful places such as a brook, a forest, or a meadow.

Exploring the macrocosmic organism of the earth teaches us about the microcosm that we each are. We receive this experience when we need to learn that our personal way of evolving and regulating ourselves has its unique rhythm and wisdom. We can go through dramatic events, illnesses, and losses, and recover from all of them. We can know peace again, just as the planet can experience an earthquake, volcano, or flood and recover afterward. The balancing and regulating capacity of the planet shows us our capacity to do the same. The life and death of the planet teach us about life and death. The organism as a whole needs all parts working together.

During integration, the goal here is to support the journeyer as they continue to deepen their resonance with nature. They can continue to reflect on their intrinsic wisdom and the ways they instinctively regulate their life. They can be reminded that all living systems strive toward equilibrium. When an organism loses its balance, there is an inner self-regulating mechanism which seeks to regain homeostasis. Our bodies consistently regulate temperature, heart rate, blood pressure, and much more in response to the changing external environment. The guide's goal is to support the journeyer in allowing his or her self-regulating mechanism to engage. The guide can track the hindrances and obstacles to this natural process and work with them therapeutically. Other possible integration practices include:

- Create an altar representing the elements earth, water, fire, air, and space
- If possible, visit people who live in close harmony with the natural world
- Read about deep ecology,[7] systems theory,[8] or author Dolores LaChapelle[9]

In an ideal state of balance with the aspect of the environment, we see and feel nature as part of ourselves, not so much something to relate to, but truly as an extension of our own organism. Our home is uncluttered, colorful, and reflective of our personal sense of beauty. We bring in branches and stones to beautify our living space. We keep flowers on the table. We tend a garden and grow our food. We tend bees and make potions from the healing properties of the plants we nurture.

We feel the beauty of nature, as well as the pain she endures due to our ever-expanding needs. Even if at times we feel helpless and sad, we stay open with our emotions about this state of imbalance. We do not shy away from being aware of our actions and their impact on the planet's fragile equilibrium. We pay attention to what we buy, where it comes from, how it was produced, and how it will be discarded. We agree to make sacrifices in order to act respectfully toward nature. We might not use the air-conditioning or we might buy an electric car, even if gasoline is cheap. We might donate funds to organizations that support ecological activism.

We find solace in the colors of the sunset, inspiration in spring's burst of foliage, calm in a shady meadow, and energy in the ocean waves. We bathe in rivers and sit by open fires. We hike in the silence of deserts and explore the darkness of caves. We become attuned to the seasons, daylight, and nighttime.

We recognize that the time we spend in nature is central to our physical and emotional well-being. Maybe the nourishing presence of nature is what truly repairs our deepest wounds and sense of isolation. Nature, after all, offers us the most restorative, fulfilling, and eternal sense of presence we can find, should we be so lucky to live near thriving wilderness or protected lands. Having an experience of deep communion with nature in her profound intelligence helps us remember our inherent wholeness.

✳ ✳ ✳

The entire process of integration is one of empowerment, transformation, and liberation. The role of the guide is to remember this and support it all the way through. In the last five chapters, the process of integration has been described through the lens of the Holistic Model for a Balanced Life and through the various categories of transformative experience. Clearly, whatever reveals itself during a journey is vital to the next step of someone's evolution. The content needs to be honored, expressed, and supported fully.

A thorough approach to integration touches all aspects of a journeyer's life, as it weaves in new insights and discoveries. For each healing stemming from an expanded state experience, the integration can be applied to all five aspects of life. For example, if someone experiences grief during a journey, the guide can encourage the integration primarily on the emotional level, empathizing, listening, and encouraging verbalization through written letters or other practices. Next, the expression of this grief could be explored through physical movement. Expressive arts, rituals, or prayer can bring awareness of the spiritual aspect. Sharing the experience with friends or family members will help weave it into the aspect of one's community. Finally, a restorative connection with nature can help integrate this experience of grief on the level of the environment.

In this way, integration takes place on all of the levels of one's life, including all five aspects of the Holistic Model. Whatever we connect with during a journey can be woven through the entirety of our life, contributing to profound holistic rebalancing. This helps reestablish equilibrium, supporting the wholeness and interdependence of our body, mind and emotions, spirit, community, and environment.

18
CONCLUSION
Sharing Our Transformation with the World

*If the world is to be healed through human efforts,
I am convinced it will be by ordinary people, people
whose love for this life is even greater than their
fear. People who can open to the web of life that
called us into being.*

JOANNA MACY[1]

All human beings have wounds, fears, and frailties, and all human beings know what it means to suffer. We all share the wish for peace, safety, and happiness. We wish to heal the pain of our wounds and reach a state of fulfillment and liberation. It is our heartfelt longing to reclaim our innate wholeness and know that, ultimately, all is well. Yet, the path of healing is not only about moving beyond our wounding. It is about finding our way to understanding and compassion while being able to face our pain.

I have spent my life looking deeply into my own consciousness, learning from my native teachers, and supporting others along their respective journeys, continually inspired by the possibilities that exist at the frontiers of healing. When I reflect on how I came to do this work, I see that I was seeking freedom from outer oppression and inner pain—my childhood colored by love and fear, losing my father at a young age, my brief but agonizing episode with drugs, and the near-death experience of my early twenties.

Now with more context and resources, I understand the gifts of the painful experiences I endured. My experiences of overwhelming panic and confusion taught me self-compassion and how to empathize with other people's suffering and confusion. The challenges of my life have inspired an ongoing commitment to self-exploration, through therapy and various kinds of healing rituals, and have led me to seek the guidance of my elders and teachers. Now I see that despite feelings of regret toward some of my destructive choices, my frustration with my negative patterns, and my string of unsuccessful relationships, the gems of my life were buried in the chaos of my most difficult moments. At the time, I only knew how to keep moving forward, guided by an inner force and resilience.

I learned resilience from my teachers, starting with my mother, inheriting her survival instinct to rise again and again when pushed back by circumstances. Despite the hardships she endured, she lived to the age of 97, passionate and full of life, always telling me about her friends, her community life, and the concerts she was attending. I learned resilience from Pablo, as an indigenous man on a Native American reservation with a challenging beginning, who generously and boldly shared his work with the world despite his physical hardships. I learned resilience from Julieta, who, despite being raised in poverty, sustained her life and work with spunk and vitality. Julieta was rarely found without a playful smile on her face.

Along with the many other teachers and guides along my path, they each inspired me with their warrior spirit, and although imperfect and wounded in their own ways, they each continually affirmed life in all its tragic beauty. They each taught me what is possible when life force has a clear direction. Like us all, they were driven by their survival strategies, born out of necessity. At the same time, like us all, they were guided by the radiance of the indomitable human spirit.

It is this human spirit that has kept me moving forward, and that I recognize in those who come to me for counseling and guidance. People desire to expand and grow, to learn and transform. It is that desire that inspires me to be with client after client, soul after soul, listening, reflecting, guiding, and doing my best to support each one with the same love that I received from my teachers. It is that spirit that compels me to step out and share these teachings and this method with others at this time.

❊ ❊ ❊

If you are a professional practitioner, therapist, facilitator, or guide, you now have a framework from which to guide the preparation and integration of a client, whether they are embarking upon a vision quest, a ceremony with an entheogenic plant medicine, a meditation retreat, or any other consciousness-expanding modality.

I have defined the role and responsibilities of a guide—that it is their job to gather direct personal experience, seek out extensive training in any modality they wish to facilitate, and to adhere to appropriate boundaries and ethical guidelines. Their work, as I have repeatedly emphasized, should be grounded in the qualities of wisdom, creativity, and love.

The Holistic Model for a Balanced Life and its inventories are a lens through which to explore the many aspects of a client's life and discover where the strengths and weaknesses reside. With this material, a guide now has a framework from which to help their client practically prepare for a journey, as well as a map describing the types of experiences that can occur in an expanded state, with guidance as to how to best support a journeyer in real time. Finally, the guide now has an orientation from which to conduct the invaluable integration phase following a journey, with concrete practices in their toolbox to help maximize the transformative potential of these experiences.

For the intrepid journeyer with no guide, you can use what you have learned to create your own preparation and integration framework and have reference points to support you as you decode the mysteries of your own consciousness. I hope that through these stories and teachings, you realize the transformative potential of these non-ordinary states and that this integrative method will help you approach them with care. As you may have realized, this book does not offer guidance as to how to actually conduct a journey into an expanded state experience, as that takes years of experience and training and cannot be imparted through a single book. If that calls to you, I encourage you to find a tradition that speaks to you and begin at the beginning, as a journeyer, under the guidance of a trained expert. Our capacity to support another person's experience is limited by the breadth of our own experience. If you want to help someone explore the vast reaches of their consciousness, start with yourself. That said, any trained therapist, facilitator, or guide with therapeutic training and counseling skills can support another's preparation and integration process. It is much needed.

✻ ✻ ✻

I believe every person has the right to seek healing and growth however they can, and that healing practitioners, facilitators, and guides have the right to learn from ancient healing modalities in service to helping others receive the maximum benefit on their healing journeys. Practitioners of Chinese medicine, Ayurveda, and herbalism have become more integrated into modern healthcare. With respect and acknowledgment, it is time to include the healing potential of expanded states of consciousness, as well as the living indigenous traditions that have been sustaining them. We have a society that is deteriorating. We have people suffering from anxiety, depression, and a wide range of ailments. We have a medical establishment bound by millions of rules and regulations. Regular psychotherapy is wonderful when it works, but it is time-consuming and only effective to the degree that the therapist is self-aware and has done their own healing work. Even then, many people reach their limits with what therapy can offer and need an approach that goes deeper into their psyche. I truly wish that there were more accessible solutions. It would be simpler. But what is available in the current field of healing is not transformative enough for everyone. The depth of healing accessible through expanded states of consciousness, when prepared for and integrated well by a trained guide, is sublimely life-changing.

These experiences open uncharted territories, but ultimately it is up to each individual to do something with that which is discovered within themselves. This path is not a solution unless someone responds with determination, following the guidance of their own soul as to how they can embody healthier ways of living their life.

The shifts that are possible through expanded states of consciousness aren't limited to the conceptual or intellectual realm. They are deep and thorough, affecting a person's physiology and changing their vibrational field. These shifts affect how someone shows up in all of their interactions and relationships, as they begin to pull the threads of unhealthy family dynamics apart. I have seen time and again with my clients, that when one person sincerely chooses the path of healing through increasing consciousness, choosing to resolve the deep wounds that hold them back and open them up to a direct experience of the sacred, the effects are felt throughout their entire family.

* * *

Though we each have our unique version of what it looks and feels like to be lost, the longing to heal unites us all. It is through opening to our own personal suffering and the suffering of others that we learn compassion and the power of love. As we each do our own healing work, and we loosen our identification with our suffering, we create an inner space within, where new possibilities can arise. As understanding dawns and compassion rises, something fundamental relaxes and our coping mechanisms dissolve. We can bring peace to the conflicts within us. Instead of being stuck in unconscious ego strategies, we can intentionally choose the path of increasing awareness, realizing that there might be an underlying intelligence to the unfolding of life.

While we all wish to be happy, to enjoy our life's journey, and to deepen our personal connection with the divine, I believe that we also wish to help others toward their respective healing and growth. Once we feel comfortable being the unique, whole being that we are, we do not feel inhibited or held back by fear. When we are confident and satisfied with our lives, we naturally want to support the well-being of others. As more life force becomes available to use creatively, we become more curious toward others and more available to listen and appreciate one another. This in turn helps our partnerships, families, and communities thrive with more solidarity, joy, and love. Whether we know it at first or not, we do our healing equally for our self and for others.

Most of us eventually discover that we wish to affect the larger world beyond our family and community. We realize that we are not isolated; we are part of a greater whole. It is our own inner healing that opens our eyes so that we can see ourselves in the other. When the great Indian sage Ramana Maharshi was asked, "How should we treat others?" he replied simply, "There are no others."

We realize that we are interconnected beings, interwoven in the great web of life.

As we wake up and perceive the state of the world and how we are all impacting it, we realize the need to think globally. How do we bring the increasing clarity in our personal world to the outer world? How do we translate our awareness into actions that positively affect others? How do we offer our gifts to the world? Our inner journey inspires us to work for the entire human family. We may choose to act locally, but we must also think about national and international policies as well as our entire planet. Our current world, laden with challenges, desperately needs inhabitants that are conscious, creative, and compassionate.

It is only in healing our individual consciousness that we can aspire to evolve as a species. The exploration can be challenging, but the courage we call forth to take the plunge into our inner world is our victory over fear. Though the path undoubtedly twists and turns, our clear intention directs us toward wholeness. Our longing for harmony leads us to compassion. Along the way, we learn to take our place in the human family and to translate the gifts of our inner explorations into actions in the outer world.

No matter where we were born or the upbringing we had, we are all native to this earth, receiving her teachings and wisdom. We are of nature; made of soil, water, fire, air, and spirit. We are living, growing, and evolving, and like the natural world, our life is a dance of cycles. Wherever we come from, each of us is a human being with a body, a family, dreams, fears, vulnerabilities, and a longing for safety and peace. Although in the modern, industrialized world we may have lost connection to the rituals of our ancestors, we can respectfully learn from indigenous cultures with their unbroken lineages of wisdom in our efforts to remember what has been lost.

As we end this time together, this is what I would like to say to you, dear reader. If you want to live a truly fulfilling life, first get to know yourself. Face what lies within you. We all receive a complex inheritance and can only try to do the best with what we have been given. We know we are not perfect, and it is through our imperfection that we realize that we belong to the human family. Learn the truth of who you are—your past, your present, and your aspirations for the future. Learn to accept yourself, your scars, your fragilities, and your imperfections. Learn to celebrate your strength and your beauty. Lastly, learn to love yourself in all of your complexity, completely and unconditionally. The path of discovering yourself is a deeply human endeavor.

Our time on this earth is brief, filled with magnificent and utterly challenging adventures. We can look to the earth as our teacher. She teaches us to be generous, creative, and how to live in balance and reciprocity. After all, who is the most steady and loving presence for us all throughout our entire lifetime? As Julieta would so often say, "When we eat the Niños Santos, it is the earth herself that heals us. Her sacred plants teach us how to live. She knows what we need. She is our mother."

BIBLIOGRAPHY

Danzico, Matt. "Brains of Buddhist Monks Scanned in Meditation Study." *BBC News.* April 24, 2011. Accessed October 15, 2018. www.bbc.com/news /world-us-canada-12661646.

Eisenstein, Charles. *The More Beautiful World Our Hearts Know Is Possible.* Berkeley, CA: North Atlantic Books, 2013.

Eliade, Mircea, and Willard R. Trask. *Shamanism: Archaic Techniques of Ecstasy.* Princeton, NJ: Princeton University Press, 1964.

Estrada, Álvaro. *María Sabina: Her Life and Chants.* Santa Barbara: Ross-Erikson, 1981.

Garrison, Kathleen A., Thomas A. Zeffiro, Dustin Scheinost, R. Todd Constable, and Judson A. Brewer. "Meditation Leads to Reduced Default Mode Network Activity beyond an Active Task." *Cognitive, Affective, & Behavioral Neuroscience* 15, no. 3 (2015): 712–20. https://doi.org/10.3758/s13415-015-0358-3.

Harner, Sandra. *Ema's Odyssey: Shamanism for Healing and Spiritual Knowledge.* Berkeley, CA: North Atlantic Books, 2014.

Hirshfield, Jane, ed. *Women in Praise of the Sacred: 43 Centuries of Spiritual Poetry by Women.* New York: Harper Perennial, 1995.

Josipovic, Zoran, and Bernard J. Baars. "Editorial: What Can Neuroscience Learn from Contemplative Practices?" *Frontiers in Psychology* 6 (2015). https://doi.org /10.3389/fpsyg.2015.01731.

Kurtz, Ron. *Body-centered Psychotherapy: The Hakomi Method: The Integrated Use of Mindfulness, Nonviolence, and the Body.* Mendocino, CA: LifeRhythm, 2007.

Lewis-Williams, David. *The Mind in the Cave: Consciousness and the Origins of Art.* London: Thames & Hudson, 2004.

Lewis-Williams, David J., and Jean Clottes. "The Mind in the Cave—the Cave in the Mind: Altered Consciousness in the Upper Paleolithic." *Anthropology of Consciousness* 9, no. 1 (1998): 13–21. https://doi.org/10.1525/ac.1998.9.1.13.

Oliver, Mary. *Why I Wake Early: New Poems.* Boston: Beacon Press, 2005.

Pollan, Michael. "My Adventures with the Trip Doctors." *New York Times,* May 15, 2015. Accessed October 15, 2018. www.nytimes.com/interactive/2018/05/15 /magazine/health-issue-my-adventures-with-hallucinogenic-drugs-medicine.html.

Riso, Don Richard. *The Enneagram: Discovering Your Personality Type.* London: Thorsons, 1995.

Uzunov, Blagoy Angelov, and Maya Petrova Stoyneva-Gärtner. "Mushrooms and Lichens in Bulgarian Ethnomycology." *Journal of Mycology* 2015 (October 2015): 1–7. https://doi.org/10.1155/2015/361053.

NOTES

Front Matter

1   María Sabina (1894–1985) was a Mazatec *curandera* who first shared the mushrooms with a non-Mexican person in 1955. During her night vigils called *veladas*, she would speak spontaneous poetry, expressing the language of the mushrooms.

Introduction: Weaving Worlds

1   See, for instance, Richard E. Schultes, Albert Hofmann, and Christian Rätsch, *Plants of the Gods: Their Sacred, Healing, and Hallucinogenic Powers* (Rochester, VT: Healing Arts Press, 2001).

2   Dr. Salvador Roquet (1920–1995) was a Mexican psychiatrist who led individual and group healing sessions that integrated psychotherapeutic interventions with the use of LSD, ketamine, psilocybin mushrooms, and morning glory seeds. Read more in Alberto Villoldo, "An Introduction to the Psychedelic Psychotherapy of Salvador Roquet," *Journal of Humanistic Psychology* 17, no. 4 (1977): 45–58.

3   Developed in the late 1970s by Ron Kurtz, the Hakomi Method of Experiential Therapy is a mindfulness-based, body-centered approach that blends Eastern and Western psychology. The Hakomi Institute continues to offer trainings to therapists and bodyworkers around the globe. Find out more at hakomiinstitute.com.

Chapter 1. Original Rituals: Expanded States of Consciousness for Healing and Growth

1   Pema Chödrön, *When Things Fall Apart: Heart Advice for Difficult Times* (London: Thorsons Classics, 2017), 1.

2   See, for instance, Vincenzo Formicola et al., "The Upper Paleolithic Triple Burial of Dolní Věstonice: Pathology and Funerary Behavior," *American Journal of Physical Anthropology* 115, no. 4 (2001): 372–79. See also Leore Grosman et al., "A 12,000-Year-Old Shaman Burial from the Southern Levant (Israel)," *Proceedings of the National Academy of Sciences of the United States of America* 105, no. 46 (2008): 17665–69.

3 See, for instance, Johnjoe McFadden, "Conscious Electromagnetic (CEMI) Field Theory," *NeuroQuantology* 5, no. 3 (2007): 262–70.

4 See, for instance, Shelli Joye et al., "The Pribram-Bohm Holoflux Theory of Consciousness: an Integral Interpretation of the Theories of Karl Pribram, David Bohm, and Pierre Teilhard De Chardin" (PhD diss., California Institute of Integral Studies, 2016), ProQuest Dissertations and Theses.

5 See, for instance, Mirza N. Baig et al., "The Eastern Heart and Galen's Ventricle: A Historical Review of the Purpose of the Brain," *Neurosurgical Focus* 23, no. 1 (2007): E3.

6 J. W. N. Sullivan, "Interviews with Great Scientists. VI. Max Planck," *The Observer,* January 25, 1931, 17.

7 "This brief overview argues that the evidence of the images themselves, as well as their contexts, suggests that some Franco-Cantabrian Upper Paleolithic cave art was, at least in part, intimately associated with various shamanic practices." From David J. Lewis-Williams and Jean Clottes, "The Mind in the Cave—the Cave in the Mind: Altered Consciousness in the Upper Paleolithic," *Anthropology of Consciousness* 9, no. 1 (1998): 13–21, https://doi.org/10.1525/ac.1998.9.1.13. See also David Lewis-Williams, *The Mind in the Cave: Consciousness and the Origins of Art* (New York: Thames & Hudson, 2004).

8 *Bufo alvarius* toad, also known as the Sonoran Desert toad or the Colorado River toad, native to Northern Mexico and the Southwest United States, excretes a milky venom that contains 5-HO-DMT, a tryptamine similar to psilocin (4-HO-DMT) and DMT. Many books have been written about documenting people's experiences with this powerful substance such as James Oroc's *Tryptamine Palace: 5-MeO-DMT and the Sonoran Desert Toad* (Rochester, VT: Park Street Press, 2009). Scientists can learn more by reviewing Alan K. Davis et al., "The Epidemiology of 5-methoxy-N, N-dimethyltryptamine (5-MeO-DMT) Use: Benefits, Consequences, Patterns of Use, Subjective Effects, and Reasons for Consumption," *Journal of Psychopharmacology* 32, no. 7 (2018): 779–92. The secretions of a frog native to the Amazon rainforest, *Phyllomedusa bicolor,* also called Kambo or Sapo, are used for cleansing and purging through the application of its toxin under the recipient's skin.

9 See, for instance, B. Lowy, "New Records of Mushroom Stones from Guatemala," *Mycologia* 63, no. 5 (1971): 983–93.

10 UNESCO World Heritage Centre, "Tassili N'Ajjer," *UNESCO World Heritage Centre,* whc.unesco.org/en/list/179; Brian Akers et al., "A Prehistoric Mural in Spain Depicting Neurotropic Psilocybe Mushrooms?" *Economic Botany* 65, no. 2 (2011): 121–28. Bulgarian ethnobotanists Blagoy Angelov Uzunov and Maya Petrova Stoyneva-Gärtner, note that, "According to our search, on the territory

of Bulgaria the use of mushrooms as entheogens dates back to the Neolithic and Bronze Age." "Mushrooms and Lichens in Bulgarian Ethnomycology," *Journal of Mycology* 2015, October 2015, 2, https://doi.org/10.1155/2015/361053.

11 While the term "shamanism" is thought to have originated in Siberia or Northern Asia, the exact origin is unknown. Plants, mushrooms, herbs, drumming, dreams, or other modes are historically used to access shamanic states of consciousness. See, for instance, E. Crundwell, "The Unnatural History of the Fly Agaric," *Mycologist* 1, no. 4 (1987): 178–81. See also Henry N. Michael, *Studies in Siberian Shamanism No. 4* (Toronto: Published for the Arctic Institute of North America by University of Toronto Press, 1963).

12 Harrison Pope, "Tabernanthe Iboga: An African Narcotic Plant of Social Importance," *Economic Botany* 23, no. 2 (1969): 174–84.

13 See, for instance, Dennis McKenna, "Ayahuasca: An Ethnopharmacologic History," in *The Ayahuasca Experience: A Sourcebook on the Sacred Vine of Spirits*, ed. Ralph Metzner (South Paris, ME: Park Street Press, 2014).

14 See, for instance, Francisco Javier Carod-Artal and Carolina B. Vázquez-Cabrera, "Mescalina y Ritual Del Cactus De San Pedro: Evidencias Arqueológicas y Etnográficas En El Norte De Perú," *Revue Neurologique* 42, no. 8 (2006): 489–98.

15 See, for instance, Pokharia et al., "Neolithic–Early Historic (2500–200 BC) Plant Use: The Archaeobotany of Ganga Plain, India," *Quaternary International* 443 (2017): 223–37. See also Ethen Russo, "Cannabis in India: Ancient Lore and Modern Medicine," in *Cannabinoids as Therapeutics*, ed. Raphael Mechoulam (Basel, Switzerland: Birkhäuser Verlag, Milestones in Drug Therapy, 2005).

16 Daniele Piomelli and Antonino Pollio, "In Upupa O Strige. A Study in Renaissance Psychotropic Plant Ointments," *History and Philosophy of the Life Sciences* 16, no. 2 (1994): 241–73. See also Michael J. Harner, "The Role of Hallucinogenic Plants in European Witchcraft," Ch. 8 in *Hallucinogens and Shamanism* (Oxford: Oxford University Press, 1973, reprinted U.S.A., 1978), 125–50.

17 See Clark Heinrich, *Magic Mushrooms in Religion and Alchemy* (Rochester, VT: Park Street Press, 2002). See also Jerry B. Brown and Julie M. Brown, *The Psychedelic Gospels: The Secret History of Hallucinogens in Christianity* (Rochester, VT: Park Street Press, 2016).

18 Raymond A. Bucko, *The Lakota Ritual of the Sweat Lodge: History and Contemporary Practice* (Bloomington, IN: Published by the University of Nebraska Press in Cooperation with the American Indian Studies Research Institute, Indiana University, 1998).

19 Nicholas J. Conard et al., "New Flutes Document the Earliest Musical Tradition in Southwestern Germany," *Nature* 460, no. 7256 (2009): 737–40.

20   Dr. Zoran Josipovic, a research scientist and adjunct professor at New York University, who has been conducting fMRI brain scans on Buddhist monks, explains, "When one relaxes into a state of oneness, the neural networks in experienced practitioners change as they lower the psychological wall between themselves and their environments. And this reorganisation in the brain may lead to what some meditators claim to be a deep harmony between themselves and their surroundings." Matt Danzico, "Brains of Buddhist Monks Scanned in Meditation Study," BBC News online, April 24, 2011, accessed October 15, 2018, www.bbc.com /news/world-us-canada-12661646. See also Zoran Josipovic and Bernard J. Baars, "Editorial: What Can Neuroscience Learn from Contemplative Practices?" *Frontiers in Psychology* 6 (2015), https://doi.org/10.3389/fpsyg.2015.01731.

21   "Now, shamanism—that most ancient of spiritual practices, long obscured by powerful state religions and politics—is reemerging and opening the doors to individual direct spiritual experiences. While lost in much of the world, it tenaciously survives in a few remote frontiers." From Sandra Harner, *Ema's Odyssey: Shamanism for Healing and Spiritual Knowledge* (Berkeley, CA: North Atlantic Books, 2014).

22   "Transgenerational Trauma" refers to fascinating studies that demonstrate how the effects of trauma and stress are inherited by the next two generations. See, for example, Rachel Lev-Wiesel, "Intergenerational Transmission of Trauma across Three Generations: A Preliminary Study," *Qualitative Social Work* 6, no. 1 (2007): 75–94.

23   William James (1842–1910), considered the father of American psychology, included the study of spiritual states and mystical consciousness in his research.

24   Abraham Maslow (1908–1970), the American psychologist and professor known for developing Maslow's hierarchy of needs, included the research of peak experiences in his studies, which he defined as "moments of highest happiness and fulfillment" in his book *Religions, Values, and Peak Experiences* (London: Penguin Books Limited, 1964).

25   Stanislav Grof (b. 1931) is a Czech psychiatrist whose decades of research and clinical work has focused on the healing potential of non-ordinary states of consciousness. Together with Anthony Sutich (1907–1976), they birthed the term transpersonal psychology, which began to appear in academic journals in 1970. Further reading on Transpersonal Psychology: Michael Daniels, *Shadow, Self, Spirit: Essays in Transpersonal Psychology* (Exeter: Imprint Academic, 2005); Harris L. Friedman and Glenn Hartelius, *The Wiley-Blackwell Handbook of Transpersonal Psychology* (West Sussex, UK: John Wiley & Sons, 2015).

26   The Multidisciplinary Association for Psychedelic Studies (MAPS) is a nonprofit organization founded by Rick Doblin that is committed to developing "medical,

legal, and cultural contexts for people to benefit from the careful uses of psychedelics and marijuana." More information on current and past research can be found at maps.org/research.

27   Roland R. Griffiths et al., "Psilocybin Can Occasion Mystical⊠Type Experiences Having Substantial and Sustained Personal Meaning and Spiritual Significance," *Psychopharmacology* 187, no. 3 (2006): 268–83.

28   In recent years, newspapers like the *New York Times* and *The Guardian*, magazines like *Oprah, Playboy, Rolling Stone*, and *Time*, and websites such as chacruna .net, erowid.org, maps.org, and vice.com have published or collected many articles written for non-specialists on the guided use of entheogens. See also Rick Doblin, "Ending America's War on Drugs Would Finally Unleash the Therapeutic Potential of Psychedelics," *Time*, May 30, 2018, accessed October 24, 2018, http://time.com/5295544/war-on-drugs-ptsd-mdma-rick-doblin/. Tom Shroder, "Can Psychedelic Trips Cure PTSD and Other Maladies?" *Washington Post*, November 17, 2014, https://www.washingtonpost.com/national/health-science /can-acid-trips-cure-ptsd-and-other-maladies/2014/11/17/3eaeb59a-5ded -11e4-8b9e-2ccdac31a031_story.html. Michael Pollan, *How to Change Your Mind: What the New Science of Psychedelics Teaches Us about Consciousness, Dying, Addiction, Depression, and Transcendence* (New York: Penguin Press, 2018).

29   See, for instance, Alex Gamma et al., "3,4-Methylenedioxymethamphetamine (MDMA) Modulates Cortical and Limbic Brain Activity as Measured by [H215O]-PET in Healthy Humans," *Neuropsychopharmacology* 23, no. 4 (2000): 388–95.

30   See, for instance, Torsten Passie et al., "The Pharmacology of Psilocybin," *Addiction Biology* 7, no. 4 (2002): 357–64.

31   See, for instance, Fernanda Palhano-Fontes et al., "The Psychedelic State Induced by Ayahuasca Modulates the Activity and Connectivity of the Default Mode Network," *PLoS One* 10, no. 2 (2015): e0118143. See also, Robin L. Carhart-Harris et al., "Neural Correlates of the Psychedelic State as Determined by FMRI Studies with Psilocybin," *Proceedings of the National Academy of Sciences of the United States of America* 109, no. 6 (2012): 2138–43.

32   See, for instance, Véronique A. Taylor et al., "Impact of Meditation Training on the Default Mode Network during a Restful State," *Social Cognitive and Affective Neuroscience* 8, no. 1 (2013): 4–14. See also, Kathleen A. Garrison et al., "Meditation Leads to Reduced Default Mode Network Activity beyond an Active Task," *Cognitive, Affective, & Behavioral Neuroscience* 15, no. 3 (2015): 712–20, https://doi.org/10.3758/s13415-015-0358-3.

33   See, for instance, J. Trost et al., "Rhythmic Entrainment as a Musical Affect Induction Mechanism," *Neuropsychologia* 96, no. C (2017): 96–110.

34 See, for instance, Susan A. Jackson, "Toward a Conceptual Understanding of the Flow Experience in Elite Athletes," *Research Quarterly for Exercise and Sport* 67, no. 1 (1996): 76–90. See, for instance, J. Nakamura and M. Csikszentmihalyi, "The Concept of Flow," in *Handbook of Positive Psychology*, ed. C. R. Snyder and Shane J. Lopez (New York: Oxford University Press, 2002), 89–105.

35 R. Griffiths et al., "Psilocybin Can Occasion Mystical-Type Experiences Having Substantial and Sustained Personal Meaning and Spiritual Significance," *Psychopharmacology* 187, no. 3 (2006): 268–83.

36 Stanislav Grof, *Realms of the Human Unconscious: Observations from LSD Research* (New York: Viking Press, 1975), 6.

37 More information on the results of MDMA studies can be found at maps.org /research/mdma. For a collection of personal reports by trauma survivors who have healed in part due to MDMA therapy, the reader might find the following book of interest: Anne Other, *Trust Surrender Receive: How MDMA Can Release Us from Trauma and PTSD* (Austin, TX: Lioncrest Publishing, 2017).

38 Term coined by John Welwood. John Welwood, "Principles of Inner Work: Psychological and Spiritual," *Journal of Transpersonal Psychology* 16, no. 1 (1984): 63–73.

39 Sweat lodges are sacred healing rituals facilitated by native leaders or those formally trained and given direct permission to lead them. It can be difficult to find public information about how to attend. You can ask your local yoga studio, permaculture farm, or dance community if they know of anyone who hosts them. Beyond that, an online search may help you find a local group offering sweat lodges to newcomers.

40 Check out 5Rhythms, Biodanza, Soul Motion, or Ecstatic Dance. They offer events around the world.

Chapter 2. Midwifing the Soul: The Role of the Guide

1 Lynn Wilcox, *Sayings of the Sufi Sages* (Washington, DC: M.T.O. Shahmaghsoudi Pub., 1997), 36.

2 According to Mircea Eliade, "The word comes to us, through the Russian, from the Tungusic šaman." Mircea Eliade and Willard R. Trask, *Shamanism: Archaic Techniques of Ecstasy* (Princeton, NJ: Princeton University Press, 1964), 4.

3 "The 5Rhythms—Flowing Staccato Chaos Lyrical Stillness®—are states of Being. They are a map to everywhere we want to go, on all planes of consciousness—inner and outer, forward and back, physical, emotional and intellectual." "5Rhythms | What Are the 5Rhythms," The 5Rhythms, www.5rhythms.com /gabrielle-roths-5rhythms/what-are-the-5rhythms/.

4 Sensory Awareness consists of "simple sensory experiments to help [students] become more deeply attuned and responsive to the felt sensations and dynamics of gravity, breathing, balance, energy, movement, and more." "About Us," Sensory Awareness Foundation, sensoryawareness.org/about/. For further reading, see Charles V. W. Brooks et al., *Reclaiming Vitality and Presence: Sensory Awareness as a Practice for Life* (Berkeley, CA: North Atlantic Books, 2007). Developed by Stanislav and Christina Grof, Holotropic Breathwork integrates short, intense breaths followed by long, deep breaths to induce a trance-like state in which healing can occur. Practitioners report accessing non-ordinary states of consciousness complete with visions, insights, and healing. There are workshops offered around the world by trained facilitators and can be found at www.holotropic.com. See Stanislav Grof and Christina Grof, *Holotropic Breathwork: A New Approach to Self-Exploration and Therapy* (Albany: State University of New York Press, 2010). Ilse Middendorf was a German respiratory therapist, author, and founder of the Breathable Breath. She taught her students to observe their breath in order to gain deep insight into personal habitual patterns. Her work is recognized throughout the world by actors, doctors, psychotherapists, and healers. See Ilse Middendorf, *The Perceptible Breath: A Breathing Science* (Paderborn, Germany: Junfermann-Verlag, 1990).

5 "Code of Ethics for Spiritual Guides," Council on Spiritual Practices, csp.org /docs/code-of-ethics-for-spiritual-guides.

Chapter 3. Illuminating the Path:
The Holistic Model for a Balanced Life

1 The Enneagram is a complex model of the human psyche, a typology of nine personality types and the relations among them. While its roots are obscure, the current understanding of the system comes from the work of the philosopher Gurdjieff (1866/77–1949) and the psychiatrist Claudio Naranjo. See Don Richard Riso, *The Enneagram: Discovering Your Personality Type* (London: Thorsons, 1995).

2 The term *Mitakuye Oyasin* is spoken within the Lakota people as a recognition of oneness and harmony with all forms of life. Translating to "All My Relations" or "We Are All Related," it is spoken during prayer and ceremony as a recognition that all beings on the planet are one—spirit, plant, animal, rock, river, and so on. It is not a casual greeting and the direct words *Mitakuye Oyasin* should only be spoken by those who have permission or blessing by the Lakota to do so.

3 Alvaro Estrada, *María Sabina: Her Life and Chants* (Santa Barbara, CA: Ross-Erikson, 1981).

4 Nisargadatta Maharaj and Sudhakar S. Dikshit, *I Am That: Talks with Sri Nisargadatta Maharaj* (Durham, NC: Acorn Press, 2012), § 57.

Chapter 4. Leaving Home: The Essentials of Preparation

1 Timothy Leary, *The Psychedelic Experience: A Manual Based on the Tibetan Book of the Dead* (New York: Citadel Underground, 2017), Introduction.

Chapter 5. Flesh and Bones: Physical Preparation

1 Martha Graham, *Blood Memory* (New York: Doubleday, 1991), 7.

2 While the composition of the *kykeon,* the beverage that broke the sacred fast at the climax of the Eleusinian mystery rituals is unknown, the case for ergot is made in R. G. Wasson, Albert Hofmann, and Carl A. P. Ruck's, *The Road to Eleusis: Unveiling the Secret of the Mysteries* (Berkeley, CA: North Atlantic Books, 2008).

Chapter 6. Turning Inward: Mental and Emotional Preparation

1 Naomi Shihab Nye, *Words under the Words: Selected Poems* (Portland, OR: Eighth Mountain Press, 1995), 43.

2 See, for instance, Barbara Tedlock, *Dreaming: Anthropological and Psychological Interpretations* (Cambridge, UK: Cambridge University Press, 1987); David Dean Shulman et al., *Dream Cultures: Explorations in the Comparative History of Dreaming* (New York: Oxford University Press, 1999).

3 The *I-Ching* or *Book of Changes* is both an ancient Chinese text and a divinatory system to discover the will of the divine. One of 64 hexagrams and its associated interpretation passages is invoked by casting coins or yarrow stalks.

4 Peter A. Levine, *Waking the Tiger: Healing Trauma: The Innate Capacity to Transform Overwhelming Experiences* (Berkeley, CA: North Atlantic Books, 1997); Peter A. Levine, *In an Unspoken Voice: How the Body Releases Trauma and Restores Goodness* (Berkeley, CA: North Atlantic Books, 2010); Bessel van der Kolk, *The Body Keeps the Score: Brain, Mind, and Body in the Healing of Trauma* (New York: Penguin Books, 2015).

5 Somatic Experiencing is a body-based approach to resolving trauma founded by Dr. Peter Levine. Learn about training or find a practitioner at traumahealing.org.

6 Mindfulness-Based Stress Reduction (MBSR) is an eight-week training program of meditation, body awareness, and movement, developed by Jon Kabat-Zinn in 1979, to address stress, pain, and other conditions.

7 Jack Kornfield, *The Wise Heart: A Guide to the Universal Teachings of Buddhist Psychology* (New York: Bantam Books, 2009); Jack Kornfield, *Path with Heart: A Guide through the Perils and Promises of Spiritual Life* (New York: Bantam, 1993); Jack Kornfield, *After the Ecstasy, the Laundry: How the Heart Grows Wise on the Spiritual Path* (New York: Random House Publishing Group, 2000). Jon Kabat-Zinn, *Wherever You Go, There You Are: Mindfulness Meditation in Everyday Life* (New York: Hachette Books, 2014); Jon Kabat-Zinn, *Full Catastrophe Living: Using the Wisdom of Your Body and Mind to Face Stress, Pain, and Illness* (New York: Bantam Books Trade Paperbacks, 2013); Jon Kabat-Zinn and Stan Richardson, *Mindfulness for Beginners: Reclaiming the Present Moment—and Your Life* (Boulder, CO: Sounds True, 2016). Tara Brach, *Radical Acceptance: Embracing Your Life with the Heart of a Buddha* (New York: Bantam Books, 2003); Tara Brach, *True Refuge: Finding Peace and Freedom in Your Own Awakened Heart* (New York: Bantam Books, 2016). Thich Nhat Hạnh, *The Heart of the Buddha's Teaching: Transforming Suffering into Peace, Joy & Liberation: The Four Noble Truths, the Noble Eightfold Path, and Other Basic Buddhist Teachings* (New York: Harmony Books, 2015.); Thich Nhat Hạnh, *Peace Is Every Step* (New York: Bantam/AJP, 2013). Pema Chödrön, *When Things Fall Apart: Heart Advice for Difficult Times* (Boulder, CO: Shambhala, 2016); Pema Chödrön, *The Places That Scare You: A Guide to Fearlessness in Difficult Times* (Boston: Shambhala, 2005). Byron Katie and Stephen Mitchell, *Loving What Is: Four Questions That Can Change Your Life* (New York: Three Rivers Press, 2003); Byron, Katie, *A Thousand Names for Joy: Living in Harmony with the Way Things Are* (New York: Three Rivers Press, 2008).

8 *Metta* is a Theravada Buddhist practice, though its roots pre-date Buddhism. It aims to awaken the heart's capacity for love and compassion. It includes a visualization and a benevolent prayer or intention for one's own well-being, which extends to include others.

9 C. G. Jung and Marie-Louise von Franz, *Man and His Symbols* (Paw Prints, 2009); C. G. Jung and Sonu Shamdasani, *The Red Book = Liber Novus: A Reader's Edition* (New York: W. W. Norton, 2012); C. G. Jung and Aniela Jaffé, *Memories, Dreams, Reflections* (United States: Stellar Classics, 2013).

10 Joseph Campbell, *The Hero with a Thousand Faces* (Novato, CA: New World Library, 2008); Joseph Campbell, *Myths to Live By* (New York: Penguin Compass, 2003); Joseph Campbell and Phil Cousineau, *The Hero's Journey: Joseph Campbell on His Life and Work* (Novato, CA: New World Library, 2014).

11 Stanislav Grof and Christina Grof, *Holotropic Breathwork: A New Approach to Self-Exploration and Therapy* (Albany: State University of New York Press, 2010); Stanislav Grof, *LSD: Doorway to the Numinous* (Rochester, VT: Park Street Press,

2009); Stanislav Grof, *Healing Our Deepest Wounds: The Holotropic Paradigm Shift* (Newcastle, WA: Stream of Experience Productions, 2012).

12 Michael Meade, *The Water of Life: Initiation and the Tempering of the Soul* (Seattle, WA: Greenfire Press, 2006); Michael Meade, *The World behind the World: Living at the Ends of Time* (Seattle, WA: Greenfire Press, 2008); Michael Meade, *Fate and Destiny: The Two Agreements of the Soul* (Seattle, WA: Greenfire Press, 2013).

13 Ariel Spilsbury, *The 13 Moon Oracle: Journey through the Archetypal Faces of the Feminine Divine* (San Rafael, CA: Mandala Publishing, 2006).

Chapter 7. Approaching the Altar: Spiritual Preparation

1 The 13 Indigenous Grandmothers was a council of elder ambassadors from various indigenous communities and traditions. They hosted ceremonies and rituals, traveling the world teaching about the sacred and indigenous ways from the feminine perspective. Their focus was on healing the rift between the ancient and the modern, nature and urban life, in regard to environmentalism and human rights.

2 Day of the Dead, or Día de los Muertos, is a Mexican holiday when families gather to honor deceased loved ones. Families create altars with photos, mementos, and possessions of the deceased. It is celebrated during the first couple days of November.

3 Among many, the ancient religions of Mesopotamia, the polytheism of ancient Egypt, the Druids of pagan Celtic Europe, the Eleusinian Mysteries of ancient Greece, Mithraism of pre-Christian Rome, Old Norse religion of North Germanic peoples, etc. Among the living traditions, Zoroastrianism from Persia, the often animist and shamanic indigenous traditions surviving from pre-Columbian America, pre-Christian Polynesia, and sub-Saharan Africa, as well as, of course, Hinduism of India, Confucianism of China, Shintoism of Japan, Buddhism in its many incarnations, etc.

4 See, for instance, the work of Marija Gimbutas (1921–1994). Marija Gimbutas and Miriam R. Dexter, *The Living Goddesses* (Berkeley, CA: University of California Press, 2005); Marija Gimbutas, *The Language of the Goddess* (London: Thames & Hudson, 1989).

Chapter 8. Tending the Web: Community Preparation

1 Malidoma Patrice Somé, *Of Water and the Spirit: Ritual, Magic, and Initiation in the Life of an African Shaman* (London: Penguin Books, 1995).

Chapter 9. Nourishing Our Roots: Environmental Preparation

1 John Muir, from *Alaska Days with John Muir,* ed. Samuel H. Young (New York: Fleming H. Revell Company, 1915), 216.

2 See, for instance, Tasian Tein et al., "Alaska Native Collections—Sharing Knowledge," Arctic Studies Center, National Museum of Natural History, Smithsonian Institution, 1996, alaska.si.edu/culture_ne_siberian.asp?subculture=Yupik(Asiatic Eskimo)&continue=1.

Chapter 10. Entering the Unknown: Journey into an Expanded State

1 Izumi Shikibu, from *Women in Praise of the Sacred: 43 Centuries of Spiritual Poetry by Women,* ed. Jane Hirshfield (New York: HarperPerennial, 1995).

Chapter 12. Returning Home: The Art of Integration

1 Eleanor Roosevelt, *You Learn by Living: Eleven Keys for a More Fulfilling Life* (New York: Olive Editions, 2016), foreword.

Chapter 14. The Truth Within: Integrating Mind-Centered Experiences

1 Developed by Francine Shapiro in the 1990s as a psychotherapy to address trauma. Francine Shapiro, *Eye Movement Desensitization and Reprocessing (EMDR) Therapy: Basic Principles, Protocols, and Procedures,* 3rd ed. (New York: Guilford Press, 2018).

2 Introduced by Gary Craig in 1995, EFT is a self-administered form of energy psychology that uses tapping and affirmations to address trauma and other psychological difficulties. Gary Craig, *The EFT Manual* (Fulton, CA: Energy Psychology Press, 2011).

Chapter 15. The Farthest Shore: Integrating Spirit-Centered Experiences

1 Gnostic Nag Hammadi, from Gnostic Gospel: Nag Hammadi Library (2nd–4th c.); Jane Hirshfield, "The Thunder: Perfect Mind," in *Women in Praise of the Sacred: 43 Centuries of Spiritual Poetry by Women,* ed. Jane Hirshfield (New York: HarperPerennial, 1995).

2   See, for instance, Stephen Ross et al., "Rapid and Sustained Symptom Reduction Following Psilocybin Treatment for Anxiety and Depression in Patients with Life-Threatening Cancer: A Randomized Controlled Trial," *Journal of Psychopharmacology* 30, no. 12 (2016): 1165–80.

3   See, for instance, Daisetz Teitaro Suzuki, *An Introduction to Zen Buddhism* (Seattle, WA: Stellar Books, 2014). Dzogchen: See, for instance, His Holiness the Dalai Lama, *Dzogchen* (Boulder, CO: Shambhala Publications Inc., 2004). Mahamudra: See, for instance, Dakpo Tashi Namgyal, His Holiness the Dalai Lama, and Lobsang P. Lhalungpa, *Mahamudra The Moonlight—Quintessence of Mind and Meditation* (Somerville, MA: Wisdom Publications, 2014). Kashmiri Shaivism: See, for instance, Christopher D. Wallis, *Tantra Illuminated: The Philosophy, History, and Practice of a Timeless Tradition* (Boulder, CO: Mattamayūra Press, 2013). Advaita Vedanta: See, for instance, Prabhavananda Śan□kara, and Christopher Isherwood, *Shankara's Crest-Jewel of Discrimination (Viveka-Chudamani)* (Hollywood, CA: Vedanta Press, 1978). Kabbalah: See, for instance, Arthur Green, *Ehyeh: A Kabbalah for Tomorrow* (Woodstock, VT: Jewish Lights Publishing, 2016).

Chapter 16. The Beauty of Interdependence: Integrating Community-Centered Experiences

1   Charles Eisenstein, *The More Beautiful World Our Hearts Know Is Possible* (Berkeley, CA: North Atlantic Books, 2013), 201.

2   Gestalt Therapy, developed by Fritz Perls (1893–1970) and others in the 1940s, and especially at Esalen Institute in the 1960s, is a psychotherapeutic approach that emphasizes experience in the immediate present, in the context of the person's situation and relationships. Frederick S. Perls et al., *Gestalt Therapy: Excitement and Growth in the Human Personality* (Gouldsboro, ME: Gestalt Journal, 1994).

3   Family Constellation Work, developed by Bert Hellinger, is a group therapy process that works on unresolved intergenerational family traumas as they are experienced by the seeker, with the help of others who represent the significant family members. Joy Manné, *Family Constellations: A Practical Guide to Uncovering the Origins of Family Conflict* (Berkeley, CA: North Atlantic Books, 2009).

4   From delos-inc.com: Voice Dialogue, developed by Hal and Sidra Stone in 1972, "is the basic method for contacting, learning about, and working with the many selves that make up each of us" in aid of fostering freedom, choice, and wholeness. Hal Stone et al., *Embracing Our Selves: The Voice Dialogue Manual* (Novato, CA: New World Library, 1998).

5 Nonviolent Communication, developed by Marshall Rosenberg (1934–2015), is a practice that recognizes that all people share the same needs and the capacity for compassion, that all actions are attempts to meet needs, and that feelings point to needs met or unmet. NVC allows people to listen with compassion to the needs and feelings of others, which often fosters connection, choice, and peace. Marshall B. Rosenberg, *Nonviolent Communication: A Language of Life*, 2nd ed. (Encinitas, CA: PuddleDancer Press, 2003).

6 From restorativejustice.org: "Restorative Justice is a theory of justice that emphasizes repairing the harm caused by criminal behavior. It is best accomplished through cooperative processes that allow all willing stakeholders to meet . . ." This approach, drawn from North American, Maori, and other indigenous traditions, stems from the ability of community circles to bring balance between those who have been harmed by crime and those who have committed crimes.

Chapter 17. Nature's Mirror: Integrating Environment-Centered Experiences

1 Mary Oliver, *Why I Wake Early: New Poems* (Boston: Beacon Press, 2005), 3.

2 The Work That Reconnects is a methodology for group process. From their website, https://workthatreconnects.org, "The central purpose . . . is to bring us back into relationship with each other and with the self-healing powers in the web of life, motivating and empowering us to reclaim our lives, our communities, and our planet from corporate and colonial rule." See Joanna Macy and Molly Young Brown, *Coming Back to Life: The Updated Guide to the Work That Reconnects* (Gabriola Island, BC: New Society Publishers, 2014).

3 Charles Eisenstein is an American philosopher, writer, and public speaker, who brings a scientifically informed spiritual perspective to topics such as economics and climate change. He seeks to help his audience reframe how they view the largest problems we face and to move humanity from tragic separation from the natural world, and our own nature, to reunion. See, for instance, Charles Eisenstein, *Climate: A New Story* (Berkeley, CA: North Atlantic Books, 2018); Charles Eisenstein, *The Ascent of Humanity* (Berkeley, CA: North Atlantic Books, 2013); Charles Eisenstein, *The More Beautiful World Our Hearts Know Is Possible* (Berkeley, CA: North Atlantic Books, 2013).

4 Naomi Klein is a Canadian social activist and critic, filmmaker, and professor, who speaks and writes on economics, corporate capitalism, and climate change. She is the Gloria Steinem Endowed Chair in Media, Culture and Feminist Studies at Rutgers University-New Brunswick since 2018. See, for instance, Naomi

Klein, *The Battle for Paradise: Puerto Rico Takes on the Disaster Capitalists* (Chicago: Haymarket Books, 2018); Naomi Klein, *Will the Flower Slip through the Asphalt: Writers Respond to Capitalist Climate Change* (New Delhi: LeftWord Books, 2017); Naomi Klein, *This Changes Everything: Capitalism vs. the Climate* (New York: Simon & Schuster, 2015).

5   The Pachamama Alliance is an organization focused on ecological and economic empowerment of groups living in the Amazon Rainforest. They organize workshops and intensives that integrate indigenous wisdom with teachings on environmental sustainability, social justice, and spiritual practice. You can find more at www.pachamama.org.

6   Bioneers is an environmentally oriented nonprofit that produces media and events and is most well known for their annual conference in Northern California, bringing together leading voices from around the globe on climate change, permaculture, restorative justice, and progressive politics: www.bioneers.org.

7   Deep ecology is a term coined by Arne Næss (1912–2009) in the 1970s. A philosophy that views all of nature and life as having its own value and equal right to exist, beyond human use. See, for instance, Alan R. Drengson and Inoue Yuichi, *The Deep Ecology Movement: An Introductory Anthology* (Berkeley, CA: North Atlantic Books, 1995); Andrew Dobson, *The Green Reader: Essays Toward a Sustainable Society* (San Francisco: Mercury House, 1991).

8   Systems theory is the interdisciplinary study of natural and man-made systems. This orientation of looking at synergies and emergent behaviors among interdependent parts informs scientists and philosophers in many fields. See, for instance, Gregory Bateson, *Steps to an Ecology of Mind: Collected Essays in Anthropology, Psychiatry, Evolution, and Epistemology* (New York: Ballantine Books, 1972); Ludwig von Bertalanffy, *Problems of Life: An Evaluation of Modern Biological Thought* (London: Watts & Co., 1952).

9   Dolores LaChappelle (1926–2007). Skier, mountain climber, researcher, author, philosopher; a leader of the Deep Ecology movement. See Dolores LaChappelle, *Sacred Land, Sacred Sex: Rapture of the Deep: Concerning Deep Ecology and Celebrating Life* (Kirkland, WA: Finn Hill Arts, 1988).

Chapter 18. Conclusion: Sharing Our Transformation with the World

1   Joanna Macy, "Schooling Our Intention: A Talk by Joanna Macy," *Tricycle*, Winter 1993.

ACKNOWLEDGMENTS

We want to thank our families, teachers, advisors, friends, and students who have supported the gestation and birth of this book. We specifically want to thank Hisae Matsuda, Catherine Hiller, Naama Grossbard, Chris Mays, and Jed Fox for their creative support and diligent help refining the manuscript. Thank you to Jacques Rossouw for his help with the cover design.

ABOUT THE AUTHORS

Françoise Bourzat is a consciousness guide and counselor. She has a master's degree in Somatic Psychology from New College of California and is Hakomi Trained. Residing in the San Francisco Bay Area, she has been weaving the healing potential of expanded states of consciousness and psychology together in her practice for over thirty years. After traveling the world as a young woman, Françoise found her way to San Francisco in the early 1980s. It was there she met her first teacher, a pioneer exploring the intersection of indigenous healing and psychotherapy. She later met her teacher of the last twenty years, an indigenous Mazatec woman leading healing ceremonies with sacred mushrooms in the high mountains of Southern Mexico. Drawing from years of close apprenticeship with her Mazatec teacher, as well as training in other indigenous traditions, Françoise has developed a comprehensive approach that bridges Western and indigenous modalities for healing and growth. She trains therapists and facilitators, teaches at the California Institute of Integral Studies (CIIS), and lectures internationally.

Kristina Hunter is a healing guide, writer, and Certified Hakomi Practitioner living in the San Francisco Bay Area. She has spent over ten years traveling the world, studying the transformative potential of expanded states of consciousness. Her work explores the intersection of psychology, plant medicine, and Buddhist meditation. She offers individual counseling and integration support for psychedelic and initiatory experiences. She also offers mentoring and consultation to healing practitioners who wish to integrate expanded states of consciousness into their practice.